AROUND
ICELAND
ON INSPIRATION

AROUND
ICELAND
ON INSPIRATION

Riaan Manser

JONATHAN BALL PUBLISHERS
Johannesburg & Cape Town

Ísafjörður

Siglufjörður

Dalvík

VESTFIRÐIR

Patreksfjörður

Sauðárkrókur

NORÐURLAND VESTRA

Stykkishólmur

Ólafsvík

VESTURLAND

Borgarnes

Akranes

1

SUÐURLAND

Reykjavík

Hafnarfjörður

Keflavík

2

Selfoss

Grindavík

1 HÖFUÐBORGARSVÆÐI
2 SUÐURNES

START/
FINISH
Húsavík

Akureyri

NORÐURLAND EYSTRA

Egilsstaðir ●

Neskaupstaður ●

Eskifjörður ●

AUSTURLAND

Höfn ●

ICELAND

© Text – Riaan Manser 2012
© Photography – Richard Mills 2012

Published in 2012 in trade paperback by
JONATHAN BALL PUBLISHERS (PTY) LTD
A division of Media24 Limited
PO Box 33977
Jeppestown
2043

ISBN 978-1-86842-481-8
ebook ISBN 978-1-86842-541-9

Reprinted in 2012

Edited by Willem Steenkamp and Alfred LeMaitre
Cover and text design by MR Design, Cape Town
Proofreading by Lesley Hay-Whitton
Set in Palatino
Printed and bound by Paarl Media

Twitter: www.twitter.com/JonathanBallPub
Facebook: www.facebook.com/pages.
Jonathan-Ball-Publishers/298034457992
Blog: http://jonathanball.bookslive.co.za/

CONTENTS

Introduction

This was almost a book about paddling solo around the rugged coasts of Greenland. How and why it ended up as a story about paddling around *Iceland* instead, with a companion who not only had almost no real kayaking experience but also suffered from a serious physical disability, is not simple to explain. But that's what happened.

One thread of that decision was my philosophy as an adventurer. A philosophy is something a true adventurer needs, because often it will be the only thing that sustains him when times are hard – and if there is one sure thing about adventuring, it is that sooner or later you are going to fall on hard times.

So, my philosophy is simple. Everyone talks about what it takes to see things through. But not many would-be adventurers actually *manage* to see things through: either they keep their dreams at the talking stage, or they actually venture forth and then give up part of the way along. That's where the great divide opens up between the doers, who actually achieve what they set out to achieve (and sometimes die in the attempt), and the ones who don't. You might say that there is an ocean between saying and doing.

Which is exactly what I was telling my friend Dan Skinstad over coffee one day. Dan had approached me many times to ask if there was some sort of 'boot camp' I could involve him in. I had always said yes, that I would try to involve him in my next effort, and I meant it. But it was more complicated than that. I was seriously considering a circumnavigation of Greenland (my plans had not yet crystalised at that stage), and what I envisaged was an extremely difficult and dangerous trip, not to be undertaken by any except seasoned kayakers.

The problem was that Dan had no experience of open-sea kayaking, especially in bad conditions, and on top of that suffers from mild cerebral palsy, which affects a person's muscle control, so that his every action is more difficult or more painful, or both, than it would be for a non-sufferer. It also affects his balance, and balance is a crucial part of paddling a typical narrow-gutted kayak. I found it difficult to summon up the guts to take responsibility for someone else's life. And that was the crux of the matter. It was not even a matter of whether he could manage the Greenland trip, but of whether he could survive it – and that might depend on me.

Then there was me. I had undertaken a solo bicycle trip around Africa, which had turned out to be a physically gruelling, wildly interesting and frequently hair-raising venture that had brought me close to death and disaster on a number of occasions. Then I paddled all the way around Madagascar, which had provided another dose of the same. Yet, each time, I had crossed the mental point of no return after about 20 seconds of deep, decisive thought. That's all it took. No crowds, hurrahs or razzmatazz telling the world about my plans. Just 20 seconds.

That happened to me once more when I headed up to the icy north with my long-suffering but greatest supporter, my girlfriend Vasti. An American exploration company, Quark Expeditions, in association with its South African partner, Unique Destinations, offered me two places aboard the Russian Arctic exploration ship MV *Akademik Shokalsky*, which was to visit the world's biggest fjord, Scorbesund, on the central-eastern coast of the gigantic, ice-bound island of Greenland. There would also be a few days in Iceland on either side of the trip.

When Vasti and I set off, I was already considering a trip around Greenland, and I hoped the journey would help me to make a final decision. It was a mind-boggling and sometimes surreal journey, epic in its own right. We saw a polar bear and her cub, hiked across ancient valleys and paddled in brash ice (this is an accumulation of floating ice fragments up to two metres across) a few hundred metres from monstrous glaciers waiting to 'calve', or give birth to icebergs. When the airport at the famous Constable Point was snowed in, we had no option but to tackle the seven-metre seas in search of a more southerly airport. It was an amazing adventure, one that I feel privileged to have experienced.

Vasti and I soaked up the local culture in Iceland's capital, Reykjavík, for a few days before returning home, and we spent some of the time discussing my next big venture. We agreed that it must be Greenland. I was excited at having reached a decision and set about preparing to speak to potential sponsors, first among them my friends at Windhoek Lager, who had supported my earlier ventures.

I knew it would not be a pushover: I would have to work hard to convince them to back me once again. If I could do that, I knew, the year would be an amazing one. I would attempt to battle an entirely new and different part of the world, a long way in every sense – geographically, climatically and terrain-wise – from my stamping ground in Africa. On the other hand, I had a good track record; I had undertaken two harrowing world-first trips and had come back in one piece, having achieved what I had set out to do.

So Greenland it was. What I didn't know, however, was that in fact I hadn't had those 20 seconds of decisive thought yet. But they would not be long in coming.

On the day of our departure from Iceland's Keflavik International Airport, we boarded the Boeing 737, buckled up and settled in for the flight back to South Africa. The aircraft rose gently off the tarmac and started climbing. Entranced, I watched more and more of the icy volcanic coastline revealing itself as we gained height. The intricate shape of the Reykjanes Peninsula came into sight, and I found myself imagining what it would take to paddle safely around it.

Man alive! My heart began beating faster, and I knew that the 20 decisive seconds were about to strike. I sank into a comfortable self-discussion, which was partly a no-holds-barred pep talk and partly an argument with myself about why the trip had to be about Greenland, rather than Iceland, and why it absolutely had to be another solo trip. The debate went something like this:

Riaan, this journey doesn't need to be about the gorilla beating its chest. It doesn't have to be about you. If you buy into even a fraction of an ounce of what people tell you when they say that you inspire them, then you need to up your game. Come on, man! Tell a story about someone who doesn't have what you have, someone whose life would change because of a journey with you. And, above all, tell a story of real *inspiration; the world is clamouring for stories like that – it* needs *them.*

There was no arguing with that. And so the 20 seconds were upon me, and I decided on three things. Firstly, it was going to be Iceland, a country about which I knew virtually nothing; secondly, it was going to be on a kayak named *Inspiration*; and thirdly, I was going to work everything around creating an opportunity for Dan to prove himself.

CHAPTER 1

PREPARING FOR ICELAND

VESTFIRÐIR

Húsavík

NORÐURLAND EYSTRA

NORÐURLAND VESTRA

VESTURLAND

AUSTURLAND

Reykjavík

SUÐURLAND

1 HÖFUÐBORGARSVÆÐI
2 SUÐURNES

'And there was no doubt about where I was going and what I wanted to do when I got there: paddle around Iceland and bring Dan home alive, with stories he could bore his grandchildren with one day. It was as simple as that.'

We had about nine months to prepare. To the uninitiated, this might seem a long time, but not to someone planning to do what I intended. But I was not particularly concerned; I had had much less preparation time for either of my previous ventures. The most important priority was to work on Dan mentally, to see that he had a clear grasp of what 'no compromise' meant. That understanding would be crucial, possibly the difference between life and death.

I saw Dan at the end of September 2010 and told him what I had decided. I didn't expect anything in return at that stage except his commitment. He had some things to get out of the way, among them the need to gain admission to the Law Society, and was under pressure. That was OK by me, because I had lots to do: giving scheduled talks, setting up partner agreements and putting in time on the water with him.

He told me he had paddled a lot with his brothers, so I was confident he would be able to handle the technical side of things. But there were other things to attend to. One was the skill of getting back into the kayak after falling out. This would have to be done very quickly in the extremely cold water around Iceland. The more important question was whether Dan would have the physical endurance the journey would demand, to stand up to the seemingly endless days of grinding effort, often in rough seas, and, Iceland being Iceland, the sort of numbing cold weather that we just don't get in Africa.

I also had to do some personal planning. How could I improve on what I had done so far? Things had gone well for me. I had done two solo adventures, somehow got through both and ended up with two world firsts, two best-selling books and two *Out There* Adventurer of the Year awards. I knew that there were still a number of new adventures left in me. But I also had to be realistic.

I had undertaken my earlier adventures for adventure's sake, not for fame and fortune, and I still felt that way. But it was time to look to my personal future – and so far this was something I had failed to do. I had returned broke from my earlier trips; I had no life insurance or medical aid, or even a retirement plan. This had to change, and the obvious solution was to document this next journey more aggressively and accurately from beginning to end. That meant more than operating – conditions permitting, which they often did not – a hand-held camera or tape recorder.

At this stage, the grand idea of making a film came up. Over the years, I had developed a friendship with Professor Mike Bruton, formerly a lecturer at the University of Cape Town and, later, head of the Cape Town Science Centre at the time that it hosted my 'Legend Africa' bicycle and some other special memorabilia I had collected in my two-year trek around the continent.

Mike was a genuine supporter, and loved the commitment with which I had tackled both of my previous journeys … and it just so happened that his daughter, Tracey, was at a loose end at the time, because the production company she had been working for had had to cut back on its staff. She had told me it was a dream of hers to make films, and so I offered her the job for the Iceland trip. Tracey was ecstatic. It was good to see someone grab an opportunity like she did.

Vasti was doubtful about the extra expense, and rightly so. Our personal budget could hardly cope with the two staff we had on board already: Shea, my personal assistant – toughness and sweetness all rolled into one, someone I wanted to look after first if we came into money – and Bradley Loubser, my friend of 25 years, who had decided to leave his missionary work in London, and was now on my payroll as expedition manager. Although he was not as worldly-wise as some, Bradley had special people skills and unparalleled organisational ability. Hiring him was an expensive business, but he brought great experience and leadership to the team; I was going to rely heavily on him to manage, discipline and lead a disparate group of young people – exactly the things I didn't want to have to do after a tough 10-hour day on the water.

Then my budget received another self-inflicted blow. Dan was very short of funds, too, and needed some sort of income. He wanted a salary for the journey. Although I was a bit taken aback, I agreed. Vasti was not happy at all. We didn't have the funds. So it transpired, against Vasti's judicious advice, that Dan would be paid to undertake the journey – something I wish someone had done for me when I entered this world of adventure ten years ago!

Tracey filmed Dan and me as much as she could during this time. My instruction to him was simple: get fit. Specifically, he needed to spend as much time on the rowing machine as he could, because, as in any repetitive-movement sport, muscle memory is crucial in combating fatigue. By January, he told me he was managing to do 140 minutes non-stop under the supervision of the Sports Science Institute of South Africa, a world-class facility headed by the legendary Professor Tim Noakes. Dan also had the personal attention of David Smith, a world-champion paddler and general good bloke. In a nutshell, Dan was in superb hands, the best we could have hoped for.

I sent Bradley to Iceland to do a recce of the entire coast, and also to come back with what he thought would be a decent start/ finish point and a good date to commence our enterprise. This put a huge strain on my finances, but I believed the journey would be significantly safer and streamlined for it. Bradley went off at the beginning of winter, and so managed to see only a limited part of the coastline at first hand, because the horrendous weather blocked many roads. However, he sought out the right contacts who could give him most of the advice and support we were going to need.

Normally I would have done all this myself, but I was frantically busy. Handing over responsibility to someone else wasn't easy for me; I'd always done almost everything myself. But I was on the go non-stop, on a schedule that meant I was almost never at home. I was giving talks for corporates to earn some extra money and also promoting my book, *Around Madagascar on My Kayak*. My travels included a quick trip to London for the razzle-dazzle of the Outdoor Show at the ExCel Centre, a convention centre in the city's Docklands. There I shared the stage with legendary figures of world exploration, such as Sir Ranulph Fiennes and Sir Robin Knox-Johnston. I was amazed to see huge signs advertising the event: 'The world's greatest living explorers – Sir Ranulph Fiennes, Sir Robin Knox-Johnston and Riaan Manser.' Crazy.

Doing things purely for the recognition they bring is flawed at its foundation. But to receive recognition in a world that is littered with TV heroes like Bear Grylls and Ben Fogle is different. Fame seems to be the only thing that attracts accolades in this adventure world of mine. There was no way around it. Although this form of recognition meant very little in the larger world out there, it made me feel the effort I'd put in thus far was getting somewhere. I wanted to create a life for Vasti and me.

The London trip brought another benefit, because I got to talk with Richard Mills, the Windhoek Lager brand manager in London, whose lifelong dream was to be a professional photographer. I decided that Richard was the man I wanted to be the expedition's stills photographer. I knew this was a calculated risk, because all I had to go on was Bradley's recommendation. I did get to see some of Richard's work, though, and I believed I could see the same quality in it as Bradley had: a natural eye for people and situations.

Richard and I met at the Outdoor Show and knuckled out a deal. In addition to a salary – not a huge one – he would share the profits from my book of the Iceland trip, as well as profits from the rights to the pictures. Given the fact that it was tied to a reputation and brand

I had built up for 10 years, it was an exciting opportunity for any photographer hoping for a breakthrough.

I won't tell you what Vasti believed would happen to our finances now! People often don't understand that all my income is what I have earned personally, so taking on new team members has an effect on short-term financial stability. So Vasti was quite right in her conservative approach, as any sane person would agree. But I believed in others, believed that they saw the sincerity of what I was undertaking, believed that they knew they were being offered an opportunity to do something worthwhile. I had to trust these people.

My schedule remained chock-a-block. Soon after the London trip, I travelled to Australia to speak at the famous Golden Key Asia-Pacific Conference, a gathering of the top 10% of the region's brightest minds. For a non-academic, it was slightly intimidating, but what a privilege it was to share my stories with them. The themes I use in my presentations – courage, perseverance and attitude – resonated powerfully with them. 'His world isn't much different from ours,' I could almost hear the voices saying in their heads.

The trip was also a chance to see the great country of Australia at first hand. Many South Africans have emigrated there in the last two decades, and it was easy to see why. Safety and security is a major focus for the Australian people, and there is the same climate and outdoors-loving approach to life.

Physically, I believed I was still very strong, but I was by no means ready for the strains Iceland's environment could bring. I was about 12 kilograms overweight, and my cardio ability was seriously lacking. But I knew what it would take to get around Iceland. I was just holding thumbs that financially we would be able to see the journey out. The last thing I wanted to do was put Vasti through another year of stress and near-bankruptcy.

Canon generously helped me with all the stills and cine equipment I would need to capture the special story we had in front of us. It was a win-win deal: I would never have been able to afford such cameras, and for them the good news was that their equipment would be going somewhere very exotic, and would be tested there by a guy who had destroyed a lot of such stuff in his time. If they survived me, they would survive just about anything.

As crunch time neared, a few potential sponsor deals fell through. But I was not crushed. I'd taught myself to roll with the punches, to get up and get on my way, and to let the rest fall into place. And there was no doubt about where I was going and what I wanted to do when I got there: paddle around Iceland and bring Dan home alive, with stories he could bore his grandchildren with one day. It was as simple as that.

The trip would take three months, maybe four. On the advice of the local kayakers Bradley had consulted, our sea journey would start, in the heart of winter, at Húsavík, on the shore of Skjálfandi Bay on the far northern coast. From there, we would paddle our way clockwise around Iceland, battling our way down the windy, exposed east coast and then along the south coast to Reykjavík, after which, we hoped, conditions would be calmer. Then we would follow the coast into the northwesterly region, which is considered remote even by Icelandic standards; by late summer, we would reach Húsavík again. That meant a lot of paddling. On the first stage of 174 kilometres, for example, we would have to average 20 kilometres a day, which looks easy enough on paper, but by one calculation each such daily stretch would require more than 10 000 paddle strokes.

I planned to start in winter because it would allow us to start slowly. As the weather improved, we would cover longer distances – especially along the dreaded south coast. If we ran into trouble time-wise, I wanted a buffer of sorts before the winter rolled onto us again. Icelanders paddle for only about three months of the year (June, July and August). It is only the craziest among them who venture out on either side of these months – and mostly within the sheltered fjords.

CHAPTER 2

ISLAND OF THE ICE GIANTS

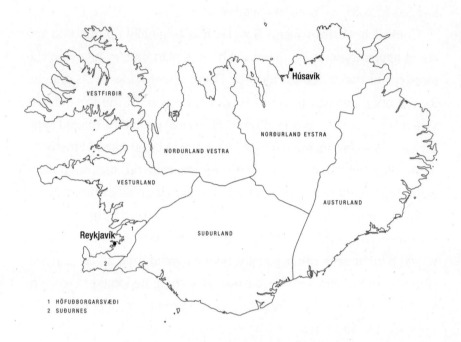

'It was like arriving in another world ... It was the first time I had ever seen so much of the white stuff, and the sight of it must have flicked the nutcase switch in my brain to "on".'

had built up a great relationship with the people at Virgin Atlantic Airways; in the past year, they had flown me to New York, London and Sydney, and now they were going to be my official expedition flight partner. They also extended their support to my newly acquired official film crew, Cooked in Africa Films. Getting all of us (and our gear) to Iceland involved a huge amount of excess baggage, and some negotiation was needed before the airline would handle this affordably. The two two-man kayaks, *Inspiration 1* and *Inspiration 2*, had left by sea two months ahead of us.

Cooked in Africa's Justin Bonello had originally approached me about appearing in a documentary he was planning, to follow in the footsteps of the famed explorer Dr David Livingstone. I was grateful for the offer, but had to turn him down because of the Iceland trip. When I told him the reason, though, his face lit up and he offered to be my partner in producing what he knew would be an incredible story.

At that time, I had had many offers from production houses wanting to work with me, but I was uneasy about all of them. None of them, I felt, truly understood where I was coming from. Justin, on the other hand, had a sincerity similar to my own, and I believed we would benefit each other equally. So we agreed on a 50-50 partnership. I would make sure the journey happened; he would make sure the 13-part documentary was filmed and produced. Needless to say, I was excited about it all.

One thing I made clear to him, though, was that Tracey had to be included as a cinematographer. Justin wasn't happy about it, because he didn't believe she had sufficient experience for the position. But I had promised Tracey something, and wasn't going to go back on that.

D-day arrived, and, like all such days, brought a burst of pre-departure activity as the crew, including Justin's team of four (only two would stay on for the whole trip), got together in manic last-minute organisational tasks at Cape Town International Airport. Things got so manic, in fact, that it took the very wise and level-headed chief of production, Wesley Volschenk, to bring it to our attention that we were about to leave without the paddles … it was an indication of the general craziness that we came near to forgetting such an absolutely vital part of our equipment. That set off a general panic, and we all started furiously checking our own baggage for obvious things like passports and money.

We divided the flight time to London between sleeping and watching the in-flight movies, and it was a somewhat tired bunch of pilgrims who arrived at Heathrow to change planes and deal with the dreaded baggage issue. Our combined baggage incurred an excess charge of £1 000, which I had to pay. Fortunately, my best friend, Troy, was there, and was able to help me out with a loan, as none of the team had the money. It was crazy how Troy got roped into the adventure, but without him we would have missed the Icelandair connection. Finally, we settled down in our seats, and, four hours later, landed without incident at Keflavik International Airport. Justin, Bradley and Richard were there to meet us, and we also met our local guide, Thor Gissuarsson.

It was like arriving in another world; the entire island of the ice giants was white, covered in metres-deep snow. It was the first time I had ever seen so much of the white stuff, and the sight of it must have flicked the nutcase switch in my brain to 'on'. As the sliding doors of the terminal opened to let us out I ran towards the parking lot, launched myself WWE-style into the air and took a low dive that landed me headfirst in the snow. This caused some surprise among the onlookers, since the temperature was -10 °C and – unlike my wiser companions – my cold-weather gear consisted of a T-shirt and flip-flops …

Anyway, welcome to Iceland, and let the adventure begin!

Our arrival at Keflavik did not, however, mean that we got straight into the uninviting water. First we had to get to Húsavík, a tough 10-hour road journey away. But before we could even leave for Húsavík we had to attend to several other pressing matters.

One of the most important was to test the specialised dry suits we'd be wearing at all times while on the water. The wetsuits worn in warmer climates allow water to filter in, which is then warmed by your body heat. But, in Icelandic waters, a wetsuit is like a suicide note. We needed to know that we could last four or five minutes in them in case we capsized or got tossed off the kayak. One very important thing to remember is to zip the suit up at the back before you put on your life jacket! In due course, Dan and I waded somewhat apprehensively into the water. To our delight, the dry suits worked even better than we had anticipated.

Another important task was to make arrangements with the Icelandic Coast Guard. We would be in contact with the team by way of cellphones, radios and GPS trackers, but, if we ran into trouble at sea, our only hope of rescue was the Coast Guard. Although they were very busy, they went out of their way to be helpful. Bjorn Helgi Ingason of the Coast Guard left us with few illusions about what awaited us, and said that they would require us to report in every six hours; if we didn't, they would assume we were in danger and mount a full search-and-rescue operation.

Then at last we shook Reykjavík's dust – well, snow, actually – from our heels and set off for Húsavík, which took us a full day.

Húsavík is an unpretentious place that has been around for a long time. According to the *Landnámabók* (Book of Settlements), a medieval Icelandic saga, it was the first place in Iceland to be settled by a Norseman, or Viking. This worthy was a Swede named Garðar Svavarsson, who arrived around the year 870. He did not stay long – just one winter, which presumably persuaded him that there were more salubrious places in which to put down roots. This is hardly to be wondered at, since the warmest months in the year, July and August, average just 14 °C, while between November and April the temperatures usually range between -1 °C and -4 °C. Nevertheless, he left his mark: the town's name translates as 'bay of houses', probably a reference to Garðar's homestead, the first houses in Iceland.

Modern Húsavík is a town with an airport and about 2370 inhabitants. It used to be the export point for silica extracted from nearby Mývatn Lake, but nowadays the town mainly lives off retail and small industry, fishing and tourism. Tourism? It's a fact. Visitors to Húsavík can gape at the different species of whales – more than 20 – that are often seen in the bay, explore the area around Lake Mývatn and take a look at Jökulsárgljúfur National Park. They can also call in at the wooden Húsavíkurkirkja, a church built in 1907.

Most of all, however, they can drop in at the Whale Museum, which also houses the Icelandic Phallological Museum, most definitely the most unusual educational facility in the world, since it displays penises from every mammal in Iceland.

For some reason, as we were to discover, Húsavík's hot water lacks the pungent sulphur smell that visitors find in the towns in the southwest. Iceland's citizens have a peculiar water situation. They have a cheap and almost limitless supply of it, but, while their cold taps provide some of the purest spring water in the world, their hot water has a pungent smell of rotten eggs, because it comes from geothermal sources and has a high sulphur content. The cheap, abundant hot water is the reason why, in spite of the climate, Icelandic towns have so many swimming pools; the only trick is to remember that the pool water is strictly for bathing, not drinking.

Bradley had arranged for us to meet the mayor of Húsavík, Bergur Elias Adustsson, who personified the warm hospitality we would receive from the Icelanders. The mayor made us the welcome offer of an unused warehouse for storing and working on our two kayaks to get them into fully seaworthy shape. Bradley collected our kayaks from the shipping agent, and, with bated breath, I unwrapped them the next morning, holding thumbs that we wouldn't have a repeat of what had happened to me on the Madagascar trip, when my kayak was so badly damaged in transit from Johannesburg that it took me more than a month to repair it.

I could have saved some money by buying my kayak locally, but I had decided I would feel safer with what I knew, and had stuck to the type built by Johan Loots's Paddleyak company in Cape Town, who had also provided my Madagascar transportation. They designed a robust model that would be able to cope with Iceland's unfriendly waters.

Reaching this decision was not as simple as it might sound. There are strong differences of opinion within the kayaking community about the best type of boat to use, and most of the Icelandic kayakers Bradley had consulted criticised my choice of a 'sit on top' boat, essentially modelled on a surf-ski, but larger and bulkier. Based on what he had been told, Bradley felt that I should follow their advice, but I persisted in my choice, and for a very good reason that few of them had considered: because of Dan's disability, it was essential that he be able to remount fairly easily if we happened to capsize, which is always a possibility when kayaking. This being the case, the ability to get out of the freezing water quickly could quite literally be a life-saver. It bothered me a bit, though, that Bradley sincerely believed I didn't know what I was doing, and was prepared to take the word of kayakers who had never been on expeditions of any sort. I didn't mention it to him, and felt he would come to see this for himself.

To my relief, the only real damage was to the boats' rudders – not too alarming, since it was something I could fix. The next step was to get the kayaks ready for sea, repairing the damage and branding them with the logos of my supporters, then rigging and testing the onboard cameras.

I had had plenty of experience of filming on board during the Madagascar trip, but this time the demands would be far greater. We would need as much good sound and visuals of both of us as possible, and no crew would ever be near us while we were on the water. That meant that they would not be able to capture the most important aspect of the adventure: how we battled Iceland's frozen waters. Justin Bonello and Zahir Isaacs, the soundman, impressed me with their problem-solving attitude. When we were done, I was confident that the cameras would withstand an acceptable amount of the abuse they would inevitably suffer.

Bradley had laid on guided tours of the town's main attractions. To my regret, I didn't have the time to visit the penis museum, whose exhibits run the gamut from the 167-centimetre fundamental organ of a sperm whale, weighing a hefty 70 kilograms, to a two-millimetre-long specimen formerly belonging to a hamster. Recently, I was told, the museum had even acquired the ultimate display item: the penis of a patriotic Icelander who had died at the age of 95 and had willed his crown jewel to the museum for permanent display. It seems that, *post mortem*, there had been great difficulty in getting the now not-so-private part to look like a healthy specimen, but I was told that if there were others out there who would like to make a similar generous offer, the good news was that, thanks to the initial struggle, the doctors were now much more experienced. Please note: any of my readers who are interested should make a direct approach to the Icelandic Phallological Museum.

The reason I didn't get round to visiting this mind-boggling educational institution was that there were so many things to do. The kayaks had to be made completely waterproof, any dangerous edges had to be smoothed out, we wanted to give the dry suits a final test – this time by going out in the kayak, not just wading into the water – and we had to practise setting up camp. This had to go smoothly, because in a typical scenario we would stagger ashore after a day's paddling and then immediately have to pitch our tents in near-freezing temperatures, and quite possibly in the middle of a storm. In that sort of situation, he who hesitated or took his time might well be lost.

The team was beginning to settle in now. The lead cameraman was a gentle and good-hearted guy named Darren Illet, young and quiet and very talented. He and soundman Zahir were totally committed to making a success of the filming. They would make up the Camera A team. Tracey Bruton would operate Camera B, and was picking up some new tricks of the trade from Justin's cinematic right hand, Sunel Haasbroek. Tracey was a capable cinematographer already, but one never stops learning, and it was a stroke of luck that she could hook up with Sunel, a perfectionist who had done some incredible work to date.

In spite of everything that had to be done, my spirit was still buoyant. In between tasks, we relaxed by meeting more of the locals. One of them was Vilborg Arna Gissurardottir, a local beauty queen who was not only beautiful but also extremely kind, and moreover one of the most connected and travelled people in Iceland. Bradley, Thor, Dan and I joined her and her friends for a fun-filled evening at a tiny little pub/restaurant in the harbour area. Dan instantly fell in love with one of her friends. I told him that without doubt she was going to be the first person on the beach waiting when we got back. Things were heating up in Iceland!

By way of final preparation, Dan and I went for test paddles, the success of which varied dramatically. One important matter was the dry suits. The first tests at Reykjavík had been successful, but of course the kayaks had not been available, and so now we needed to try them out while actually paddling.

We had done very well in South Africa, and I believed Dan would get better with every passing minute, just as I was hoping I would. The first paddle was all right, but the second one saw us battling strong winds and rough seas, although we stayed only 100 metres or so from the shore. For Dan, this was the first real test, bearing in mind that he had no experience of extreme paddling conditions, and what kayaking he had done had been in South Africa's friendlier waters.

I knew exactly what this meant, because I had learnt it the hard way. First he would have to learn what it means to be afraid, and *then* learn how to act while he was feeling that way. The unanswered question was whether he had the mental stamina to endure; it is something that, with the best will and foresight in the world, simply can't be simulated beforehand – you have to be in such a position before you find out.

We paddled along the coast for about a kilometre. Dan was rattled by the conditions, which was understandable, and froze up. I had to speak firmly to him to snap him out of it – the first time I had ever raised my voice to him. I managed to get us safely to shore, by which time we were in a very unstable state physically. Just after we landed, a wave Dan should have been alert to sneaked up on him and hit the kayak, which swung in towards him. I managed to grab it and stop it from hitting him – big, strong people have suffered broken legs in similar situations.

Dan did not make excuses or try to lay the blame anywhere except on himself, and took his failure very seriously, because, as he said, he didn't want to let the rest of us down. I told him what I'd said to him many times before: he must back himself, he was brave, and he was strong; it was all in his hands; I wouldn't want anyone else but him in the kayak, and, no matter what came our way, I would keep backing him. And I meant every word of it.

The fact was that we should have had a couple of months together in the kayak. I knew Dan understood that, when my demands on him kept getting tougher, it was because his life was in my hands, and that he was going to learn by mostly painful experience. That was what I'd had to do on the Madagascar trip (when I had no support or rescue backup).

It was not all like this, though. We had some lovely paddles, in dead-calm conditions with very little wind (conditions, I knew, that we'd probably see rarely after the trip started). We paddled twice to Lundeyisland, an island just north of Húsavík, which at low tide reveals a distinct mushroom shape. In the evenings I spent time teaching Dan the important elements of sea paddling. One thing I felt he needed to concentrate on was putting the paddle in front of him, which takes effort and is easy to neglect. This would secure his body in an upright and forward position, rather than to one side, which would have him literally falling over. We laughed a lot as we practised on the floor of the guesthouse kitchen.

I also picked up on something else I had not noticed before, and managed to rectify it. Because of his disability, Dan's knees would come together when he was seated, which affected his balance. I came up with the idea of wedging something between them to keep them apart, something that could float if it became dislodged, and could be tied to the kayak so that it would always be within reach. We did this – the wedge was actually a piece of plastic piping softened with padding on either side – and he was amazed at the immediate difference it made.

The other thing, as I said, was that we had to practise setting up our tents quickly – we calculated it should take no more than about 20 minutes – once we were ashore, especially in cold weather (or perhaps I should say 'colder than usual'). By the second night of practising with the tents in the lee of the guesthouse, I realised that this was going to be a problem. Dan was willing, but was battling to manage on his own. This placed an extra responsibility on my shoulders. At the same time, I worried that helping Dan with the tent would diminish his greatest aim, which was to show the world that he could look after himself.

It was a difficult situation, and we were getting a little tense about small things, like my constant reminders to him not to lose his tent pegs. Then I gave myself a mental shake. This was no time to get emotional. I needed to toughen up myself. People were relying on me, for goodness' sake! Yet I was filled with self-doubt.

One day, I just had to laugh when I saw a blog headline that had tried to describe what I planned to do in Iceland, and came up with 'Heading into the unknown and kicking it in the balls'. At times like this, I start to realise how frighteningly little most people understand about what I do.

My journeys around Madagascar and the African continent had created the image of a devil-may-care adventurer who was willing to spit in the face of any risk or danger, regardless of the odds. But this was not me, and here, in the debilitating -10 °C cold of northern Iceland, I felt humble as never before and doubtful of my abilities as never before. It seemed to me that I didn't know what I was doing, that this time I was out of my depth. About the only saving grace was that, as on both my earlier trips, I was honest enough to acknowledge my fears, which was the first step to controlling them.

Apart from the radically changed environment, the greatest difference between this and my other trips was the fact that I would have a travelling partner to look after. Previously, I had always known that every ounce of energy I expended would be directed towards saving *my* life in life-or-death situations, of which there were quite a few. Now this energy would have to be shared with Dan. Because of his disability, every bit of cold or discomfort would be much worse for him than for me. Even the simplest of tasks would be a battle. Try to make a comparison of this with your average bad day, and I'll tell you there is none.

So it would be a huge responsibility to have Dan with me out on the water. It was his own courageous choice to find something he had wanted to do his whole life – find an outlet for his guts and determination. I knew from painful experience that, when we got on the water, Dan would be exposed to sheer hardship and backbreaking physical effort such as he had never before encountered or even imagined, effort that his body might not be able to handle ... And this was it. Out on the freezing seas, nothing counts except the ability to grit your teeth and stick tenaciously to the task in hand. The learning curve would be steep and painful at times.

In one way, though, Dan and I were in the same boat, figuratively speaking. Each of us had huge obstacles, both in and out of the water, obstacles we would have to tackle and overcome. But let's understand one thing: I had never been more determined to make something work. So I would leave Húsavík on the kayak and in due course return the same way, only from the opposite direction.

Now who's the fool? Only one answer to that question. On second thoughts, I decided, the writer of that headline actually had it right! Dan and I were heading into the unknown, yes, and we were going to kick the frozen north in the balls. Whether it would go down and then stay down was, of course, something neither of us knew yet.

Overlaying all this was a thin layer of incredulity. I still found it difficult to believe that I was actually in Iceland, on the brink of my greatest and most perilous adventure.

CHAPTER 3

SETTING OFF

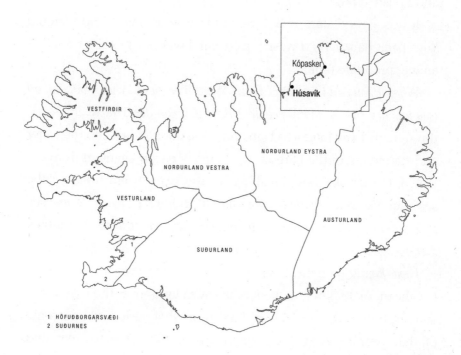

> *'The razzmatazz was over. From now on, it*
> *would be Dan and me and the environment,*
> *with seconds out of the ring and the bell*
> *clanging for the next round.'*

Launch day! We had done everything within our power to prepare for this day. Now, as you might say, we were ready to break the ice. No doubt I looked very self-confident to the crowd of Húsavíkers who had come to see us off – I was a genuine card-carrying adventurer, after all! But I was as nervous as a cat as I smiled at our well-wishers and thanked them for their help and support,

Then I dragged almost 100 kilograms of kayak into the sea, and Dan and I pushed off.

It was a good start, with little in the way of waves, and I should have been happy. But I wasn't; as usual, I was questioning myself at an inappropriate time.

What if you can't look after Dan? What if he dies? What if you fail on this journey that so many people believe you can do? The 'what ifs' ran through my head loudly as Dan and I dug our paddles into the water and started out of the harbour to shouts of encouragement from the crowd, the kayak's bow breaking up the layer of brash ice on the sea's surface. *You're pathetic; you can't be strong even when the journey is less than a kilometre old. Your mindset now, right at the beginning, dictates what will happen in the end, you idiot! Show some backbone!*

I *was* being pathetic, but I was also winding myself up for what lay ahead. As I tell the audiences in my talks all over the world, it is your attitude at the beginning of a venture that decides the outcome of that venture. And, once again, that combination of fear and aggressiveness flicked the right switch.

On that first day we covered 26 kilometres, some of it familiar from our earlier trial paddles, and some of it new. We made good time and could have gone further, but I could see a huge storm charging down from the northeast and knew it was time for us to get our heads down. We entered a small bay and I set up our tents on kelp and snow-covered rock in a relatively sheltered spot on the eastern shore. Then I ventured out onto the slippery ground to fetch logs that I used to secure the tents.

My caution paid off. The storm was a bad one, and for two days we were marooned there while the strong winds howled around us and falling snow cut our visibility down to almost nothing. On the second day, after breakfast and coffee, I went on a long walk across the ridge above the bay. It was a dangerous climb in the reduced visibility, but, once on top, I could see the mayhem wrought by the storm. Looking down at the huge, scary waves, I decided to obey my instincts. Our first day could easily have been our last!

Since this is a warts-and-all story, I have to note that at this stage I had my very first snow poo, when the strenuous walk urged my body to say goodbye to all the oats and noodles we had been eating. I built a commode out of snow, made holes in the appropriate places and sat down to survey the blizzard-beaten bay below me while nature took its course.

I can't say that what happened was pretty or enjoyable, but I certainly got in touch with nature in no uncertain terms, so that, by the time I was done, my bum was numb and my genitals distinctly compact, presumably like those of the 95-year-old Húsavík patriot. Hell! Garðar Svavarsson and his fellow Vikings must have been a tough lot to see out a winter here without thermal underwear and dry suits.

But my walk in the snow had served a purpose. Numb and shrunken I might have been as I returned to our storm-lashed little camp, but I was relieved in mind and body, and my excursion had brought that essential survival mindset to full strength. The razzmatazz was over. From now on, it would be Dan and me and the environment, with seconds out of the ring and the bell clanging for the next round.

On the morning of the third day, I studied the map, pondered the weather I had witnessed and then began to formulate some sort of plan. Quite understandably, Dan was dubious about venturing onto the open sea before the weather had abated properly, but I explained to him that once we had set off I would be in a better position to decide whether to do a short day or go crazy and head across an entire bay, which, frankly, I didn't think would be possible. The fact was that, although I didn't tell him this, I desperately needed to test myself, to see how my body could cope with the distance and the extra weight; Dan was strong, but I was still doing the bulk of the paddling.

We exited the bay and rounded a small peninsula, and suddenly we were heading for the open seas. As I'd done on the Madagascar trip, I also had a bale-out plan tucked away in the back of my head, just in case. The wind was our biggest enemy, our fatigue and health the second most dangerous; if our bodies failed us, we did not want a situation in which the wind was pushing us out to sea.

The swell was running from a northeasterly direction and turning more towards direct north inside the bay. That was good for us. An old kayakers' joke is that it is not complicated to go around a piece of land, as long as you keep that land on the same side all the time. That's how it was here as well. When in Iceland, make sure the land is always on our right. I mentioned this to Dan, who assured me he'd keep reminding me if I showed signs of forgetting.

Fifteen kilometres into the bay, I made my judgment call – a stupid one, I realised later – which was to try to gut it out, and cut straight across to the village of Kópasker. Dan was lame with fatigue at this stage and I was feeling a little tired myself, but I believed I could get us across. It was touch and go, however. I was fairly strong until the end, but, if the wind had continued building up at the rate of that last hour, we would not have made it.

It was, to be honest, an amazing feat so early on in the trip: an eight-hour, 40-kilometre paddle in weather that was anything but friendly. Dan was very emotional when we arrived, apologising for not having paddled enough. I felt great sympathy for him, but there was little I could say or do that would have been any use in the circumstances. Essentially he was learning the lesson I had been taught so painfully by my Madagascar trip: when you're out there, it's all or nothing. There is no Plan B. You can't check for the bullet after you've rolled in Russian roulette! You just have to keep going. What I was keen to do, however, was to get to dry land, stand him up, turn him around and show him where he had paddled from. That was the message I wanted to get home: he *could* do this!

Then it was on to the next step – survival. The temperature was a numbing -8 °C, and I was already cramping up. Ideally, the support crew should have been there, but for some reason they weren't, so the only other option was to beg for help from the locals. I made sure Dan was secure and headed for the harbour wall. There I found a friendly fisherman, who bundled us into his truck, turned the heater to max and took us to the village hostel, the existence of which was a pleasant surprise, seeing that Kópasker had only 148 inhabitants.

Kópasker, I discovered, subsists partly on fishing and partly on a unique tourist attraction, for which visitors flock there: seeing the results of the movement of the earth's tectonic plates. Iceland lies atop the Mid-Atlantic Ridge, the boundary of the Eurasian Plate and the North American Plate. Here the plates are pushed apart – the rate of movement is around two and a half centimetres each year – allowing volcanic material to reach the surface. Elsewhere in the world, people know about tectonic plates through maps and artists' illustrations. At Kópasker, it is different. The area forms the northern tip of the Icelandic volcanic line, which consists of more than 120 active volcanoes. The most famous – or notorious – of these is Eyjafjallajökull, whose emissions grounded air travel over Europe in 2010. All this I discovered that afternoon over a beer with our host, Bennie, after Dan and I had settled in at the hostel.

CHAPTER 4

TO THE ARCTIC CIRCLE

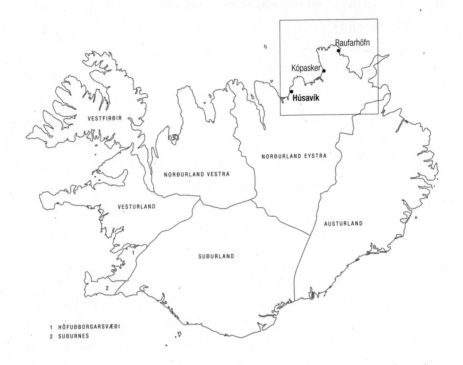

'It was a truly awesome moment when we glided across the line that wasn't there and officially became Arctic pilgrims rather than just temporary northern sojourners.'

O ur next destination didn't exist, except as a line on the map and a siren song in the ears of every explorer of the frozen north: the Arctic Circle. We did not actually need to cross the Arctic Circle, but as an adventurer it would be another notch on the butt of my revolver, so to speak. Before making a decision, I bounced it off Dan to see how he felt: this, I remarked, was the only chance he would ever have of crossing that invisible but famous line. It might be dodgy, but should we risk it? Although he did not know it, this was also part of the learning curve. He had by then had a strong taste of what a tough, risky business open-sea canoeing was, and his answer would indicate how he was shaping up.

Being a child of the warm and distant south, I hadn't known what the Arctic Circle was before getting interested in Iceland. Basically it is one of the five major circles of latitude that you see on maps of the earth. Not only is it purely a cartographer's marking, but it doesn't stay in place – exactly where it is at any given time depends on the Earth's axial tilt. Right now it is drifting northwards, according to Wikipedia, at the rate of 15 metres every year, for reasons we needn't go into here.

The reason the Arctic Circle is of interest (for rather ignorant adventurers like me, in any case) is that it is a psychologically important marking. North of it, you are officially in the Arctic, the storied 'Land of the Midnight Sun', where you have a 24-hour day and a 24-hour night, respectively, during the June and December solstices. South of it, you are only in what is known as the Northern Temperate Zone – not that the two look any different. So a few metres one way or the other would determine whether we were simply mucking about in the cold north or venturing into the dreaded Arctic itself.

For any adventurer, whether a veteran like me or a first-timer like Dan, this was, of course, an irresistible lure, and I was not surprised when he said yes. The night before we left Kópasker, we speculated about what the first question would be from our families and friends when they heard we had gone right up to the Arctic Circle, and decided that it would be something like, 'Did you paddle into the Arctic?'

Next morning, we shoved off from Kópasker beach with a small group of locals (well, it is only a small place) to see us off. One local paddler, Atti, joined us for the first few kilometres. He wasn't the most experienced kayaker I had ever seen: he had his paddle the wrong way round, and his dry suit had a big tear under the right arm. This was no minor matter: if he fell in, he would not only get wet and very, very cold, he would also drown, because the suit would fill up in seconds and he would go down like a stone. But Atti had that tough Icelandic spirit, the spirit that says, 'If our ancestors did this, then so can we. And maybe even better than them.' Far braver than me, I think!

The coastline was a lot more jagged and aggressive in its tussle with the sea than previously, although fortunately the swell was from the north, our bow side, which was distinctly better than a side-on swell. But I knew it wouldn't last: the northeasterly swell was curling around the massive peninsula on our right, and we were going to feel the consequences once we crossed the Arctic Circle ... it was going to be an interesting day, one way or another.

We took it easy, resting often so that Dan could paddle in bursts, without any pressure except to give of his best. We reached the top of the peninsula with ease, and I had no hesitation about deciding that we would head directly out to sea until we reached the point where my GPS – plotted with coordinates supplied by Bennie – showed the current position of the Arctic Circle. We worked our way nearer and nearer to the invisible line, and when we got to the last few metres I started counting down loudly for Dan's benefit.

'What are you going to tell people who ask if you've ever crossed the Arctic Circle?' I laughed.

'I'll tell them, "YES, YES, YES!"' he shouted exultantly.

It was a special moment when we glided across the line that wasn't there and officially became Arctic pilgrims rather than just temporary northern sojourners. *This journey is going to deliver way, way more than I could have dreamt*, I thought. *'Inspiration' isn't just going to be a word any more for people who have watched the Oprah show …*

Needless to say, this being the Arctic, the good times didn't last. Soon the wind was blasting us and the swell was hitting us constantly from the side, as I had foreseen; we were coming close to capsizing every 10 minutes or so. It seemed as though every natural force was against us, edging us towards the inhospitable coastline, with its rocks and pounding, icy surf. We were involved in a desperate struggle, which was especially hard for Dan, who had become so tired that he was falling backwards, his body dangerously close to the camera mounted in front of me.

This was bad news: if the camera fell off, it would be impossible for me to re-attach it in these conditions. I decided the most important thing was to keep things simple. I reminded Dan of the exercises we had done during the preparation, about how valuable it was to put the paddle in front of you and not at your side. Right now, this was what was needed, more than anything else.

The wind turned, so that the wind-swell was hitting us from the same direction on our left. The sea-swell, which is caused by the ocean's general movement, was coming from slightly behind us on the left. It made things difficult for us. Two or three times I came close to deciding that it was more dangerous to try to continue than to pack it in. Dan was lame with fatigue towards the final 10 kilometres, and I directed some harsh encouragement at him. This isn't in my character, so, when Dan reads this, I formally apologise; it was all done for the right reasons.

If I became as exhausted as Dan, I wouldn't be able to make good decisions when I guided the kayak through the rocks to the shore, and I wouldn't be able to put up the tents. I was frankly desperate, and Dan was furious because I kept telling him, shouting from pure fear: 'Please sit forward, Dan. Please just sit forward. I'll get us back. You don't have to paddle, just sit forward!'

We were moving at only three kilometres an hour, and because of the conditions I couldn't check our exact position. All I could hope for was that we were getting closer to our destination, Raufarhöfn. To make things even more desperate, the sun was beginning to set. If it went down while we still out at sea, I knew, that would be the end of the journey, and probably of us as well. I felt a sense of crushing responsibility settle over me that hit home every time I tried to think of ways to escape death. How would I be able to get Dan past the pounding surf, so that he might have a chance of survival? If I couldn't, the reality was that he would die. *Geez*, I kept thinking, *it wasn't meant to be like this.*

There was a lighter, though somewhat disgusting moment when a whale popped up when we were about three kilometres from the bay. The sea was so turbulent at this stage that all I managed to see was part of its back, and Dan some of the spray it threw up. What neither of us missed out on, however, was the stupendously bad smell when the whale either farted or burped. It didn't strike us as worth laughing about just then because we were tired and irritable, but later that night we saw the humour of it.

The sea was so rough that I miscalled three points around which the natural harbour lay. Maybe this was a good thing, because I used it to sharpen Dan's focus: *it's not far now*, I remember telling him, *it's not far, have faith in me.* Then Raufarhöfn's eight-metre rescue boat emerged from the harbour mouth.

Immediately I felt my dejected spirits perk up, so much so that I knew right away I was going to refuse my would-be rescuers' offer of assistance. We had come far on this day, in every sense of the word, and I believed we had learnt more in this one paddle than we had in the past nine months. So we went on, with the rescue boat pitching violently nearby and eventually deciding to return to port. The final three kilometres were covered in near-darkness. And then, finally – finally! – we landed gently inside the harbour on a small, snow-covered beach.

I felt for Dan. He was crying as we landed. I reassured him, telling him he had done something amazing. It was important to boost his morale in order for us to finish this trip together. I tried to shake the stress of the last 10 hours out of me. I sprinted up and down the beach like a madman … I told the camera that Dan had done well; he had paddled where no person in his situation had ever, ever dared to go. He needed to be proud of that. I don't know what Dan said to the cameras. But he was not happy with me. It was with this landing that I began to see a change in the crew. They all felt for Dan, and even Bradley took me aside to ask me to stop being hard on him. My dilemma was that, if I weren't tough with Dan, we would not make it. It seemed that no one but me understood the reality.

I was upset with myself and hurt that I had to be tough on Dan. All I wanted was for him to tell me honestly what was going on. Up to that point, he had communicated nothing to me. I needed honesty from him, and especially honesty that addressed the reason he had asked to come with me on the journey.

It was the wrong time of the year to see the aurora borealis, or 'northern lights'. But that night, around 22h00, while Bradley was hanging up washing and I was working inside writing my articles for Independent Online in South Africa, the sky lit up with an extraordinary light show. The aurora borealis occurs when nitrogen and oxygen gases clash with charged particles in the solar wind, and the resulting display is prominent in high latitudes because the magnetic field around the poles is weakest here. Green and orange indicates the presence of oxygen, while blue and purplish hues stand for nitrogen. Being colour-blind (as I am) didn't lessen the effect: I was mesmerised. I woke up everyone else and we stood in the freezing cold for nearly two hours: Darren and Richard came out to film, while Dan got dressed for the cold. Photography was difficult in the low light, but I was impressed with what Darren and Richard managed to capture. Dan came out to catch a glimpse, although he missed the most spectacular dancing of the clouds. I was glad I'd woken him up. I hoped it would remind him of the reason he was here in the first place. Magic is going to happen whether you like it or not.

Justin and his team had decided to ignore my request to train Tracey. He had booked flights for a new cameraman to replace her. The message about her replacement had somehow trickled through the grapevine before I could chat to her the next evening. I could see she had been crying, and eventually Bradley came to me to explain.

'Eish, what can I do? Justin says we won't have a doccie if she does Cam B.'

I was tired of carrying everything on my shoulders. We were only two weeks into the four-month journey. Bradley was going to have to help share this load. He didn't know what to do, so I went to Tracey and said to her that I didn't care what Justin had decided. She would shoot until the new cameraman arrived; I guaranteed her she would still have her job and could do what she wanted. I believed she was a hard worker and just needed some training, but Justin felt that training was still a risk. I think Tracey perked up and was energised by my commitment to her. How I was going to sort out what I promised, I didn't know. But I knew I'd stick to my promise.

Drama was following me, but I was about to start learning lessons the best way, the hard way.

Justin called me to say that Cooked in Africa had been unable to raise the funds to cover their expenses. Our agreement was that they could approach my partners, as well as other potential partners they found on their own. He said he didn't think they could carry on with the expedition unless they received money from somewhere. The problem here, though, was that he had contributed very little financially, compared with my outlay in getting everyone over to Iceland. I didn't need him threatening to pull out of the show or saying that he would have to inform my partners at Windhoek Lager. After all, I had committed to a documentary for Windhoek Lager. I recall Justin's words to me that early morning: 'It will be the honourable thing to do to let them know the documentary is not going to happen,' he said.

I could just see him sitting there in his office back home, glum and proud, with his coffee, milk and two sugars, warming his hands. Surely it would have been the honourable thing to do. Justin then added another issue: he said he was worried about how I was managing the crew's morale. I was astounded. Were the crew actually finding things to complain about? Did Justin not trust me enough to manage this? Justin said that I needed to learn to lead and to build morale. He suggested that taking the team out for a few beers would do wonders. It amazed me how little faith he had in me. I needed support, not instruction.

We went out for a few beers, played pool and got drunk.

Just writing this down brings back that jelly-like feeling in my legs. How could so many things come down on me like this? I was giving it everything I had – and more. But everyone was unhappy, and I was expected to fix it. Then, as I always do, I had a short, hard talk to myself. This was no time to feel sorry for myself. Make this journey happen – no matter what.

Ahead of us was the Langanes Peninsula, a craggy, needle-like finger of land that juts in a northeasterly direction into the Norwegian Sea. The peninsula is rimmed with cliffs that make landing impossible. The Icelandic newspaper *Morganblaðið* had said they would give us a cover picture once we had rounded this formidable challenge. We had proved nothing yet, they said. It was classic, but too true. Dan and I took this as a challenge. Cliffs, thousands of birds and spectacular scenery awaited us.

CHAPTER 5

LOOKING FOR A BREAKTHROUGH

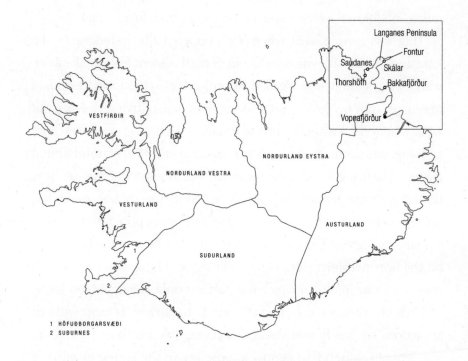

'The task itself hadn't changed. It would take
thousands of paddle strokes to get us to the
day's Point B, and we needed them now ...'

People sometimes try to convince you that you have enough experience to tackle a difficult project or venture, and sometimes your own mind attempts to do the same, but the fact is that, unless you are an insane optimist, you will always have a bit of doubt about whether you are really up to it. It might not overwhelm your self-confidence, but that small shadow will always be there when you have to take a minor decision purely on instinct or gut feeling. What I have been able to achieve is not due to mere physical prowess, but rather intellectual savvy – and, of course, a good dose of luck.

This was how it was when we pondered the rounding of the Langanes Peninsula, which sticks out of northeastern Iceland like a fist, with a long, skinny finger (called Fontur) pointing out to sea. I studied the maps until my head hurt and my eyes itched, trying to work out what was 'normal' when it came to Iceland's winds and swell direction.

Langanes (Long Peak) is an inhospitable and almost uninhabited place. Measuring 40 kilometres from southwest to northeast, it is dotted with the remains of abandoned settlements, some old and others relatively new. These days, almost its entire population lives in the small village of Thorshöfn, tucked into the base of the peninsula on the northwestern side. We're talking *small* here, since the entire regional municipality of which it is part has only about 480 residents.

Unlikely though this might sound, Langanes is not without attractions for hardy tourists. At Sauðanes, just north of Thorshöfn, is a very old church that is now a museum. In the spring months of May and June, guillemots and kittiwakes lay their eggs on the high cliffs, while bird-watchers roll up in considerable numbers because the peninsula is the world's third-largest nesting place for gannets.

But, in truth, Dan and I had more pressing things to think about. For 50 kilometres, according to Bradley (who was quoting the opinion of a local kayaker), there was simply no safe place to land anywhere along the peninsula. So I had to take an alternative approach, and work out a course of action that would pose no more than reasonable danger, as opposed to almost certain death. Just say we had to swim ashore. I was a good swimmer, and Dan told me he was, too. But being a good swimmer simply would not be enough if the breakers were smashing us onto a line of rocks.

I decided not to take the local expert's advice at face value, and insisted that we drive along the coastline and recce the peninsula for ourselves. It was no cakewalk, since snow and ice still lay thick in places, but we managed to struggle through right to the end. It was a spectacular but dismaying trip: endless stretches of ocean, thousands of birds and a parade of intimidating cliffs falling hundreds of metres into the sea.

We found a spot about 20 or so kilometres from our departure point, however, into which I believed I'd be able to navigate us safely. In essence, this meant that the 50 otherwise-unlandable kilometres could be divided into two manageable, and therefore safer, legs.

And this is what we did. We covered the 20-odd kilometres without a problem, came ashore and set up camp, although the wind was so strong by the time we were on dry land that it eventually began snapping our tent poles. We were thrown about so much that I reckoned it was almost inevitable that sooner or later Dan, with his mobility problems, would fall against a tent pole. And he wasn't the only one – although I had full mobility, I had to be ultra-careful not to fall over while wriggling into my tent.

With me inside the tent, there was almost no space to spare, what with all the food and cooking gear crammed into it as well. This was unavoidable. The tents had to be as small and light as possible; on a kayak, it is crucial to save on space and weight wherever you can. Even so, we already weighed over 250 kilograms at this point. Crazy! Theoretically, all that weight should have made us super-stable at sea, but unfortunately it didn't.

I gave up the unequal struggle after the third pole snapped, and we sought refuge with the crew, who had put up in Thorshöfn. Their temporary refuge was a guesthouse that offered a little more luxury than what they were rapidly becoming accustomed to. It also had free wi-fi internet access, which they considered the biggest bonus, I realised. The hostess, whose name was Fanney, made us welcome; I think she appreciated the company as much as the business, seeing that it was well outside the tourist season.

The weather did us no favours. Overnight the sea got up, and stayed that way. It was a frustrating business – by now, bad weather had cost us nearly two weeks. In the light of our recent experience I was more cautious than I had been, and not so ready to make snap judgment calls. I wanted perfect conditions, and, without thinking twice, I called off three attempts to leave after catching a glimpse of the murderous surf breaking onto our launch site. I had tackled some pretty bad surf in Madagascar, but here it left no room for debate. I was in new and untested territory, for sure, and I had to look before I took a potentially fatal leap.

The perfect conditions I longed for did not happen, and so we had to take what we could get. I can't say I was confident as we headed into the water, battling the harsh two-metre shore-break. Dan needed some help here, so the plan was that I would accompany him through the surf, then go back to grab the kayak and get it into the water, after which he would climb on.

I waded with him into the surf as it crashed down on the beach's small rocks and pebbles and then went into a carefully timed dive, literally shoving him forward in what must have looked like a very unkind way to the onlookers. But I knew, and so did he, that this rough handling saved him the loss of a front tooth or two. Once I had Dan through the major impact point, I swam him a few metres to calmer waters and then made my way back to the shore at my best speed.

The shore-break was becoming even more dangerous as I plunged into its clutches. I fought my way through it, acutely conscious of two things: I couldn't afford to waste a moment in getting back to Dan, and I couldn't risk damaging my dry suit. By this time I was operating on pure instinct, because I had never done anything like this before.

I was pretty far gone as I tried to run out of the sea and up the beach, my lungs and head burning from the chill of the icy water. I had a terrible feeling that control of the situation was slipping away from me, and that Dan would look shorewards and conclude that I wouldn't make it back to him any time soon while he drifted around beyond the line of surf. I grabbed the front of the heavily laden kayak with my frozen hands and started pulling it down to the water, but that was only the start: I still had to get the timing exactly right for launching it into the crunching surf. And if I got *that* right, there was still the matter of getting Dan on board.

And I was running out of time. Dan was already drifting parallel to shore and towards a deeper impact zone; I simply had to get to him before the surf did and tumbled him onto the rocky beach. Rational thought was beyond me as I fought my way through the surf, mounted the kayak and wrapped my frozen fingers around the shaft of the paddle. I was hyperventilating, forcing my stiffening muscles to do their job. I had to get to Dan – fast – and then, when I did, I would have to stabilise the kayak so that he could climb on.

In my weakened state it seemed an impossible task, but our practice back in South Africa paid off, and after only a couple of attempts Dan made it … and at last we were off. I remember thinking: *Where are the papers now? We should've made the front page for the launch alone!*

The conditions were superb as we set out. The high cliffs, which protected tens of thousand of nesting birds, shielded us from the wind and sea swells coming from the northeast, a common weather direction for this time of year. It meant, however, that we would be smack-bang in the middle of the turmoil halfway through our paddle. But I was on a high, and paddled with purpose; every minute we saved on the good-weather side would be a minute saved on the bad-weather side.

As always, I started the day by reminding Dan that there was no pressure on him, that all he had to do was concentrate on the main task I expected of him. I felt this was a good strategy: there would be no diffusion or waste of effort, and between us we would be able to get from Point A to Point B. The task itself hadn't changed. It would take thousands of paddle strokes to get us to the day's Point B, and we needed them now, in the good times, which would help us to survive when we hit the bad conditions later on. He always seemed to manage it for the first few minutes as we left the shore but from there I imagine he felt it was not as important.

But this required the right kind of paddling, with the paddle held to the front and not to the side. Dan was still struggling with this, starting out to the front but gradually inclining to the side. I knew it was something that we would simply have to correct, because we had a very long voyage ahead.

An Iceland Sea Rescue rubber duck had decided to join us for the trip around the peninsula, and dawdled comfortably behind and alongside us as we made the 14 kilometres to Fontur, the tip of the 'finger'. The view was majestic, with the sheer cliffs rising straight up out of the crystal-clear, green seas. Local people told us they had a seasonal concession to harvest seabird eggs from the nests on the cliffs, and sometimes gathered as many as 70 000. Getting hold of the eggs involves abseiling down the cliffs and nicking as many eggs as they could carry – a daunting occupation, except, perhaps, to the lion-hearted Icelanders.

As we neared Fontur, I spotted one of the camera crews waiting for us on the cliff top. They were so tiny in the distance that we were reminded once more about just how isolated we were. This inspired Dan to renew his efforts … strange how the sight of a TV camera can motivate you! I didn't care – motivation is motivation. And here I was treating him as an equal. It was not that he wasn't able to put the paddle in front of him; I was just providing the wrong encouragement. It seemed that the film crew was the cue. I had to be honest with Dan and tell him that this could not continue.

On top of the motivation issue, we still had to sort out this business about the paddling. Dan was a full member of the crew; on a two-man kayak traversing Iceland's forbidding waters, there is no room for a passenger, and that was the way he wanted it. He had begged to go on this trip because he was a man with a personal mission. That meant he would have to solve his problem. That was the reality.

And that reality hit us hard as we rounded Fontur's lighthouse. The sea was slamming into us from the front left, and the swell from our exact left; if ever we needed the best possible balance, it was at this moment. As if that was not bad enough, the Sea Rescue rubber duck came alongside and informed us that they would have to leave us for the time being, because their fuel was low and they couldn't risk running dry in such sea conditions. That meant we would be paddling alone into the teeth of the turbulent seas for another 12 kilometres before reaching our next landfall, a fishing village named Skálar, abandoned since 1946.

At this stage, I honestly didn't know if we could make Skálar; every minute brought a fresh struggle against the elements, and Dan was seriously fatigued – to the point where he had difficulty keeping his seat. I kept up my urgings, but I couldn't help asking myself if I was crazy to carry on. My request remained for the paddle to enter the water in front him. I knew he was able to do this.

For the next four hours, I didn't even look up properly as I slogged away, fighting not only the sea but the numbing cold. I kept stops to an absolute minimum because if we lost way the wind blew us backwards. It was a battle just to stay in the boat, never mind paddling with enough force to progress against our powerful enemies. I remember once checking my GPS and seeing we still had another five kilometres to go; we were averaging only about two and a half kilometres an hour and it just seemed like a bridge too far.

We were in extreme danger. If we crashed or capsized, we would be on our own. The Sea Rescue boat had gone and the camera crew would not be able to reach us; all we would have to look forward to were cliffs, rocks, thundering surf ... and death.

But we made it somehow, and I can honestly say that this was one of the times when I saved my own life – and Dan's as well. There was nearly a last-minute disaster as we approached Skálar's harbour, when a wave hit us, carried us along and eventually rolled us out onto the boulders that lined the shore. The crew was waiting for us, and Bradley came in like the champion I knew he was, sliding and skidding around on the wet rocks to help us retrieve the kayak while it was still in one piece.

'The water's actually not *that* cold,' Bradley teased us, but he got no reaction; I was just too tired to take the big guy for a swim. I felt gloomy as we settled down for the night. *I'm not as tough as I maybe thought I was,* I reflected. *After today I'm feeling useless. Will I be able to stay strong enough for another four months?*

Rounding the Langanes Peninsula left Dan and me with some special memories. Apart from our ordeal – there is no other word for it – we will not soon forget the frightening but wonderful scenery, the majestic flocks of birds, and the wild horses that still roam the middle section of the peninsula. It is all a photographer's dream, and lots of souvenir postcards feature the wild horses with their long manes flying in the wind, picturesque old farmhouses and the like. But the best memory, though, was the fact that we had taken on a huge challenge and won, without any help or support whatever.

Skálar was a ghost town, a collection of crumbling buildings with a weather-beaten red rescue hut. It had been founded early in the 20th century and was flourishing by the 1930s, but in the 1940s other villages captured the local fishing quotas and, inevitably, the labour force as well. I found the place fascinating. It reminded me of Kolmanskop, the abandoned diamond workings near Lüderitz in Namibia – albeit with the slight average temperature difference of about 50°C! I love history, and my journeys have taught me that, wherever I go, brave and charismatic men and woman have almost always preceded me.

Somewhere or other, I am sure, there are some stories about Skálar that deserve to be retold. Our previous night's host, Fanney's grandfather, for instance, actually hails from Skálar. It would have been great to spend more time with that family and hear their stories. One thing is sure: today's Icelanders have inherited the adventurous spirit of the pioneers who first settled this remote place. And, thanks to this ancestral gift, they thrive in conditions that would daunt many other people.

Impossible paddling weather gave the team enforced time off, and the opportunity to visit one of Iceland's major waterfalls, Goðafoss, in the Mývatn district. Fed by the Skjálfandafljót River, it is not all that high by African standards – about 12 metres – but it has a spectacular horseshoe shape, and it has a good story attached to it.

In the year 999 or 1 000, a prominent Icelander, Lawspeaker Þorgeir Ljósvetningagoði, converted to Christianity. Among other things, a lawspeaker had to know the laws by heart, act as a judge, put into suitable language the laws that had been passed, see to their proper administration and safeguard the people's civil rights. Ljósvetningagoði was clearly not a man who did things by halves, because, when he declared Christianity the official religion of Iceland, he threw all the statues of the Norse gods into the waterfall; hence its name, which means 'waterfall of the gods'. This being out of season, the crew saw Goðafoss as few tourists see it. Richard took some pictures that left us breathless.

Eventually, the sea conditions calmed to the extent that we could make our second attempt to launch, and I held thumbs that the surf at Skálar would have diminished enough in the meantime. It had, although 'diminished' was strictly a relative term as far as Skálar was concerned. The weather was still bad, and, even though the surf was smaller, it was still high enough for Dan and me to run the risk of being smashed onto the rocks.

Dan was now back on the learning curve. It was as steep as ever, but I left him to it. I know the crew thought I was being unfair; for a man with his condition, even small physical acts – right down to preparing a meal or making his bed – were a problem. It wasn't an easy decision, but I knew it was what Dan had signed up for: the responsibility of looking after himself, come what may, to prove to himself and the world that a physical disability like his needn't mean that a man couldn't stand on his own two feet, It was going to be tough, since he was going to battle with even minor tasks like carrying the paddles down to the beach, but he had asked for that responsibility and there was only one way for him to win his spurs; helping him with everything would not do him any favours.

People talk endlessly about 'breakthrough moments'. I needed one of those moments with Dan soon. He didn't have to do anything but put the paddle in front of him. I have to be honest and say that

I didn't have the energy to keep repeating the words 'put the paddle in front of you' every time we got into the water. I don't know who would.

Being so tough on Dan depressed me. I knew that, besides the two of us, only his family would understand. The burden of misunderstanding, and the guilt of stepping back and letting him struggle through every day, really weighed me down. But there was no alternative for either of us. Back at Thorshöfn, he and I had had a solitary, very sincere and gentle chat about what lay ahead. I had explained what I was about, and why it was now time to rise to the challenge. I had asked Dan if he fundamentally and sincerely believed he was privileged to have this opportunity, to which he had answered an emphatic 'Yes'.

That was good. I believed he needed to see himself as special and, regardless of the circumstances, still privileged. I told him about the time I had spent with brutalised, raped and maimed innocents in Liberia and Sierra Leone. I dredged up terrible memories that I found difficult to share with anyone, memories of people who had never had any opportunity in their lives, who did not have Dan's education and never would, and who had not undergone the operations and gruelling physiotherapy he hated so much. Dan agreed with me that he needed to show the world how privileged he has been and, above all, how grateful he is.

I was moved by his commitment. Though I have never had a real family, with the love or support so many people take for granted, I've always felt that there were people who were much worse off than me, and that I needed to over-perform to show gratitude for my few gifts. It was a breakthrough moment, and it was great to see Dan so passionate, emotional and sincere about these same feelings. He really is such a good guy.

It all came down to one question: in this cruel world we live in, who deserves a reward for doing nothing? The answer is simple. Nobody. That was why I had hung a sign on my bike during my African trip saying 'NO FOOD FOR LAZY MAN'. I had lived by this motto my entire life (and still do), and for the next few months it would be Dan's as well. Would he be able to manage it? I didn't know, and neither did he. We were venturing into uncharted waters in every sense. That's what separates the adventurers from the armchair explorers.

Now we made our last preparations on the beach at Skálar. I swam Dan out as before and returned as quickly as possible to haul the kayak into the water and pick him up. My carefully calculated gamble paid off, and before long we were away on our next leg, another huge 40-kilometre paddle, across Bakkaflói Bay. Fortunately for us, the weather was good by Icelandic standards, with a low-lying, chilly mist during most of the day, which was much better than it might have been. I was well rested, and put every ounce of energy into my paddling. I didn't hassle Dan about paddling: I wanted him to concentrate on the safety aspect, specifically the old problem of keeping his paddle in front of him, and I made sure to compliment and encourage him. He was still struggling to learn all the safety tricks, and I wondered if I was failing to get the message across. It was all second nature to me – thanks to the Madagascar trip – but not to him.

The weather kept smiling on us, more or less, throughout that long, tiring venture across the big bay, gliding past some stunning scenery and being jerked back to less pleasant things by the sight of an abandoned radar station on the mountainside. The installation had once been able to scan the entire Norwegian Sea, poised to give early warning of any approaching Soviet ships. How the world has changed since the end of the Cold War! It was a grim reminder of where we had been just two decades earlier.

Late that afternoon, with the wind beginning to rise, we ducked into a rocky cove just east of the fishing village of Bakkafjörður, which nestles on the eastern shore of a small fjord leading out of Bakkaflói Bay. Bakkafjörður is small – at the time of our visit the permanent population numbered just 72 – but it is the regional service centre for the Skeggjastaðahreppur district in the Norðurland Eystra region. The village's wooden church, built in 1845 by Hóseas Árnason, is the oldest in eastern Iceland.

Leaving the beach required a short climb up a steep, rocky incline, and here I became fully aware of just how much frustration at his unresponsive muscles had built up in Dan. I helped him out of the kayak and up the slope. Dan had not yet developed an instinctive knack for taking in his surroundings, and as a result he was not giving enough attention to the ground and where to put his feet, and I found myself continually reminding him, every time we slipped and he nearly smashed his head open, that he wasn't doing what he himself had said he should be doing. After about the twentieth reminder, Dan blew up.

'Fuck you, man. Can't you just shut up for a change?'

I called Bradley and asked him to take over the job of helping Dan up the slope. I continued on my own, deeply hurt. Everything I had done, and was doing, was for his safety, without insulting him by pitying him and making allowances for him; I deserved more than disrespect, even though I had been pushing him hard.

Our next stage would take us around a bulge called Urdir into the next bay, Vopnafjörður. At this stage, the weather closed in again and the crew secured some wonderful little cottages in Vopnafjörður Bay so that we could sit it out. I decided to spend the time usefully, getting Dan to overcome one of his weaknesses: his failure to hold the paddle in front of him.

For this purpose, I enlisted the help of Zahir, whose maturity and relaxed demeanour I had come to trust. Zahir agreed to do what I requested. He would speak to Dan, stressing the fact that my only aim was to contribute to our safety, namely, by proper handling of his paddle. I was worried that Dan might start thinking I was simply harassing him, making him feel like the victim, instead of just getting him to focus on what was needed. Then Zahir would get Dan into the boat to handle it on his own.

Zahir wasted no time. That same afternoon, he had Dan afloat in the calm waters of the bay. I stayed away on purpose so that Dan could feel empowered. It was a good idea in principle, but then things nearly turned ugly once he was on the water. From my cottage window, I could see from the wind pattern on the surface of the water that there could be a problem if Dan got pulled out too far, so I abandoned my stance of 'no involvement' and ran down to the beach.

Sure enough, Dan was being pulled out into the bay by the force of the river running into it, because he had remained in this current instead of heading for the shore immediately on entering the bay. I knew this was my fault; I should have supervised the launch instead of stupidly leaving the risk to someone else, when the responsibility was all mine.

Zahir was making a staunch effort, wading deep into the water to relay shouted instructions to Dan, who was now almost unable to steer the kayak in any direction and was heading out towards the open sea. Zahir was encountering his own difficulties, because the extremely cold water was pouring into his waders. I did a rapid review of the situation and concluded that the only thing to do was to get Bradley to call the Sea Rescue people, who were on standby at Vopnafjörður village.

Fortunately, the wind that was adding to the river flow now

subsided, and I screamed to Dan to stop fighting the current and instead to head towards the shore at right angles to the flow. At the least, it would mean that, even if he had to run some way down the coast, he would not be in danger from the rocks that littered the next 30 kilometres of shoreline. We had only a few hundred metres of rocky beach left to get Dan to shore. Dan had to paddle hard.

Our luck was in, and Dan made it to the last stretch of beach available. He was tired and a bit rattled, but I reckoned he needed to build on the adrenaline he had pumping through his body. So, instead of calling it a day, I encouraged him to keep paddling along the shore as far as he could. He did, and did amazingly well, even happily fighting his way through a short stretch of white water. I was encouraged beyond words. Zahir, Dan and the crew seemed to come together with me. We were in this together, and together we would overcome.

The next leg consisted of travelling along the coast from Bakkafjörður to Svartanes Point, then turning southwards to hug the land to our next destination, Strandhöfn, near the entrance to Vopnafjörður Bay. The weather and sea conditions fitted in with my frame of mind as we set out. I didn't plan a long day's paddle, and the sea was as flat as a pancake as we crept up towards Svartanes and its landmark lighthouse, although the wind and chop hit us as we began heading down the eastern part of the bulge.

In the meantime, Bradley and the crew were on the road, scouting out potential landing places where they would be able to get to us at the end of the day's journey. The map indicated that the farmhouses dotted here and there seemed to present the best opportunities for landing.

We suffered with balance again. In fact, it was non-stop imbalance from the word go. It seemed that Dan refused, no matter what tone I used, to do as I asked. I guess I had accepted having him in the seat in front of me, and I had to accept the responsibility of him being stubborn. I probably would have been even more stubborn with myself if it came down to it. Dan obviously had an idea of how he would paddle around Iceland, and blatantly refusing to make small changes seemed now to have become part of his plan. I was running out of solutions.

After a while, we arrived at Strandhöfn. For me, this was an extra-special landing spot, not only because it was a stunningly beautiful natural rock harbour but because of its associations with both the distant and recent past. In ancient times, fishermen had launched and landed their boats here. Bradley told me that, when he had visited the nearest farm to ask for permission to cross it to the launch site, the owners had told him that, 34 years earlier, the first people ever to kayak around Iceland – two crazy bearded young men, as they described them – had landed right where we had come ashore!

On our way back, we stopped over at the farmhouse and had some coffee and cake, and I asked if I could see the guest book that these guys – Geoff Hunter and Nigel Foster – had signed. The owners produced it, and Dan and I became a tiny part of Icelandic history by signing it as well. Our visit had stirred some nostalgic memories for the farmers, but to me it meant more than that; those kayakers had been part of their own journey, but now they were part of mine as well. And they must have been true hard-core adventurers: they did not have a fraction of the resources we had, and from very recent painful experience I knew just how tough the journey was, even for a well-equipped paddler.

I knew I would love to meet them and have their story included in our documentary, so I asked Richard to take a photo of their details and then asked Tracey to Google them so that we could get in touch.

Needless to say, I managed to have a good look around on shore. Vopnafjörður, like most of Iceland's coastal villages, is a small place – under 700 permanent inhabitants – but its typically energetic citizens make their living from things like fish processing, agriculture and tourism and other services. It has an airport from which scheduled flights leave on certain days, a bank, a clinic and two schools.

Its balmy climate – for Iceland, that is – two famous salmon rivers and natural attractions have brought all manner of foreign tourists to its rocky shores, among them celebrities like the Prince of Wales, former President George Bush, Sr, golfing legend Jack Nicklaus and Queen Paola of Belgium, not to mention a range of artists.

The village has been around a long time. The first settlers were Vikings in the late 9th century – Vopnafjörður means 'weapon fjord' or 'weapon bay' – who, being Vikings, spent some time fighting among themselves in the absence of anyone else to cross swords with. Naturally, the village has its own set of myths and legends. The main one has it that an ancient seafarer sailed into the bay and came across its guardian, an enormous dragon with a large entourage of lizards and insects, who drove all strangers away by breathing fire on them. The dragon became one of Iceland's four mythical *landvættir*, or guardian spirits, and is featured on the national coat of arms. The highlands around Vopnafjörður even helped Halldór Laxness to win a Nobel Prize for Literature in 1955, by providing the setting for his novel *Independent People*. Not bad for a small village whose entire population would fit into one suburban commuter train elsewhere, with plenty of room to spare.

I set off on our next leg in an optimistic frame of mind. Dan and I had sorted things out, and I believed he was going to do what he had set out to do: managing the hard yards, to show the world – and, more importantly, himself – what a man of determination could do, cerebral palsy or no cerebral palsy. I believed that the team would see now that my commitment to Dan was unwavering and my leadership necessary. He wouldn't disrespect me and he would get what he had asked me for when we left South Africa: the chance to change what he said to me was his poor self-image.

Did I think the crew would make it as a team? Yes, I did, even though by now almost every single one had expressed his or her dislike of one another to me. I had anticipated this. Did I believe the crew would see that my commitment to Dan was unwavering and my leadership necessary? Yes, again. Would the guys at Cooked in Africa stick to their original agreement and pay their own way without threatening me with withdrawal every chance they got? I sincerely believed they would. It only makes sense to do what you said you would, especially if the other party is delivering.

I was keen to get back on the water as soon as possible and paddle to our next stop, the island of Bjarnarey (Bear Island), which lies off the headland of Kollumuli between Vopnafjörður Bay and its neighbour, the long, shallow bay of Héraðsflói. This leg seemed quite manageable, since it was only 25 kilometres or so. How wrong I was about this! But of course I didn't know that, and so I kept a careful check on the weather, and made sure Bradley was in the loop. He was eager to understand more about why I made certain choices about timings, choices that sometimes seemed odd – in this case, getting up at 03h00 with the intention of being on the water by 05h00 or so to make an early start.

ABOVE: Originally, I was considering paddling around Greenland. This photo shows Vasti and I in Greenland, after an awesome paddle in Scorbesund. But Greenland wasn't to be; the next journey would be around Iceland with Dan Skinstad.

LEFT: For most South Africans, snow is a foreign concept. When we arrived at Keflavik, I was so excited at the sight of the white stuff that I just dived in – right outside the terminal!

THESE PAGES: The little town of Húsavík (above) was our base of operations as we prepared for departure. Spring comes late to northern Iceland, and the wintry conditions presented us with a major challenge. One of Húsavík's landmarks is its picturesque wooden church, shown here behind Dan and me (left). The entire team, including the film crew (top right), was on hand as Dan and I donned our dry suits and waded into the frigid waters off Reykjavik to test them (right).

ABOVE AND LEFT: Bradley had sourced excellent maps of the Icelandic coastline, but route planning and locating potential landing spots was often a matter of trial and error. Plans have a way of changing once you get on the water and have to face the treacherous Icelandic weather. Our two double kayaks, both named *Inspiration*, were built in Cape Town by Johan Loots and his team.

RIGHT: Our time in Húsavík allowed us to practise getting the kayak in and out of the water, something that proved to be a challenge throughout the journey. The black sand consists of tiny particles of volcanic material. The local Sea Rescue crew was on hand as we prepared to leave Húsavík.

And then we were off! But the first few
paddles showed how much work was
needed before Dan and I could really make
progress. The film crew could not follow us
on the water, so the kayak-mounted video
cameras were invaluable. Once we were out
at sea, we were just that – all on our own.

ABOVE: Rounding the Tjornes Peninsula (above), soon after leaving Húsavík.

LEFT: Dan and I had many chats about the kind of commitment I wanted from him.

RIGHT: By the time we reached Raufarhöfn, reality had set in for me. Things were going to have to change.

TOP RIGHT: Each day it took me an hour to pack all our gear into the kayak.

Not much can prepare you for the awesome spectacle of the aurora borealis, better known as the 'northern lights'. It was a rare privilege to see this cosmic light show, and Richard managed to capture some amazing shots.

THESE PAGES: As we made our way round the Langanes Peninsula, we faced challenges both physical and psychological. Dan's disability meant that each launching and landing had to be negotiated with extreme care. Throw in the metres-high surf and strong winds and you've got a recipe for disaster.

THESE PAGES: The relatively low freeboard of the kayak should have added to our stability. However, Dan's tendency to paddle to the side instead of leaning forward meant we often ran the risk of capsizing (above). Sometimes, there was no helping it, and over we went! It was a great source of frustration for both of us. For Dan, getting ashore on smooth, slippery rocks was a major challenge (left).

ABOVE: When bad weather made paddling impossible, we paid a visit to the mighty Goðafoss waterfall. The name means 'waterfall of the gods', and the site has a special significance in Icelandic history.

LEFT: At Skalár, Dan and I visited an abandoned settlement, one of many in this part of eastern Iceland. The harsh climate makes farming difficult on the island, and, over the years, many of its people have left the land to move to the towns or overseas.

CHAPTER 6

DAN OVERBOARD!

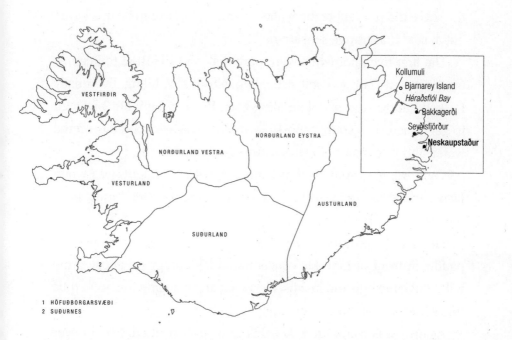

'I told myself to stay calm. Nothing would come from panic. This is when the reality hit me, smashed me between the eyes: "You will never find him."'

O ur early start wasn't a pleasant experience. It was very cold (surprise, surprise) and getting ready to venture out – dressing, feeding, packing – seemed to take a long time. But eventually we were ready and we slid through the floating kelp towards the open sea. As soon as we were away from the shelter of the shoreside rocks, we found ourselves heading into a lapping chop, with the wind coming from dead ahead. This wasn't pleasant either; I remember this as one of those paddles where the view from the shore did not reflect the reality of what it felt like to be in a kayak out at sea … a strange sensation.

The first five kilometres were pure hell, and I battled to keep us on the water. Dan was still struggling with his paddling. Eventually I asked him to stop paddling altogether. It was rough, but I wanted to get us across as soon as possible and not waste a good day on the water, and it was part of Dan's learning curve.

Then came a moment that I can see, with hindsight, was when Dan decided to dig in his heels. He was going to rebel. I must have touched on a sore point.

He blankly refused to respond to any of my requests to put the paddle in front of him. He concentrated his energy on abusing me with foul language and insults. He swore at me, telling me numerous times that he was tired of me bullying him.

Again I was astounded, but this time also insulted. I had never disrespected Dan or personally abused him in any way. I was furious. I stopped paddling immediately. I took out my phone and called Bradley. We were turning around. I had never seen Dan this disrespectful. I couldn't believe this was the same kind, smiling and meek-mannered guy I thought I knew.

I didn't say a word as we got out of the boat. I just apologised to the team, who I knew would be frustrated at the wasted effort that had been put in. We would have to try again the next day. I would have a lot to think about that night.

I went straight to bed, while Dan, Bradley and the crew socialised for the rest of the day and into the night. I'm sure the day's events and my discussion with Dan came up once or twice.

It can't be that complicated, Riaan. Simplify it back to basics, take the emotion out of it, and get on with your job. It's that simple. My little voice was putting me to sleep with the best advice.

It was time for a one-on-one. I asked Dan if he was willing to hear honesty from me. I was nervous but relaxed – angst and calm all in one.

'Dan, do you think you try hard enough?' I started.

Dan kept quiet.

'Do you think you are showing the commitment that you and I have spoken about so many times?'

'I am trying!' was his reply. I knew, though, that Dan was not trying hard enough or we would not be having this tension. I reminded him again that I expected nothing physical from him; all I expected was that he make the effort of putting the paddle in front of him – something that I was asking on average 500 times a day.

'Has anyone ever pressurised you to perform, without excuses?' was what I wanted to know. It was important for me, because it could tell a lot about his reaction to tough love.

'Yip, many people.' he said. 'Bob especially, man. You have no idea how hard Bob has been on me. Sometimes brutal.' Although I believed his brother was hard on Dan, I was not sure that any of his circle of friends had ever had to be as honest as I was going to be with him.

'I know it's hard being disabled, Dan, but what I think you really need to address is your willingness to be lazy. Everything gets done for you. Everyone is too scared to treat you as an equal when it comes to responsibility. I'm sorry it sounds harsh, but, Dan, I believe you are lazy and that you are like that because you get away with it.'

Dan kept quiet for a while, and then told me he didn't want to speak any more.

I felt I had been brave to approach him on this level. It was tough, as I felt I had risked hurting his feelings. But two things were for sure: firstly, I was being honest, and, secondly, my advice could literally change his way of seeing his life.

The next day was ideal, weather-wise, and our second attempt, like the first, started well. But again the good times didn't last, and I had to make a huge effort in very dangerous winds to get us to Bjarnarey. Why is it called 'bear island'? Probably because polar bears had been seen there in the past. Bjarnarey has lots of vegetation and is richly fertilised by the many thousands of birds that nest there. From time to time, I had been told, it had been inhabited; as early as 1703, two families had eked out a living on the island, and local people had continued to come here to fish, collect eggs and catch birds until the late 20th century.

But right now the island's only 'inhabitant' was the unmanned lighthouse, which had been built in 1917 and renovated in 1946. I had the key to its accommodation hut in my pocket so that we could spend the night in relative comfort.

I was stuffed, both physically and emotionally, from the previous day's turn-around paddle. I wasn't keen on dealing with two people's mental weaknesses. But I had seen far tougher things in my life. I was going to make this work, no matter what.

The crew were taking some strain over Dan's and my issues 'on water'. It was unfair to them, so I had tried to make as much available to them as possible. Cooked in Africa were still not contributing financially, while my budget was under pressure. I told Bradley to make sure the crew were fed well and stayed in the most comfortable places I could afford. He agreed that this would help.

I remained almost wordless with Dan from the start of this paddle. The previous night, I had decided to work through this: less emotion, more going through the motions. I believed the best day, weather-wise, had also just arrived and would set the scene for reconciliation. I was hopeful.

But, on the contrary, Dan had now prepared himself. He had watched the previous day's footage with the crew and had also discussed the scenario with them. He felt he understood the reality of our situation. Dan started his conversation when the cameras had been turned off. He asked me whether I believed I was here to learn things from him, and also why all the focus of growth as an individual had to be on him. We were paddling well together that day, oddly enough.

Of course I should learn from him, he said. Not for a second did he acknowledge the fact that I had been only patient and supportive. I had never doubted him and had never given up on him. Instead, we were now discussing Riaan Manser's personal growth with Dan Skinstad around Iceland, instead of dealing with Dan's disrespect and inability to make us safer in dangerous seas. I had to explain that I was humble enough to want to learn something on this journey with him. His laziness and lack of respect were familiar by now. It was a crazy scenario, but Dan was a shrewd and thoughtful strategist. He was not going to be cornered.

It was unfair of him, but I kept quiet. I was not going to get into an argument. Instead, I tried to be positive. I made a huge effort in very dangerous winds to get us to the island. The crossing went better than most of our earlier paddles, but now, at the gulley between Bjarnarey and the Kollumuli headland, we could barely make two kilometres an hour. I aimed for a small inlet, with a boulder-laden beach, that I hoped would shelter us. The surf was small, and was breaking on golf-ball-sized rocks. First I helped Dan to safety, next secured the kayak, and then began searching for the hut that would give us shelter for the next few hours. We were tired and needed rest.

I moved Dan to a sheltered area out of the wind before I set off to investigate the island. The hut was next to the lighthouse, but I had problems with the door key, which was rusted into the lock. The door hadn't been opened for nearly nine months, and I almost snapped the key into the lock as I tried to turn it. My back was cramping and my body shivering in the -2 °C chill. I tried a few tricks, but it took me an hour to get the door open. Then I ran the few hundred metres over uneven, moss-covered lava fields, dodging panicked puffins, to get back to Dan and begin the job of getting him safely to the hut. I had to help him up a slope, but felt he could move himself slowly across the uneven terrain if he was careful. I know others would not have left him to do it alone. I ran back to the kayak and began unloading our clothing and food so I could get us warm and fed. Dan slowly made his way over the rocks, while I carried the bags alongside him. It was an adventure of its own to get to the hut.

Once inside, I made us coffee and soup. Then I made sure Dan had a dry change of clothes and helped him get comfy in one of the bunk beds.

We slept for four hours and awoke with the idea of crossing Héraðsflói Bay, whose broad expanse was lined with a beach of black sand. This was not to be, though, as a headwind had picked up. The only option was now to tuck inside the northwesterly corner of this grand bay. I believed the landing would be safe, as the swell was not too big.

The black beach landscape was surreal. The beaches of Héraðsflói were formed from deposits of lava debris carried by the numerous glacial rivers. These silt deposits have created a huge delta of shallow streams and marshland. In fact, the bay itself is becoming smaller each year due to the constant deposition of lava debris. The crew had driven ahead to the eastern corner of the bay, where they came across what they thought was a beached humpback whale. Apparently whale strandings are common in the bay because of the inflow of debris.

Two days of rest, including getting caught up on the never-ending admin, settled me tremendously. Dan and I were not speaking that much, unless the matter was crucial. I wanted this to change, and when I had the first opportunity to speak to Dan alone I used it to have another heart to heart. I wanted him to tell me how he felt, and I hoped to get across to him what I was feeling. I also sensed that the crew were antagonistic towards me because of my perceived impatience. I hoped Dan would notice this and, off his own bat, nip it in the bud. It could get very dangerous for us as a team if the crew sided with one or the other of us.

Dan explained to me that he was happy but wanted more encouragement. I asked him not to lose focus on what needed to be done. I could see he was sulky, and I didn't want him to feel sorry for himself instead of acting brave and taking responsibility for his failings. We also agreed that he would address the crew, that night at dinner, to explain that I wasn't being unfairly harsh on him and that he wanted to be given a chance to do things on his own. Dan agreed with me that this would be far better coming from him. Unfortunately, at dinner the vibe from the crew was too jovial for a serious chat like this. I suggested we try another time, but I shouldn't have backed out. We needed to clear the air.

The following morning was special for me in that, for the first time, I really let go of the negative emotions I had inside me. The winding drive over a snow-laden mountain pass was exhilarating. Bradley had some music on his iPod that I had listened to while on my Africa circumnavigation. It was by Hillsong Church in London. The songs have deep meaning and are, above all, about humility. I sat in the front passenger seat and cried while this profound feeling of relief came over me. One song that was playing, 'This is for You', speaks about a person doing everything they do for God. It reinforced the belief that *nothing* I have, talent-wise, have I earned. I'm undeserving. It reawakened that gratitude in me. I needed to allow Dan space to grow and space for me to forgive. It was difficult, as I sat there, to wipe away the tears without being seen by Bradley or Tracey. I really felt refreshed and, more so, at peace. Dan was handicapped and I wasn't; I had to remind myself of that. He needed all my support and all the love he could get. Reconciliation was within me and was in my hands.

I put my arm around Dan when we arrived at the launch site – he had got there before me – and told him I was eager to make this journey work and eager to see him succeed. 'Let's start afresh' was my commitment to him.

It was an exciting paddle across Héraðsflói Bay. I didn't know how strongly the rivers were flowing out to sea, and so, to play it safe, we headed parallel to the coast for the first 10 kilometres and took drift readings every two kilometres. This way I could estimate the direction in which it would be most effective to paddle. At one stage, we found ourselves paddling into a current running strongly at four kilometres per hour. I worried that we might encounter whirlpools created by the clashing of the tide and the river. The upside would be that, as we neared the easterly side of the bay, we could almost be assured of the current assisting us. Once we rounded Kogur lighthouse, the stunning fjord scenery offered glimpses of what we could expect later in the journey. The inlet of Borgarfjörður pierced the aggressively rising mountain to form a bay, which had low-level clouds hovering in it. The snowcapped peaks were so neat as to be almost cartoon-like. It had been a long day, but I had so much spirit in me that I sprinted the last five kilometres of the 40 kilometres we did that day. Dan was very tired, so I told him not to paddle those last few kilometres as I was feeling great. The boat was moving at 12 kilometres per hour at times, so I definitely was combining mental vigour with physical strength.

Bradley had found a shallow rocky inlet around Landsendi Point, five kilometres north of Bakkagerði. The crew were in high spirits, and had hung the Riaan Manser Adventure banner across a section of low cliffs. It really moved me to see that, and I felt appreciated, big time. Dan knew he hadn't put in a big effort, and even apologised to me at the end. I didn't care. I felt new and free of the stress we had built up over the last few weeks. I hoped the positive affirmation would help. I never, ever spoke about Dan failing on the water to anyone, or even to the cameras. I believed he noticed that, if I ever had reason to take something up with him, I would do it in private.

By now the ice was melting, and I can remember for the first time taking serious note of how much more of the land one could see. Bakkagerði was small, and its 100 or so inhabitants were mainly involved in fishing and a bit of tourism. The place was still sleepy because of the time of year. We stayed in some unfinished flats that were just left open for us, without any follow-up or supervision. It showed either incredible trust or, if you want to be negative, naivety on the part of the locals. Bradley had caused a stir in a previous town because he hadn't yet paid our accommodation bill. I was afraid that, with his schedule and movements and the landowners' lack of availability, we might build up a bad reputation in Iceland. We still had a long way to go and I wanted only good words to precede us.

Dan was very excited. He knew that his father and brother Andy were arriving the next day for a visit. In a way, I was jealous. Having a family to share your successes with must be amazing. That feeling of making someone proud – someone who loves you unconditionally – must be unparalleled. The high I was on, and Dan's eagerness to see his family, combined perfectly to make me believe we could take on the gale-force tailwinds expected the next day.

We had now covered 318 kilometres and were one seventh of the way around Iceland. But actually we had covered a lot more than that, since we were more or less following the very uneven coastline and being swept about by the ocean swell. Our big hope was that, with winter nearing its end, paddling conditions would improve. But painful experience had already taught us that Iceland's weather was not something you bet on.

It was just as well that our expectations weren't too high. Sure enough, the waves that had looked so deceptively small from the shore proved to be much larger and more difficult to handle. But the wind behaved itself, and Dan and I were working well, so we made good progress. After about three hours, we had pretty much covered the allotted distance, and when we came abreast of the team I called to Bradley: 'Watch us closely, we're moving our arses, baby!'

We were making such good time that I decided now to push on around the Glettingsnes headland for another 24 kilometres or so to Seyðisfjörður, at the head of a fjord also called Seyðisfjörður. Like most human habitations in Iceland, it had ancient roots, although the present town, with its 660 or so citizens, is quite young by Icelandic standards: it was settled and built by Norwegian fishermen only in 1848, but traces of earlier settlement go back to the 9th century.

Isolated and thinly populated though it is, the area has had its moments. From 1864 to 1866 the world's first industrial whaling station operated near the town. The first telegraph cable between Iceland and Europe reached Seyðisfjörður in 1906, and for half a century it was an important part of the world's telecommunications network. During the Second World War, there was an Allied air base here, traces of which remain to this day, among them the old landing strip and a tanker that was bombed and sunk in the fjord, where it is still visited by wreck-divers. When the local fish-processing plant closed down, Seyðisfjörður reinvented itself as a tourist destination, although it remained a well-equipped fishing port.

As we paddled towards Seyðisfjörður, the team left us to get on with it and headed inland to Akureyri airport to meet Dan's father and brother Andy, who had tackled the long haul from Cape Town to visit their family adventurer. Having dropped them off at a guesthouse in Bakkagerði, Bradley returned to the team's main job of supporting the paddlers.

Bradley's plan was to go to the tiny settlement of Húsavík (not the same place as our starting point), which he calculated we should be nearing … except that we weren't. Unbeknown to Bradley and the rest of the team – not to mention the newly arrived Skinstad family members – what we were actually doing was trying to work our way through the worst crisis we had encountered so far.

We had made a cold and windy start. The wind was slightly side-on from our left, but I calculated it would swing to our backs 15 kilometres into the day. We had to be tough and determined for the first two hours, and then we would reap what I believed would be a huge reward: a very strong tailwind and accompanying swell.

Man alive, it was tough going. I was in a determined mood and remember telling Dan that we had our work cut out for us. It was another 40-kilometre day, this time in dangerous seas. We would be skirting the most isolated and the most dangerous coastline we had been pitted against to date. I knew we were in for adventure after the first few kilometres. The mist was so thick that I could not see land for long periods. I navigated mainly by using the swell direction and the sound of the waves crashing into the cliffs to our right.

All good maps of Iceland maps show the locations of rescue huts for shipwrecked sailors. These huts are dotted along the coast. Never had I taken such note of them mentally as I did on this day's journey. Usually I photocopy and memorise the day's planned coastline, with as much detail to support it as possible. This information provides what I believe is the crux of saving your life in time of need: 'options'. I knew the positions of all the little coves where rescue huts were situated, as well as how the weather factored into the geography. Not one of the crew, and neither Bradley nor Dan, understood the risk we were taking today. Not that I expected them to, but there definitely is something to be said for sharing the load and responsibility. If anything went wrong, no one, but no one, would be able to save us. All the factors needed for drama were here: thick mist, freezing temperatures and gale-force winds. Never mind that we were in a five-metre kayak and that Dan has cerebral palsy. Adventure doesn't come any purer. Dan, I think, was now mixing his determination, his bravery, with the ingredient I have often relied on the most: naivety.

I still needed Dan to listen to me when it came to putting the paddle in front of him, and not at his side. This created 99% of our balance issues. I was a strong paddler and could take the physical responsibility, but the never-ending wobbling in rough seas gnawed away at me physically and mentally, hour after hour after hour.

Again, I started out gently in the way I asked Dan to put the paddle in front of him, but after a few hundred requests it was wearing away at my positivity again. Even though the conditions were stressful, I knew my resolve had to endure.

The sea had now become so rough, with the wind gusting at 70 kilometres per hour from the north, that turning back was impossible. As we neared the Glettingsnes lighthouse, though, I did mull over the idea a few times. Turning in a southerly direction, I thought that our going would get significantly easier. It didn't. Our average speed had increased to over 12 kilometres per hour, but Dan with his paddle at his side threw us off balance numerous times. I countered as best I could, but eventually, while we were surfing a big wave for a hundred metres or so, we capsized.

It was a furious impact, as we were going at quite a speed. In such conditions, the frigid water rocks your senses, almost freezing your hands and brain. I grabbed the boat firmly, and then lunged forward with my right hand to get a grip on Dan, who was trying to right himself in his air-filled dry suit. The nose of the boat was drifting more quickly than the tail, putting us in a favourable parallel position to the wind and swell. I reminded Dan not to let go of the boat, no matter what. We had practised this drill many times. We both needed to get back on, and first needed to round the respective front and rear points. I moved quickly around my side with the goal of stabilising the boat for Dan to get in. We were both getting cold at this stage. Dan was moving slowly, but doing well. By the time I had hauled myself onto the kayak and was seated, he had made it to the nose, and was about to turn around it onto the windward side. I reminded Dan again not to let go of the boat. I didn't mind how long he took. Just never let go of the boat. Never. It was his security and his safety. Without the boat, we would drift aimlessly and die.

'Take your time. Just don't let go of the boat,' I shouted into the wind.

Dan's eyes were wide with what I presume to be many emotions: fear, anxiety and panic. Never mind the -2 °C temperature. I was feeling the same. He now had to do what was probably the most difficult part of getting into his seat: rounding the nose of the boat in these choppy conditions. He negotiated this precarious position in one movement, and reached the windward side of the kayak. All he needed now was to move slowly along this side to his seat, a maximum of two metres. The wind still gusting strongly from his back.

I started with 'Remember to hold ...', but couldn't finish my sentence.

Dan let go of the boat.

It was unbelievable. He drifted away so quickly. One metre became five, and then five metres became 20. I went into panic mode immediately, and acted with instinct and aggressive determination. The situation demanded it. Every second meant more distance between us.

To the average person, the simple solution would be this: paddle the boat to Dan and pick him up. It was not that simple, though. I had to get the kayak paddle ready and keep myself stable in the harsh winds. Dan's paddle was on its leash and trapped under the kayak. It would very difficult to get it out of the water and to secure it somewhere on the boat. I had to solve this before any thought of paddling could begin – while not losing sight of Dan.

'You'll be OK. Stay calm. I *will* come get you,' I shouted loudly to reassure him. I was screaming because it seemed so noisy around us. It probably wasn't. My heart was beating furiously.

Once I had my legs in the cockpit, I realised just what was in store for me. The nose of the kayak was pointing upward. With my weight pushing down the rear, it meant that the nose was above the waterline, catching the wind like a sail. Dan had now moved even further away from me. I knew the worst thing that could happen was for me to lose sight of him.

Dan was about 50 metres to my diagonal left; there were high cliffs at my back and white seas ahead and all around. I stepped as hard as I could on the left rudder pedal, hoping to swing the kayak nose left and to face both the wind and Dan. I didn't believe it was a futile effort at the time, but I can remember thinking how the rudder was too small to turn the kayak in those winds. I thought at one stage that the rudder cable was going to snap, because my left foot was applying so much force. But the kayak, even with this effort, managed to stay only perpendicular to the wind. I was not even making a slight left-hand turn. In Madagascar, I had used the original technique of kayak steering that Johan Loots had taught me, that of leaning the boat, or rather tilting it, with your hips. If you tilt to the left, you will turn right. And vice versa, of course. I attempted this, too. It didn't work.

'I'm coming to get you now. Stay calm. I'll get you now!' I screamed in Dan's direction, doing my best to keep him reassured. At this point, I did not feel confident about keeping this promise. I couldn't even turn the kayak in his direction, for goodness' sake! Having spent an interminable two minutes paddling away from Dan, I now realised the 50 metres had become 150 metres. I glanced back over my left shoulder now every five strokes to keep him in sight. It was non-negotiable in my mind: keep him in sight.

And then I lost sight of him.

That was when the pain I felt in my shoulders and back turned to pain in my stomach. *Keeping him in sight was all you had to do, Riaan. Nothing else. Fucken stupid idiot. You're an idiot. Fucken idiot,* I kept saying firmly to myself. I normally don't even curse. I couldn't help it then.

It was decision time. No matter what I tried, I couldn't turn the kayak into the wind. It was impossible. Not that I had tried it before on a double kayak, in such conditions. But I had an idea, a brain surge, to attempt something that made the smallest bit of sense to me then. If what I needed was to turn the kayak around, then I needed to make this priority number one. Forget everything else.

Turn right and go with the wind and sea, gain momentum, and as you surf one wave use that burst of speed to throw the nose as hard as possible into the oncoming wind. With the momentum so created, I believed that the weight of the boat – if one wanted to employ simple physics out here in the Norwegian Sea – would almost double the brute force it produced. Would this work?

I was now doing the unimaginable. Taking a hundred steps back (away from Dan) hopefully to take a few forward? I ran fast with the wind and the swell, all the time the voice in my head reminding me that if I capsized now I would be in even bigger trouble. I was scared. Still talking to myself and giving myself constant but harsh motivation, I did what I didn't think I could do: I turned the boat around. I think, in hindsight, that the wave I managed to ride down acted as a shield, holding off the wind just enough for the nose to swing to windward.

My hands were burning with cold, almost frozen in position. I had no time to put my mitts back on. I shortened my paddle stroke so the wind would not catch the paddle blades, and it also upped my rhythm. Geez, I was moving slowly. Amid the spray and mist I could see nothing but a grey expanse in front of me and the faint outline of the cliffs to my left, no more than a kilometre or so away.

I probably looked and sounded calm as I spoke to myself, asking what I was going to do now. I had no visuals of Dan, and no sound bearings from him either. I convinced myself that, taking our approximate capsize spot into consideration, I was generally moving into the right area.

Just stay focused and calm like you always do, I said to myself.

When I've been in difficult seas before, I've been fortunate enough always to get sight of something that would assist me in getting a bearing. In this case, I just wanted to spot Dan. I scanned from right to left in a 30- to 40-degree scope, so as not to rush my eyes over the sea and to remain balanced.

It felt like forever, each stroke and breath lasting an eternity. I told myself to stay calm. Nothing would come from panic. This is when the reality hit me, smashed me between the eyes: *You will never find him. You're trying to stay alive yourself. How do you think you'll help someone else?*

I continued, grimly, in the same vein: *Originally when Dan fell out, you could search for him in a 50-metre by 50-metre area. Just by the few turns and distances you have gone, you will be searching for him in an area of more than a square kilometre! You don't even know where you are, idiot!*

The only geographical reference I had at that moment was the spot where we had capsized, which I estimated to be one and a half kilometres from the cliffs. And that was a thumb-suck. It was crazy!

Do you know what you are going to be doing tonight? What are you going to say tonight? I knew I was going to have to tell Dan's family that I had lost him at sea and that he would not be coming home alive. I knew, without doubt, that this was the fact. I was so nauseous; I wanted to vomit my guts out as I began to absorb this reality.

Who are you going call, Riaan? Who will be the best person to break the news to? Not his mom, no ways. I could never. I don't know Andy that well, nor his dad. I'll have to call Bob. That was my logic at that moment. I was numb inside, my body on the exterior fighting with all it had just to keep crawling forward. I could not believe this day was happening. This could not be real.

Then, as bipolar as I think I can be at the best of times, my mind took another line of thought: *Riaan, you will paddle until you cannot any more; you will paddle until you find Dan or until you die. Bottom line: it's not over. You will keep paddling and looking.*

And I did just that for a little while longer, scanning the sea to the front right-hand side of me. Then, as if a light flashed, I noticed the yellow of Dan's dry suit about 400 metres away to my right. I caught the bright yellow in my peripheral view, and, even though at first I thought I had imagined it, I kept my eyes trained on the area. *Geezlike, it is him.* He came up again with one swell, and then again a few seconds later with another.

I shouted as loud as I could, but there was no way he could hear me.

I cannot tell you how the tears welled up in my eyes with relief. It wasn't a done deal yet, but I had 100% more hope/chance than I had had 15 seconds before. If I could just keep Dan in sight, we both might make it.

The challenge, besides the obvious ones of paddling and balancing in the wind, was to choose the right time to turn the kayak nose from parallel to perpendicular to the wind. Once I made that choice, I would not be able to head upwind again. I had no strength for that. Once I had paddled near enough to Dan, I would have to stop some 20 metres upwind of him, throw my legs out for stability, and hope that the drift and the wind would miraculously bring us together.

Dan was drifting in what looked like a comfortable position on his back. His dry suit had plenty of air inside and had created sufficient buoyancy for him. What I was surprised to see was that he had done what I think was the last thing he heard from me: he had lifted his hands out of the water. Dan didn't look too stressed. Hands in the air, lying on his back, he looked as though he were patiently waiting for me to pick him up.

I chose a spot to stop paddling, about 15 metres upwind. I threw my legs over the side and waited to see what would happen. If the nose of the kayak did not pass within 50 centimetres of Dan, he would never be able to reach it. We needed luck. And we got it, too. The kayak drifted straight into Dan, hitting him hard in the chest and startling him somewhat.

'Hold on, hold on hold on!!!' I was shouting.

This time he did. He pulled himself to the windward side of the boat, and I leaned forward to grip the back of his life jacket. I summoned the last drop of adrenaline I had in my body and pulled him in. He lunged and made it back to where I wanted him – safe and sound.

If you think this is where I told Dan how proud I was of him, you are wrong. I screamed at him with all the strength I could muster. Something about him never, ever, ever doing that to me again. I was drained.

The biggest reality of this journey had just set in. Riaan Manser the fool knew nothing about doing. All Riaan Manser did was talk about how he had Dan's life on his shoulders. Things changed that day, though.

Eventually we came into a pocket of cellphone reception and I got hold of Bradley. By this time we had overshot our designated landing place by about a kilometre. On shore, this created another problem for Bradley, given the team's difficulties in just getting down to the beach. But our luck turned, and we finally made it ashore, very cold, very shaken, very alone … but very alive. That was what counted.

Bradley booked us in at a local guesthouse and set off to fetch the Skinstads. An hour and a half later, he returned with them. It was a good end to a near-disastrous day. I reckoned it was just the moment when Dan needed his family: now that we were safe on shore, the reality of what could have happened began to sink in. He said it very well himself when the team turned the camera on him: 'It's a very sobering and very frightening thought to think, you know, that they might have been here two minutes after I was gone, and it would have been an absolute catastrophe.'

We took a day off, partly to rest up after that misadventure and partly to give Dan some time with his father and brother, who would soon have to return to South Africa. I knew that, with the best will in the world, they would find it very hard to comprehend fully what it was like to be paddling a very small kayak on a very large ocean, and an extremely hostile one at that.

CHAPTER 7

END OF A FRIENDSHIP?

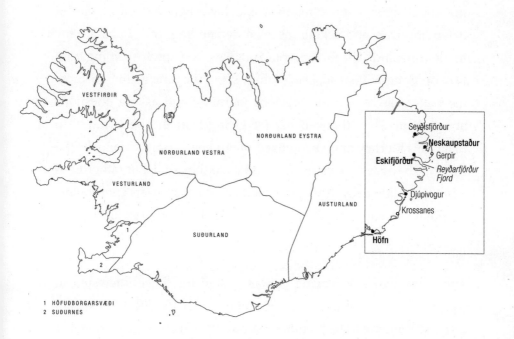

*'We didn't have a proper conversation from that
moment, the last being the morning I fired him.
The entire crew were by now avoiding me.'*

It was good to spend some time with Dr Skinstad and Andy, and
to have them experience first-hand – sort of – what their son and
brother was going through. From what I could see, they are a
loving and caring family, and humble to the core. I can imagine the
pressures of having one son with special needs and another who is a
world-famous sporting icon.

For me, what meant the most in those few days was the fact that neither Andy nor his father felt it was necessary to have a talk with me about what I think many would have believed inevitable: of defending Dan and asking, or even demanding, that I change my modus operandi. The picture could not have been pretty coming from Dan or the crew. Instead, Dan's family spent the time getting to know me better, discussing my previous journeys, and asking questions about them. They thanked me for giving Dan the opportunity to make this journey and encouraged me to keep going. Strangely, the support they gave me came not from what they said, but rather from what they didn't say. It would have been so easy, even appropriate, for them to lecture me. They didn't, and for that I'm grateful.

The lodge we were staying at was geared for those interested in Iceland's unique birdlife. I learnt plenty about the local birds from Izzi and Paul, the lodge's enthusiastic and super-intelligent caretaker duo. They shared many details of the spectacular annual migration of Arctic birds, and even showed me how to recognise the feathers of the eider duck. I'd always known eider down to be the Rolls-Royce of duvet fillings, but never knew what it looked like. One day when I can afford it, I will get myself a duvet filled with eider duck down!

Our Icelandic guide, Thor, had other ideas for me, though, and they didn't include keeping animals alive. Thor is a man's man, and I mean this in a nice way when I say that he loves the things men are presumed to love: drink, women and hunting. I will only criticise what I've tried or have experienced first-hand. Otherwise my opinion is just that – one person's view. Thor decided to take me fox hunting.

The story began when Thor and I were having a cold beer in a warm pub, waiting to watch the Seyðisfjörður ferry depart – quite a sight for those who time it right. We were minding our own business when one of the locals, who was reading the newspaper and drinking beer, shouted something in Icelandic at me. I went over to speak to him, and eventually, through Thor's translation, worked out that he had seen Dan and me on TV and wanted to wish us well. We chatted and laughed for a bit, and then I returned to my seat while Thor continued talking with the man. Twenty minutes later, as I headed towards our vehicle, Thor appeared with a gun bag slung over his shoulder. Beaming, he announced proudly: 'We have a gun to hunt with now! Tonight you will hunt your first fox!'

I wasn't sure how he had managed to borrow a gun, or whether it was all above board. But whenever any of us questioned Thor, he would just put one hand in the air and say 'This is how Iceland works'. Leave it to him, was the message. That was what I liked about Thor: he made things happen.

So there we were, hunched low, climbing over the hills, the sun setting slowly. We were hoping to catch a glimpse of a white fox, which Paul had told us was, along with the mink, one of the only huntable animals on the reserve. Thor even confirmed there was a formal bounty from the government of 3 000 krónur per tail!

I tried my best to act like a hunter should – tough, focused and determined – but we spotted nothing at all in those two hours of hunting. Afterwards, I asked myself honestly how I would have felt about shooting a fox. Firstly, I believed what I was told, namely, that foxes are in abundance and not endangered. Secondly, we kill many things for our benefit, and only a hypocrite would question my actions as any more cruel or barbaric than commercial meat farming.

The visiting Skinstads displayed a talent for shooting. We set up a few beer cans about 50 metres off the track leading into Seyðisfjörður, and some of us managed to hit a standing can a few times. Thor was furious that his shots missed, though, considering his Icelandic blood. To make things interesting, we decided to aim for the cans that had fallen over. Only the bottom circumference area was visible to us. I missed three times, while the Skinstads nonchalantly piled every one of their six shots through the bull's-eye. I'd definitely go on a hunting trip with them.

It was a relief to be leaving Seyðisfjörður. It seemed that the decision I had made regarding the conditions we would venture out in might come back to haunt us. I had enough money for a three-month expedition, four months if I cashed in some investments. I didn't want to do this to Vasti again, but it looked like everything we had would go into making this journey possible, although she didn't know this at the time. So, it was a relief to head out of Seyðisfjörður and resume our journey.

The sea was calm, and the promise of another 40 kilometres off the total was attractive. We aimed, with grand ambition I must admit, first to pass the milestone of Gerpir, Iceland's easternmost point, and then to find the best landing spot possible inside Reyðarfjörður Bay. I knew it was ambitious. If we were successful, we would have covered 55 kilometres. Our last paddle made this even more challenging.

Dan, I think, saw for himself how adventure keeps no schedule and never considers your plans. The swell was smallish in the morning, but by midday I noticed a dramatic increase in swell size. The first bale-out option I had in mind I wilfully ignored as we crossed the bay. I told Dan we would give it huge effort for another two hours, and then I'd make a call. The time for decision came sooner, though. Thick mist had again accompanied us most of the way. I didn't want a repeat of our capsize day, when the GPS battery was drained by the end. We needed to know roughly where we were in this mist.

We barely noticed we had rounded Iceland's easternmost point. I made a quick mention of it to Dan as Gerpir's majestic 300-metre-high cliffs loomed out of the mist to our right. Then it was concentration and effort time again. When I managed a quick peak up at them through the mist, all I could think of was Frodo Baggins and his friends hiking up steep mountains. I'm sure they are almost identical!

This day was another huge wake-up call. It was time to pull up our sleeves and prepare for a beating.

Bradley and the team had dealt with various administrative matters in Seyðisfjörður and then set off after us, and this time they kept a close eye on our progress. There were no mishaps, however, although there was very low-level cloud and lots of fog as we approached the landing place … or what we *thought* was the landing place. I tried to call Bradley, but there was no cellphone reception.

In the meantime, as I discovered later, the team was lagging behind us, because of a really bad road and almost impenetrable fog. All this was quite serious. Even if we were heading for the right place, we'd need help to get the kayak safely ashore, because there was now a heavy swell running. I tried the radio, and eventually got through to Richard, the photographer. He told me that he thought he had reached the right place, but he couldn't see us anywhere.

One capsize later, I started to worry. We'd been paddling around in circles for half an hour by now, trying to stay warm, and we were at risk of getting overtired. Then Richard came up with another scheme. He had tied an orange bag to the end of Zahir's mike boom; could we see it? We couldn't, but then Richard called back to say Zahir had spotted us; they were going to pull back a little to meet up with us.

All my thoughts were on the landing place, which was partly obscured by the fog. After failing to satisfy myself about what lay ahead, I called Richard: 'If we go straight from where we are now, is that a beach or is that a rock?'

'You have a surf-break and then a little bit of a beach-break as well,' he replied.

So far, so good. 'OK,' I asked, 'where do we land, right of Zahir or north of Zahir?'

'To your left, right of Zahir –'

'That's Zahir!' Dan exclaimed. 'I can see Zahir with the boom.'

Good enough. I told Dan that, if we capsized again, he was to hang on to the kayak and wait for the waves to pull him ashore. As for me … well, I'd have to let go and take my chances with the waves, because two of us hanging on might make the kayak too heavy. It wasn't a plan I fancied. But once again my options weren't exactly plentiful.

Thankfully it didn't come to that. We barrelled in through two-and-a-half-metre surf, made it safely to shore and staggered out of the water, tired and freezing cold after spending the better part of an hour trying to find our landing place. According to Bradley, part of the problem was the unexpectedly swift progress we'd made that day – so swift that we'd got ahead of the team.

But there was not much time to rest on our laurels. While the team went to visit the local Sea Rescue, I drove down the coast to look for another launch site. The wind was howling and the surf wild – and this was in a fjord, which was supposed to be quieter than the open shoreline. We were quite obviously not going to be able to get off from where we had come ashore, even though conditions were expected to improve next day.

I found a launch site about 45 minutes away, which meant another early start, because I wanted to be on the water at 07h00; I got an encouraging message from the team's scouts to say the sea there looked flat and calm. I was really excited. This was a day's paddle that we really could pull off. It would be a 60-kilometre paddle, to Djúpivogur, and we were going to do it a little differently: land halfway through, have a two-hour rest in a tent the team would set up ahead of time, and then do the rest.

The first stage went well, and we got a little shut-eye in the tent while Thor went ahead and found the final landing place. It worked like a charm. The short sleep in the tent left me feeling like a new man, as if I were starting the day's paddling. We got going, while on shore the team got the campsite ready at Djúpivogur and started making the food.

It was the most stunning scenery in which I've ever landed a kayak. The purples and blues and, later, intense pinks blended together seamlessly. There seemed to be almost no differentiation between the water, the snowcapped mountains and the sky. It was a fine reward after a long and tough day on the sea. Note to self: stick at it no matter what; the reward is *always* part of the deal. Hard work, in the right direction, delivers rewards.

Djúpivogur is another of those little Icelandic towns that have been around since the year dot. Its hardy inhabitants started trading and fishing there in 1589, and their descendants now also run a nice little tourist industry that makes good use of the area's natural and cultural assets.

The media had come out to interview Dan and me. It was good to see such interest in our efforts, particularly among the locals, and I was happy for Bradley to set up as much PR as possible. Our campsite had electricity, and was probably the best environment for us to test out the camping rigs we had spent so much money on. The site lay in the shadow of the pyramid-shaped Búlandstindur (1069 metres above sea level). We had heard a lot about this mountain, which is said to be a source of cosmic power.

Our arrival in Djúpivogur was not the only source of excitement for the locals. The country's entry into the Eurovision Song Contest, Sjonni's Friends, had made it to the final. This was obviously a proud day for Iceland, but all the more so because the band had surprised everyone by singing only in Icelandic. (Most Eurovision contestants sing in English to have broader appeal.) Bradley, Dan and I were swept up in the euphoria, and we seemed to meet hundreds of people – in a village with a population of 35 or so. A fact that someone shared with me that night was that Djúpivogur holds the distinction of being the hottest place in Iceland: the temperature has reached the mystical 30-degree mark here. It was difficult to believe, considering we were still waking up to sub-zero temperatures.

Icelanders love to party, and they party the whole night. I have a feeling that, in a place where daylight can last 24 hours, you cannot be expected to follow a clock when you're having fun. As a result, Bradley and I got only a few hours of sleep. We had a small paddle scheduled for that day – 20 kilometres on calm seas – and it wasn't easy. I had definitely learnt my lesson.

Our stay in Djúpivogur also brought a resurgence of the problem between Dan and me. I was lying down in Bradley's tent (I didn't have a place to sleep!), writing my next article for Independent Online back in South Africa. Zahir and Dan were standing at the food area alongside the tent, unaware that I was inside. They were discussing the footage the crew were busy downloading from the cameras. The footage showed me having stressful discussions with Dan.

'Geez, it's bad,' Dan began. 'You won't believe what it's like in real life with him on the water. He never fucken shuts up.'

'Naa, man, I can see and hear!' Zahir now replied. 'It must be tough, I mean that laugh of his would fuck me off. It's so irritating!'

They laughed and continued chatting about how difficult it was for Dan with me on the water.

It did hurt my feelings but I understood where it came from. I was an irritation to Dan, and I would not want to look at that footage either. I was disappointed that Zahir was saying things like that. My stupidity had led me to believe he understood that my approach, although flawed in some ways, was necessary.

I tried not to let this incident affect my mood, but it did. That morning, Bradley had also come to me to tell me that the crew were unhappy about camping in these conditions. I asked what he meant, and he said they were ice-cold and battling to get any sleep. Bradley said Richard in particular was struggling to stay warm. He warned me that I needed to do something before things fell apart. Ouch. I had been under the impression that Bradley was leading the group. I also thought that giving them the best gear would help their morale. I was wrong. Even when I brought it to Bradley's attention that I was sleeping in the open air, inside the wind flap of his tent, and that I had only my sleeping bag to protect me from the icy ground and wind, he said something to the effect that not everyone is as tough as me.

Something was wrong, and I didn't know what. I wanted a happy crew and I wanted them to see the goal as clearly as I did. I needed to try harder.

From Djúpivogur, our next paddle would be about 25 kilometres as the puffin flies, so to speak, to a spot called Krossanes. The team would range ahead to prepare a landing place. After that, we would head for Höfn, a little over 35 kilometres further down the coast. I suppose this was something of a milestone, because we would be travelling southwestwards, towards the lower tip of Iceland's land mass.

We got to Krossanes all right, but it was an unhappy start in the new direction. It was at this time that the simmering tension between Bradley and me broke into the open. Bradley and I had never had a boss-employee type of relationship. It had never been tested in an environment where there was no 'out'. All I could do was hope that Bradley would read between the lines. It was obvious that he was delivering Dan's version of events to all those around him. For me, the worst-case scenario would be to lose Bradley's support. I desperately needed for Bradley not to side with Dan and become anti-Riaan, as the whole team currently was.

But it happened. Bradley got into a sulk, and would suddenly have an issue if I asked about something or questioned anything. Obviously, this was not what I needed, considering what I had to deal with on the water for 10 hours a day. I needed support, and Bradley was the only person I could trust and rely upon. He was my only support.

I approached Bradley a few times to ask what the problem was, but got only the default answer that everyone uses to avoid conflict: 'Nothing, everything is fine.' This type of response makes you pause for a second and question yourself.

It turned out that Bradley was hugely upset with me for not allowing him to leave the expedition to attend his friend's wedding in Canada, an event which happened to coincide with our trip. We had spoken about it long before he even accepted the Iceland job.

Although it is unlike me to be difficult (just ask Vasti how easily I give in!), I felt I had made the right call by asking for his total commitment to the adventure. At the time, he agreed unwaveringly and said he would work it out. That wasn't the end of it, though. The week we arrived in Iceland, he had joked that he couldn't miss a wedding at which he was to be the best man. I remember responding firmly, but I was disappointed that he was emotionally blackmailing me at a time when I really needed his commitment to the expedition. Of course I knew the wedding was important and special to him, but I was disappointed in him for bringing it up when we had already agreed on the issue.

It was ominous, though, how angry I became with Bradley when he asked me again if he could go away for the wedding. We had just driven back from the launch site outside Höfn, after checking the sea conditions, and were parked at the T-junction in front of our farmhouse accommodation. Bradley's timing was bad. He decided to dig up what was a sensitive subject for me. I was in a very lonely place and was upset, and I shouted at him for putting me on the spot at that time. I cannot remember my exact words, but I told him that if he was not committed any more then he must get out. He was more of a hindrance to our objective than the leader I needed him to be.

We didn't have a proper conversation from that moment, the last being the morning I fired him. The entire crew were by now avoiding me. They would all squash around a little table and leave me sitting eating dinner on my own. Bradley also played up his resentment of me in front of the crew. He blatantly showed how he was able to ignore me, and essentially become part of the 'other' side. It's something most people are probably guilty of: it's easier to join the group and feel safe and have a sense of belonging.

I was sad, confused and angry. Sad because a friend of 25 years was siding with people whom he had met barely a month ago. Sad because he knew me, and knew what I was about. I was confused because I considered Bradley one of my real friends. I have never believed in the false world of a million acquaintances. Believe me, none of my acquaintances know what my real friends know about me. If I say I would die for my friends, I don't say it to impress. I really would offer my life up in exchange for theirs. Bradley is one of these friends.

That Wednesday night, I got the group together and suggested, because the sea conditions were so poor, that we film elsewhere. They had visited a glacial lake at the tip of the Hoffelsjökull glacial tongue, northwest of Höfn, and believed we could shoot some memorable iceberg footage. My spirit was outwardly upbeat, and I made sure we had direction as a team. If I showed weakness, it meant I was weak; nobody follows a weak leader. I was going to stay strong – inside!

The following morning was one I will probably never forget. We were close to departure, dressed and packed for our iceberg excursion, when I decided to check with Bradley if all was OK. He had uncharacteristically closed his door, so I had to knock before I could go in. He was sitting behind his desk, his laptop open in front of him and paperwork spread across the table. He didn't even turn his head towards me or ask what I needed. He just continued as if I weren't there. I had wanted to ask him to lunch after the excursion, so that we could talk things over. I didn't want to fight with him. I was hurting too much already.

But it's strange when I try to explain how my instinct kicked in at that instant. Before I was kicked again, while figuratively still on the ground, I was going to defend myself. I didn't deserve this treatment, and also couldn't handle it any longer. I needed support.

'Is this going to carry on much longer, Brad?'

'Carry on what?' was his reply, with a scoffing frown on his face.

'Brad, we can't go on like this any more. Something needs to change.'

Again, he pretended not to understand and denied anything was wrong.

'You are being childish now, and you know it. It's putting huge strain on me when I am already stressed beyond belief.'

'I don't like the way you speak to me. You treat me like a child.' He had decided to open up with me.

Well, I had no argument for him. I was his boss and he had been slack in his job. His work required intelligence above what is needed to operate a camera or do physical labour. It takes special mental and leadership toughness, not getting caught up in the emotions of the moment. Above all, it means staying focused. Of course I was going to be straight with him. We weren't on a holiday, an all-expenses-paid trip to magical Iceland. But maybe I had it wrong … maybe some people in the crew did see the journey as a holiday?

I didn't know where to begin; I wasn't going to get into an argument at that moment.

'Brad, we have a tough journey ahead of us; it's just begun and you're a crucial part of its success. You need to understand why I need to be harsh on you when you're not doing what you should be. I have never moaned at you unless you have not done your job. I've never disrespected you or treated you badly.'

'The whole crew know how you treat me. Tracey told me the other day that I am your bitch. They feel exactly the same way. It has to change.'

And I guess this is where it did all change. I was the only one on the trip that knew what was needed to get Dan home alive, and, so help me God, I was going to make the decisions myself if Bradley didn't know how to, or chose not to, make the right ones on his own.

'That's where you have it wrong, Brad. Change your shit rebellious attitude or go home. We don't need you if you're acting like this.' I closed the door and walked back to my room. As I got to my door, which was only 10 metres away, I stopped and paused.

I couldn't believe that Dan could create such a rift between me and one of my best friends. There was bad blood between us that I felt was the direct result of what Dan had made the crew believe about me: that I was just a plain bully. But what Dan hadn't grasped was that I wanted to make a hero out of him, and that something like that doesn't come without hard work, dedication, blood, sweat and tears. It is difficult to put this into words, but I think it's just human nature. Who would side with a 'tough' adventurer against a person with a disability? It's a strange thought, but, if you really think about it, nobody could imagine that maybe a disabled person might also have personality flaws just like able-bodied people. I saw some flaws in Dan that others didn't see – flaws that Dan wanted to hide.

'Geezlike, I wish I could rather send Dan home. He's responsible for all this hatred and angst between us.' There is no way people will side with a tough, uncompromising leader when a handicapped guy with tears in his eyes pleads for mercy. Of course people are going to hate me. I have to deal with it. I would probably feel exactly the same. After all, I've been on that side with Dan. I always felt that, when he told me a story about someone who was an arsehole, it was a simple, clear-cut case. There was no way this guy wasn't an arsehole, especially if Dan said he was.

It had just gone horribly wrong for me. *I* was *that* arsehole now, and I was just about to make the first big decision of the journey. I was going to fire Bradley.

I turned around and calmly walked back to Bradley's door, knocked, and opened the door halfway. I didn't step inside the room, but leaned forward and said: 'Pack your things, book the next flight home, and get out of here. We can't have you behave like this.'

Bradley didn't look surprised, but just said 'OK, if that's what you want, then I'll do it.'

I closed the door. The one thing I hadn't wanted to happen on this journey, or ever, had just happened. I still felt relieved, though. The right decision is not always the easiest decision.

I grabbed my life jacket and, on the way out, as I passed Bradley's door, I noticed he was now talking to Thor, telling him what had happened. I asked Bradley when he would be leaving, and was stunned to hear that he had already booked a flight for that afternoon at 17h00. I was surprised. I felt Bradley, like me, was also relieved and wanted an out. Perhaps he wasn't cut out to manage this expedition, or maybe he just really wanted to attend his friend's wedding. I did believe, though, that he would decide to change his attitude and see this thing through, but it turned out I was giving him too much credit

Thor then added the icing on the cake for me that morning. He stopped me as we were walking out and said he wanted to chat alone.

'I know this is a bad time,' he said, 'but I need to discuss something with you.'

I can remember telling him just to get to the point.

'I got a job offer in Greenland; it pays one million krónur and any person would be mad not to take it.'

I didn't hesitate, and calmly replied: 'It's fine, Thor, please just hand over the keys to Tracey and make sure she is up to speed with everything you do. Good luck.'

Thor was feeling slightly bad, and tried to reaffirm his decision to me: 'I'm sure you understand, it's a lot of money and I'm sure you would've even taken it.'

No, Thor, I wouldn't have. I would have stuck by the people who I'd committed to – the people who gave me a job when I was suffering without any income. I wouldn't do what you are doing. I was disappointed in Thor, but he is young, and I probably acted more foolishly when I was his age, when I thought I knew everything.

It felt like a blessing in disguise to have Thor out of that oppressive environment. The entire crew, every single one of them, had behaved two-facedly towards him. They would speak badly behind his back, but no one had the guts actually to say to him what they felt so they could resolve their feelings. Say what you want; talking about someone behind his back says less about him and a hell of a lot more about you.

From the outset, Thor had been what I had now become: an outsider. He would never be part of their circle. He was a good guy thrown into a tough situation. He wanted to prove himself and show he was worthwhile, like anyone tries to do in a new social circle. He was always on a hiding to nothing. I'd like to see him again under different circumstances. I feel the conversation would be less pressurised.

The paddle on the glacial lake was incredible, to say the least. I took direction from Darren and the crew and navigated my way through what is actually a very, very dangerous place. The truck-sized icebergs that have calved off the main glacier are unstable and can flip over at any time.

Bradley's imminent departure was gnawing away at the back of my mind, but, to be honest, I believed he would stay. I was very wrong, though. He came down to the edge of the lake, walked over to the crew, and explained to them he was leaving and why. Later, back in South Africa, I saw the footage that the team recorded of him saying goodbye: he said he was tired of being treated like an animal, and he wished them all strength in dealing with me. It hurt my feelings tremendously, and felt like another twist of the knife in my back.

When Bradley finished talking to the crew, he walked back with Thor and Tracey, who was going to take them both to the airport. Dan and I had stepped onto one of the massive islands of ice to get the feel of it. I couldn't believe what was happening at that moment. Dan made a comment about how something was going on and he wondered what it was. At that moment, I looked Dan square in the eyes and asked him if he was living in a dreamland. Of course everything was not OK, and *he* was the reason it wasn't OK.

The world felt surreal, and I had no choice but to play along. No cracks in the armour. Lead bravely no matter what. This was the most unreal moment of all my journeys. And I had no one to turn to. Bradley had gone.

That night, I could hear the crew laughing and having fun in the dining room while they downloaded the day's footage and watched movies. I went to bed, and, yes, I cried. Actually I didn't cry; I sobbed as though a friend of mine had died. I couldn't believe I had had to do what I'd done, and I couldn't believe Bradley had made that choice. I wasn't feeling sorry for myself. I knew I was doing what was required for the success of the expedition. I was just sad and hurting. It's not fun to lose a very special 25-year friendship amid so much hatred.

I needed Vasti, and I needed Troy. I needed help. But help wasn't coming, only more challenges.

That Saturday – Bradley left on Thursday – I was looking at a South African news website, and saw a short article, with no names or much detail, about a spearfisherman who had been killed by a shark off Cape Vidal. I told Darren how I had learnt to spearfish there as a teenager. Something like this felt close to home, I told them. Little did I know how close to home it was.

Later that day, I had just returned from the supermarket and was sitting in the vehice outside the farmhouse where we were staying. I was catching up on some email, and got a message from my friend Shane Smart:

Amazon
I bring sad news my friend.
Warren has left this world, he was attacked by a shark at Vidal on
Saturday while spear fishing. Injury was just too large.
Want u to take care my friend.
Thought for the good man.
Love Shane

My head was spinning and my heart beat furiously. I felt breathless. The sense of unreality was the same as when Bradley left. Warren, Shane's brother, was the guy who, nine years back, had supported me in marketing my Africa Bicycle circumnavigation project throughout South Africa – before I'd even done one kilometre! With unmatched enthusiasm, charisma and never a complaint, Warren had stood with me at shopping centres handing out pamphlets. He was genuine and sincere, and at one stage I felt he believed in me and my journey more than I did myself. He seemed to feed off adversity. If people scoffed at this unimaginable world-first trip, he just smiled broadly, a glint in his eye, and moved on to the next lucky person.

I cried as I sat in the vehicle in the growing darkness. The crew peeked through the windows now and then, oblivious of what I was going through. I tried to call Shane, but he wasn't available. I called Vasti and had a long chat with her. She was very sad for me. I asked her to read the piece I wrote about Warren in *Around Africa on My Bicycle*. She cried as she read this to me:

> *I remember Warren's technique. He would say: 'See that guy? He's going to cycle around the whole of Africa with this bicycle in one year.' He would then pause, gauge the response to this forthright approach and wade right in with the rest of his spiel if it looked as if he had hooked a fish. The people loved him – but, more importantly, they wanted to know how they could follow me on the journey.*

Apparently, Warren had been reeling in a fish he had just shot. Before he could remove it from the spear, a shark had tried to grab it, missing the fish but getting Warren instead. When Vasti read that piece I had written so many years ago, I got an eerie feeling. Warren will be sorely missed. He was one of a handful of people who were there from the beginning of my adventure career, when so many people only wanted to show me what I didn't know and why I wasn't good enough. Warren never, ever, ever doubted me. He shared with me that naivety and bliss for life that makes us willing to take on challenges that others would decline. Rest in peace? No, I think Warren will be looking for a fishing or spearfishing spot the moment he meets the guy holding the clipboard at the pearly gates.

That night was another tough one for me. I had plenty of newspaper articles, interviews and other expedition PR responsibilities to attend to. In between this, I managed to get hold of a good friend of mine, Tracy du Plessis, also someone who had stood by me through the early days. She had gone out with Shane for 11 years, and had known Warren from a very early age, and cared deeply for him. I wanted to support Tracy, so it was a shock to hear she was not planning to attend the funeral. She felt she could not cope with the emotional trauma it would bring. I was angry with Tracy. She is a powerful woman who doesn't just speak about doing things – she does them. Now she was going to wither like a flower in the desert. She needed to be there for Shane, for Shane's family and, above all, for Warren. She promised she would go. She did. This moment proved to me once more how an honest friend's criticism can help you make a better decision.

But determination is the adventurer's most important quality. For Tracey, who had just celebrated her birthday (I gave her a box of sweets), it was also the start of an unexpected personal journey of discovery when she was appointed to step into Bradley's shoes as expedition manager. (Replacing Thor was another matter, of course.) It was the most abrupt turnaround imaginable, but she took it in her stride, although with understandable feelings of trepidation at having to take on a range of difficult tasks without any preparation whatsoever.

We removed some of the stuff from the kayak, tied it down and went on to Höfn, the plan being to come back next day and resume the paddle southwestwards. But then Mother Nature took a hand. Iceland's largest volcano had just erupted, spewing huge clouds of ash all over the place and creating havoc in airline schedules far and wide, and gale-force winds of up to 75 kilometres per hour suddenly made their unwelcome appearance. We didn't know it at the time, but we were heading into the worst crisis of the entire expedition.

CHAPTER 8

HIGH NOON IN HÖFN

> *'I treated Dan like I would everybody else,*
> *which I had promised to do from the start. To*
> *make this dream journey a reality, everyone*
> *involved needed a thick skin.'*

We spent 10 long days cooped up at Höfn. Then the weather cleared, and the team spirit revived a little. I had something else to boost my spirits: Vasti was coming to visit in a few days. But, Iceland being Iceland, we had to cope with another disaster before we could get away. When we went back to the kayak, we found it had suffered a lot of damage. Among other things, the hull was damaged and the rudder completely missing. My paddle was gone, along with some fishing gear and the mitts I wore for paddling (Zahir managed to find one, but the other had disappeared for good).

The only thing to do was to switch over to the spare kayak, which wasn't in great shape either. It had been damaged earlier in the trip when Dan and I had gone through a glacial lake; ice had scraped the bottom. At the time I had laughed it off, thinking: *Nah, this is the spare kayak, the real one's over there; this one I can just patch up when I need it.* Now the major kayak was crippled, and this was all we had left. It just shows you shouldn't take anything for granted when you're playing a high-stakes game.

Fortunately, the damage to the spare kayak wasn't anything major, but I knew hours of painstaking work would be needed to make it seaworthy. This meant, in turn, that the expedition wasn't taking off any time soon. I suspect the only person who didn't mind the delay too much was Tracey, who was still struggling to get to grips with the paperwork she had inherited so suddenly from Bradley (she had also taken over Thor's kitchen tasks, so she was pretty busy).

I made a trip to the local hardware store for repair material and got to work without delay. The problem was simple but life-threatening. If there was a hole in the hull, that would be it for us – no second chances. That meant I had to do a proper job of fixing the leak. I was confident I could do it, because, thanks to my Madagascar adventure, I was no stranger to this sort of thing.

Altogether, it took us three days, with Richard inspanned to help. This included an extra bit of work when, as I was putting on the finishing touches, I noticed that the top and bottom decks had actually separated, probably also from that bashing in the glacial lake that had caused the other damage. Well, what the hell. I whacked in a dollop of fibreglass and resin with plenty of hardener to cement the decks back together and went to do the same to the other kayak.

The damage to the kayak came at a time when the team basically fell apart. The trigger was the growing problem between Dan and me. We'd had disagreements, and exchanged some harsh words, but I felt we could work it out. I didn't think a huge falling-out was necessary. I believed Dan would see the logic of our situation. Yes, I was harsh with him, but for the right reasons – nothing else. I was never disrespectful or demeaning of him. I treated Dan like I would everybody else, which I had promised to do from the start. To make this dream journey a reality, everyone involved needed a thick skin.

Einar, one of the local paddlers in Höfn, invited us for a meal. It was amazing, with almost every Icelandic delicacy on offer: crayfish, haddock, chicken, puffin and even blackbird. Everything was prepared with such care and thought – as if we were royalty. What I believe we saw that day was the real Icelanders, not the shy ones hiding behind their layers of clothing and heated cars, but people who love to host and entertain. Einar was a seasoned river paddler, as well as a sea kayaker, but, more interestingly, he loved hunting from the water. He was very interested in our boat design, and believed it would be ideal for use as a hunting boat. I wish I could have given him a boat as a gift, but I needed them both for the journey. We still had a very long way to go!

Einar knew we had damaged our boat and would be land-bound for a while. He offered to assist with the repairs, and also gave us a rowing machine he had made. It imitated proper paddling motion, and the settings could be adjusted to suit different fitness levels. I got stuck into that machine the day it arrived and used it so much that I eventually wore out the pulley ropes. Fortunately, all it took to get it going again was replacement nylon cord.

I was surprised that Dan did not spend more time practising his paddling. He mainly hung around with the crew, going into town with them or watching YouTube clips and movies on his computer. It disappointed me that neither he nor any of the crew could see he wasn't making an effort.

This contributed to the huge blow-up that took place during our enforced stay in Höfn. The wake-up call came when I overheard Dan discussing things with one of Justin's employees during a Skype call. Dan had a room at the bottom of the house, and the rowing machine was right next door. I don't think Dan knew I was rowing, and he continued an animated conversation with Alexis Burg, the documentary producer, and the person who would decide the basis of the story of *Around Iceland on Inspiration*.

I could hear that Dan was emotional. Alexis's tone was comforting. Dan's exact words to her were: 'You guys don't understand what an absolute arsehole he is. You really don't understand!'

Alexis's immediate reply was assertive and sure: 'Dan, don't worry, we are all behind you. We all know what a fucking bastard he is. We can all see on the footage. Don't worry, we're all on your side.'

I was stunned, and stood there wiping the sweat from my face. I can't say I was entirely surprised at the feelings expressed, but it still hurt. To make the pain of hearing this easier, I repeated Vasti's tough words over and over in my head: 'No matter how badly they treat you or speak about you, they all will stay who they are. Dan will stay Dan, and you will still do something amazing for another person. That cannot change. Stick to your original plan. It wasn't your plan to change people. They are who they are.'

Geez, I felt like walking in on the conversation and asking Dan why he would talk like this behind my back. I think I was afraid of the confrontation, though.

When I got back to my room, I decided to do what was probably long overdue. We needed a team meeting to discuss the dynamics of the relationship between Dan and me. More importantly, we needed to get to the root of how this affected the team and how we could improve it.

I believed everyone needed a say, even new arrivals like Brad Theron, the replacement cameraman. So, one by one, we each stood in the centre of the circle. Everyone said Dan needed to up his effort and that Riaan needed to support Dan more. Richard believed the core problem was that we needed more practice together. It was a good point, although I felt we weren't even getting the basics right. And we would be paddling only in flat conditions from that point.

There were two things that amazed me about the crew's insights. I was impressed that they spoke a 'solutions' language throughout: they wanted to see a peaceful result and a happy ending. We all did. But what worried me was that everyone insinuated that Dan was being treated unfairly, and no one brought up the point that Dan needed to show humility and, above all, respect. His disrespect to me was never mentioned.

Then Dan had his chance. He believed he was giving his all, and made the point that I made everyone, even the crew, feel that they were never good enough. This fed into the 'me vs them' scenario. He went into a tirade of note. It was like something out of a Hollywood movie, like the coach in *Any Given Sunday*: he laid down the law that he would not be bullied by anyone – especially not by me.

What amazed me here was not just that Dan interpreted my pushing him to do his best and make a legend of his life as bullying, but that he hadn't given any thought to what I had done or achieved in my life. The reality was that I didn't need to bully a disabled guy to achieve a goal, especially this one. My gripes were simple, straightforward and unchanged. His response and self-defence mechanisms changed, though.

What I was asking for was not a demonstration of power – I was willing to paddle Dan around Iceland for his benefit – but rather an act of safety. Putting the paddle in front of him. Ever since the day I had found the courage to confront him about his laziness, he had turned ugly on me. He was willing to go to any length to convince those around him that he was being bullied, in order to deflect the focus off his laziness and show me to be a person of third-tier character.

It was probably a blessing that I didn't get to see the interview recorded with Dan around this time. I saw this only later, when shown some of the raw footage of the trip. In the clip, Dan sits in front of the entire crew, visibly agitated and furious.

He repeated to them something he had told Brad: 'If the guy says to me, listen, your disability is what is holding us back, it's a fuck, that's what it is.'

I was gobsmacked. I wish I had known what he was telling the crew at the time. Dan was right; who *would* say something like that? He was telling the crew that I had told him that it was his disability that was the reason for us not coping. Who wouldn't be antagonistic towards someone if that was what he was going around saying? He had convinced the crew that I had told him his disability was the reason we were not making it. Not one person there questioned his point of view. The dynamics of the crew were such that no one even bothered to confront me, to find out if I had said something like that, or even to speak to me about it. They all just took Dan at his word.

If he was willing to say something like this, what else was he prepared to say about me? I never said one bad word about Dan to the camera, even if I felt unhappy with him. Didn't he see that?

Dan had now convinced the crew, his family, his friends and anyone else who would listen that I was a terrible person. He convinced them that I was blaming his disability and that he was enduring inhumane treatment.

The facts had not changed. I expected Dan to put his paddle in front of him and, above all, not to be lazy. I had to be harsh with him to save our lives. I never attacked him personally, but he swore at me and said things he never should have. I didn't have time to cry and whine about the situation. I had to step up and get on with this expedition. I also had no shoulder to cry on. Based on what Dan had told them, everyone now thought I was a monster.

The crunch came a few days after Bradley and Thor left. Dan and I had an almighty screaming session in that old farmhouse. I had expected him to apologise for using foul language at me, for his disrespect towards me, and also for creating a rift in our team – a rift that had had serious repercussions in my life. But he was having none of it.

No amount of shouting will solve real problems. We were destined for something else. I had to go and sit to calm down. Fortunately, Vasti was on her way to lend support, and to work out how to categorise all the things that were going on.

The breakdown in relations with Dan was just one of my many worries. Peter Gird, Justin Bonello's business partner, was on his way to try to solve our problems in Iceland. He was coming to act as an arbitrator, which I felt was exactly what was needed. The problem, though, is that, as everyone knows, an arbitrator needs to be impartial and objective.

All this time I was holding thumbs that the good weather would last, so that Dan and I could attempt our first midnight paddle. The sea was calmer at night – the sea breezes dissipate because of the lower temperatures on land – and Iceland's proximity to the Arctic meant there was at least some light 24 hours a day. This routine would upset everyone's body clock, of course, but the benefit of dealing with calmer sea conditions made up for it. By the time we set off, the resin would have had time to cure, which I reckoned (and hoped) would be enough.

My intention was to be in the water at Hvalnes, a little promontory just south of Krossanes, by 23h30. That would give us a window of about seven hours to do the 32-kilometre paddle to the Stokksnes lighthouse, which stands on a long, skinny piece of land called Austurfjörur, actually the outer arm of Höfn's fine natural harbour. I was confident about the repairs, but I couldn't help worrying a little, too; if worst came to worst and we did take on some water, I just hoped it wouldn't be too much. But, at the same time, Dan and I had come to Iceland with the idea of doing things we'd never done before, and tonight was definitely one of them.

Dan was keen to get going. 'It's a little bit of a different start,' as he put it, 'but it's a first, hey. What the hell, it's cool.' Which it was, in every sense of the word. But I knew that we would face dangers we hadn't had to confront before. What's not funny about paddling at night, even in the bright Icelandic twilight, is that you just have to sense the sea around you. You can't see anything coming at you. On the plus side, though, there weren't too many clouds that night.

Actually getting into the water at Hvalnes promised to be a dodgy venture, thanks to the powerful surf crashing onto the rocky shoreline, but after assessing the risks I worked out a way and briefed Dan carefully on what he had to do. If I was wrong, or we didn't get swiftly over one particular place, it would be all over. It was particularly important for Dan to get into the kayak as quickly as possible so that I could push it out and scramble on myself.

Then we'd take the initiative. We would punt through each wave instead of waiting for it to hit us, and while Dan paddled as hard as he could, I'd be steering our nose into the waves. On shore, Tracey would now have yet another task – tracking our progress so that the team would always know where we were. To make this more complicated, she would have to keep a separate eye on each of us, because we were now both carrying satellite tracking devices in case we got separated again.

My tactics worked, and soon we were in the water and forging ahead. 'Well done, Dan,' I said. My heart was pumping, the way it always does when I do a successful launch in dangerous conditions. I nearly crap in my pants, but you can't beat the excitement, even though the repercussions aren't always funny.

I was too busy to look at my watch, but on shore Tracey had a moment to check, and yes, it was very nearly midnight. Meanwhile we were up to an excellent eight kilometres per hour; if we kept that up, we'd reach the halfway mark within two hours. But Dan was still struggling with his paddling, and we couldn't get the rhythm we needed.

The paddle to Stokksnes was a tough one. The sea was quite rough and it was, of course, freezing cold. Now and again, we had what Dan aptly described as 'hairy situations'; just getting around the lighthouse at Stokksnes, which stood on another jutting bit of eastern Iceland, required a struggle. About five hours later, though, we reached our designated landing place. Our first night paddle had thrown our bodies out of sync, and our exhaustion magnified my anxiety about making a safe landing, but we managed it, and the team was waiting for us. I was satisfied; we had done well.

Now it was back to Höfn to get our heads down in preparation for the next day's paddle, to a place called Skinneyjarhöfði, about 27 kilometres away. This time, we took the kayak with us. I think it was a tough moment for Tracey, since loading the kayaks and transporting them used to be handled by Bradley and Thor. Managing the expedition was a daunting task for someone who had never done it before, but she pitched in and got the job done.

CHAPTER 9

THE ARBITRATOR VS THE SUPPORTER

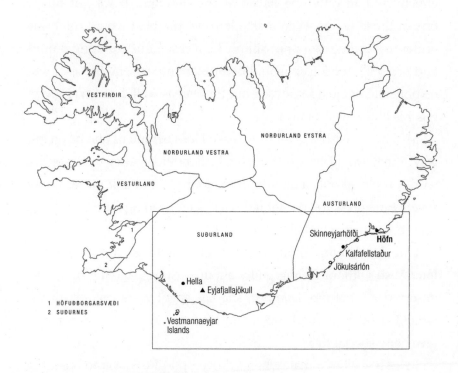

*'It was very difficult managing the radio and
the cellphone while trying to paddle. If we got
it wrong and were caught by bigger waves,
then we could be washed up on rocks.'*

B ut now the North Atlantic showed its teeth again. We found
ourselves stuck at Höfn again, trapped by monstrously bad sea
conditions: just to get into the water would have meant fighting
our way through breakers four metres high. I am willing to take a
calculated risk, even a dicey one, but I know when I'm beaten.

In addition to fighting the sheer brute power of the sea, we effectively had only one kayak at the moment. If we got hit by one of those waves, even a smaller one, the boat would roll away under us. And it would not simply be a case of us suffering bumps and bruises – the kayak would be broken into several pieces. I was responsible not just for myself but for Dan as well; I had no right to risk his life as well as my own.

My biggest wish was for us to leave Höfn behind us and be on our way – that would be worth a small celebration. After two months, we'd completed only a quarter of the journey, and that put us under severe time pressure. We should have been heading for the finish by now, but we were far behind schedule.

One good thing, though, was that I could go to Reykjavík to fetch Vasti without feeling guilty about wasting paddling time. She deserved a bit of fun. Damn it, she has spent years waiting for me while I knocked around Africa and Madagascar, and so I wanted to give her a special treat.

I was a shell of a man when I drove up to Reykjavík to meet her at the airport. She was coming for a week's visit. Apart from her supporting me in a very tough time, she was also going to be a part of my third big journey. She had seen, on other occasions, how people and relationships could turn ugly. I think the group's tense situation made her apprehensive.

Darren and Richard drove me back to the capital and on to Keflavik airport. They were good company; it was good to learn a bit more about them and have them in isolation for a change. I like surprises, and decided to spring one on Vasti. I sent her an SMS to say I had been delayed by a few hours on the road, and that she would have to catch a bus. Darren bought into the idea of catching Vasti off guard at the airport. We hid so well that when she eventually made her appearance and wandered over to the bus ticket counter, she didn't spot us. I walked quickly up behind her as she stood in the ticket queue, and stood there, just short of uncomfortably near her. She had noticed someone was behind her, but didn't want to react at once, so she attempted to look as far left as she could to try to get a peripheral view of the person behind her. She paused, smoothly glanced backward, looked me in the eyes, and glanced away as if she didn't know me. Then she let out a high-pitched shriek of surprise and spun around to face me. Man, I was happy to see her. I needed her desperately.

Darren didn't miss a second of the action. He had moved as if he were my shadow. People say it's difficult to put your finger on what makes a cameraman 'good'. It doesn't matter how much he knows; what matters is that he can capture the special moments. I was learning plenty from the documentary crew every day.

I had given Vasti the impression that we were going to go straight back to Höfn, but, paradoxical as it may seem, I *always* have a surprise in mind when I convince her I have none. I was going to hire a helicopter to fly us over Eyjafjallajökull. We would fly right over the volcano's steaming crater and hopefully land on the adjacent ridge, with views over to the Vestmannaeyjar Islands, as well as of grand old Hekla – the mother of all volcanoes, according to Icelanders.

I told Vasti we had to overnight at the village of Hella because Darren needed to collect a package sent from South Africa. I told her we would probably stay near the hotel that supposedly had the package. She was happy with the arrangement and didn't see through the surprise. In the morning, we went for breakfast at the Hotel Ranga. Darren, Richard, the hotel reception staff and I were all speaking 'code' around Vasti so as to not to arouse her suspicions.

The helicopter eventually landed, with all of us making comments about how great it must be to fly over Iceland in one. We were still waiting for the package, though. The pilot eventually gave the thumbs-up signal for us to board, but I kept Vasti in the dark by telling her that Darren had the package and we would pick him and Richard up later by helicopter.

'Bring your jacket; you might get cold,' I said. Vasti's face lit up with excitement. She didn't know what was up, but she knew now it had something to do with the helicopter. In the past 11 years I had missed nine of her birthdays. It wasn't fair. I wanted to surprise her with something special for this birthday. Although I couldn't really afford the helicopter trip, I made sure we doubled up the opportunity for Darren and Richard to get some aerial footage for the documentary.

The crater of Eyjafjallajökull was 80% intact, but the flow of molten lava had carved out a new valley on the north side. Inside the crater, the main sign of activity was steam billowing out through giant spouts. We landed alongside the volcano, on Mýrdalsjökull Glacier, to take a few photos. We couldn't stay long up here because it was so cold and the pilot felt the wind was picking up. We then flew down the valley carved out by the Markarfljót River. It was the most amazing natural artwork I have ever seen, the brown streams weaving and intertwining so delicately across the landscape. I could imagine how beautiful the sight would be in spring, with the river swollen by meltwater from the glacier.

Vasti loved the effort I had made, and agreed to sign the 10-year birthday-present-waiver contract I had waiting for her back in the vehicle.

We returned to Höfn, and to business as usual. I made it clear to Vasti that we would continue paddling, no matter what. We could not miss the opportunity to catch up time and distance just because she was there. She understood. We needed to get out of Höfn, which had bad associations for me, and we needed to get as far along the south coast as we could during the short Icelandic summer.

For the first few days, it was as if we had released a tightly wound elastic band. During the time Vasti was there, we managed four days of sea time. We covered more distance in those four days than we had managed in the preceding month. It was mind-boggling.

I think Vasti brought the happiness and the 'yes' character back to me. Determination cannot be tested if the environment is receptive and kind. Determination expects action when every other message tells you to stay put. Vasti was fully aware of how I'd been treated by the people around me, but she remained focused on our goal. People who focus on sideshows never attend the grand event. She brought focus back for me, and enthusiasm and focus for the whole team.

Dan, meanwhile, had made use of the break to train on the rowing machine. He was optimistic, or maybe philosophical, about the delay – it was an opportunity, as he put it, 'to clear my head a little bit'.

Fortunately, we were not paddling that much. Brad had now taken over from Tracey as cameraman, but there were still some staff issues for me to sort out. Tracey is a very good fix-it person. She has guts and determination and an unwillingness to give up. Even though I know she, along with the rest, hated my guts, I wanted to give her a reward of some sort. My original plan had been to bring over a replacement for Bradley and Thor from London. I had some friends who were between jobs and keen to spend a few months in Iceland. They didn't expect salaries, but only for me to look after them while they were here.

The problem, though, was that Tracey had told me that her fiancé, Chez, could not find work and desperately needed something. I had issues with this, as it would mean introducing a couple into the already-tense group dynamic, and I didn't really know Chez. But I felt Tracey had too much on her plate. Without her knowing, I called Chez and spoke to him candidly about my worries. What would happen if they argued? What would happen when I got angry with her in front of him? What would happen when she expected him to take her side? Even with the best intentions, I needed to consider these scenarios. He promised he would guarantee this would never be a problem. I asked him if he had a valid passport and how soon he could get his visa. Once we agreed on a salary, I offered him the job, and he accepted. I could hear his joy at the other end of the telephone line. Although it was going to cost me a lot to get him to Iceland, I believed it was the right decision. I really liked Chez once I got to know him; he was honest, reliable and hard-working.

I told Chez to break the news to Tracey that night, which he did. She came up to me while I was sitting having dinner – alone, of course – and whispered that she was very grateful for what I'd done for her. I really hoped she would see how I was rewarding her. I did find it odd, though, that she asked me not to tell the crew about Chez's impending arrival, as she felt it would create a divide between them and her. It was a huge risk and a massive expense to bring Chez over. I didn't want to have to spell it out.

Chez was going to do all the manual work that Thor had been responsible for. He would also cook and, as I said to him, 'be responsible' for team morale! Chez was going to be perfect for us. Tracey had no more filming responsibilities, and had taken on Bradley's duties of managing the finances, organising accommodation and planning our paddling. She still had to assist me getting visual

PR out to the media. This included a weekly video, which only she could do and which she was actually getting very good at.

Although I felt Tracey was sometimes dramatic in managing stress, I knew she could learn from this opportunity if she employed a positive mindset to confront her challenges. After all, she comes from the distinguished and proven-tough Bruton clan.

It was at this time that Peter Gird arrived, supposedly to try to resolve the problems between Cooked in Africa and me. Peter is a jovial old bear, a big man, gregarious in spirit and awesome to have around. He is incredibly wise and thoughtful, what many would term a father figure. He is calm, level-headed and good with people. I had to be open to what he was coming to try to resolve in Iceland. As I had told Vasti numerous times, I needed him and Justin to support me. I was carrying everything on my shoulders.

Peter was having personal problems at the time, with his younger sister very ill in the United States. He was going on to see her after his visit to us in Iceland. Peter was in a situation no one wants to be in. He told me the doctors did not believe she would make it to the end of the year. It was awful, and I felt for him. His job in Iceland was even more difficult, and I needed to be part of the solution.

My resolve with Peter was, at the outset of his visit, to clear up some concerns that I had. This is something I would never have done previously, as I would rather have avoided the potential conflict by a country mile. It was important for me to explain to Peter, even though he was by far my senior in terms of age and way more experienced, that I needed him to show respect to my leadership and what I'd managed to accomplish thus far. If he was going to have conversations with the crew like Alexis was having with Dan, then it would only make matters worse. He would buy us a meal and a beer or two and then jump on the plane, leaving me with a crowd that still believed what Dan had told them. I didn't need Peter to fly 20 000 kilometres to reaffirm this, so I hoped he would understand why I needed to meet with him as soon as he landed.

To my surprise, we had a great time, sipping a few beers and joking, while discussing my concerns. I felt that I sincerely conveyed my position, and that he understood the gravity of what I was dealing with. It later turned out that that was exactly what I didn't achieve – a huge surprise, I can tell you.

Peter spent time with each member of the crew, trying, as I had done in the past myself, to reassure him or her. He made sure to ask all the team members about their individual concerns, what they wanted to see improve, and how we could intervene to assist in making the situation better. I'm sure Peter employed the right strategies with each person as he felt best suited the situation. What he told me he was going to explain to Dan was that Dan, more than at any time before, needed to step up to the plate. Of course, I liked hearing this. I believed Peter understood what the journey was about and would relay the right message to Dan.

Peter had told me about a film he'd made about this extraordinary character who had cerebral palsy, much more severe than Dan's condition. This guy decided he was going to run as many marathons as he could. He never took short cuts, kept falling, and lost many teeth, but, as any superhero does, he finished every time. I hadn't seen the documentary, but just listening to Peter tell me the story gave me goose bumps. Peter wanted Dan to see this guy as an inspiration and to make himself a role model in the same mould. It inspired me, so I knew the story would inspire Dan.

Peter's message to me was that he wanted me to go easier on

Dan so we could end the journey the way everyone would love it to end – crowned with success. This wasn't easy to accept, as the problem with Dan had gone beyond a little squabble over cupcakes. The hurt he had already caused me was deep. I explained to Peter that I would not accept Dan disrespecting me as he had, and would not accept any justification from him for it. Disabled or not, Dan should fall under the same umbrella as any other friend. Was I wrong to expect this from Dan? We always read stuff like 'See the person, not the disability', and that is exactly the way I saw Dan. I treated him as I would have treated anyone on that expedition. Disabled or not. I felt that I had earned some respect through my experience and leadership.

Peter had Dan write me a letter explaining how he felt. I was looking forward to receiving it.

The second to last day of Peter's visit, though, brought a shock and a reality of its own. We were all crammed into the small farmhouse, which had prefab walls and only one toilet. The kitchen was tiny, too, but absorbed our numbers well after each paddling session. Peter and I were basically wrapping up his visit and what he felt could be salvaged from what most people considered a wreck. We chatted about how Dan had responded to his requests. He told me he had been with Dan, and that Dan had taken what he had to say to heart. He told me I was a hero to do what I do and that everyone in South Africa was behind me. He convinced me of this amazing 'thought' and I believed him. It made me feel a little bit better. But I didn't anticipate the conversation we were about to have. It centred on Peter continuing to encourage me to try harder with Dan.

I never planned to write this, but I want to convey the reality of this journey. Peter told me to be patient with Dan. He told me that Dan was not always there. Peter insinuated that Dan was sometimes very absent-minded. As I am probably more absent-minded than Dan, I took what Peter was saying at face value. Peter continued, and then shocked me beyond belief with a very derogatory comment about Dan. I won't repeat his exact words, but I was deeply shocked.

What Peter said next about Dan reduced me to stunned silence: 'We all know Dan is …,' he went on, saying something he thought was quite humorous. His words, combined with his actions, intimated some horrible things about Dan. As I said, I was shocked. This is what he and Justin and the crew and maybe even people back home believed I thought of Dan?

I responded immediately and abruptly, catching him visibly off guard: 'I'm sorry, Peter. Geezlike, I don't see Dan in that way and I never have.'

'What I mean,' Peter started again, 'is that he's just strange sometimes. He talks about the same things all the time. I mean, if I have to hear one more time about his law and his exams and those same stories, I'll go mad!' He clearly realised he had said something inappropriate to someone who didn't share his view. I had never, ever, said anything bad about any of the people involved in the expedition, not one person, even though they had bad things to say about me. If I had anything to say, I would say it directly *to* the person concerned. Doesn't this have value in our world any more? Or is it all a social game we play, with everyone aware of the other's two-faced approach to friendships? It is only with time that people are sifted and separated for who they really are. The real from the fake.

Now, I don't know where this conversation left our relationship, but I was horrified that Peter would actually say something like that about Dan to me. He saw my response and was now unsure of what he had said. We all say the wrong things now and then and don't mean it, but this situation, in its broader sense, was different and seemed to explain a few things.

Our meeting ended very uncomfortably, and I went straight to Vasti's and my room. The room was next to the kitchen, separated from it only by a thin cardboard wall. As I walked into the room, Vasti was sitting waiting for me. She had heard everything.

'Riaan, I am proud of you for standing your ground with Peter. I heard everything. You know I don't want to interfere, but I'm telling you this: if he is willing to speak about Dan so derogatorily, imagine what he is saying about you to the others.' She left it at that.

Vasti was right. But was this going to put us back at square one? No, it wasn't; I wouldn't allow it. I was going to forgive Dan and make this journey fun again. I was going to avoid having to test him any more. I would now take the danger of the challenge away. The complications of life and death had created my stress, and had then exacerbated my weakness in communicating it to someone who essentially was only trying his best.

The conversation with Peter gave rise to a few positive things for me. It showed me that Dan is a victim, and that it's not fair for him to have people around whose motives he cannot trust. I mean, he probably thought I took him on the journey because he is the brother of a former Springbok rugby captain. Nothing could be further from the truth, but perhaps he believed it. The reality is that many people who act sincere and kind in front of him are not in fact motivated by sincerity and kindness.

I needed to soften and employ logic to the problems of 'our' world. I am the person I am today because of the experiences that moulded me as a child. Dan is also who he is because of the experiences of his youth. I understood his challenges perhaps better than anyone, and I understood better than anyone how he felt about himself. I hoped that

Dan would see the truth eventually. He was targeting the only person who had *proven* himself – through actions rather than words – to him over and over again.

I was going to do something great for another human being. I would expect nothing in return. This would not change. I would finish what we had started.

At last the weather relented, and on a calm, perfect day we set off from a spot on Austurfjörur, about 10 kilometres from Höfn's harbour mouth, and pointed our bows towards Skinneyjarhöfði. The team followed us for the first bit, but then had to break away and go around the lagoon at whose seaward end Höfn lay. Conditions remained good and we motored on until we came to the landing place, where the team was waiting for us.

It was only a short paddle, really, but that was because we were planning another night journey, starting at 20h00. I wasn't looking forward to it. We would have to do about 43 kilometres to get to Skinneyjarhöfði, my back was sore, and at the end of it we'd have to land safely on a rocky and hostile coastline, although Tracey was confident that she had found a suitable place.

I was a little concerned about the launch, because that was always the time when Dan's disability left him in the lurch. Because of his unresponsive leg muscles, it was difficult for him to stand solidly in the surf. During the first stage of a launch, you have to do things as speedily as possible – get the boat in the water, climb on, drop the rudder down and then overcome the kayak's inertia. The last-mentioned was not easy because the kayak was so heavy.

What concerned me more was that the kayak had been taking on water, which would have to be removed before we could carry on.

We had to take an hour off to fix the leak. This would mean that we would miss the tide, but there was no alternative. Out at sea, any leak was potentially dangerous, and of course we didn't have a backup. This tide thing was a serious factor. From the beach, the sea looked nice and calm, and so it was. But what you couldn't see from the beach was the strong tidal flow, and that meant problems for us. I wasn't going to try anything fancy; I was just going to try to get us out alive.

We got down to fixing the leak. It was positively sweltering – by Icelandic standards, anyway – according to Richard, it was the hottest day since 1947. I decided that the best way of tackling the launch would be for Dan to swim out to just beyond the breakers; I'd meet him there and he would climb on. Dan was game, so that's what we did.

But, needless to say, it was not as easy as it sounded. As soon as we got in the water, the strong tide started pulling us away from one another; it was just another reminder of the fearful risks we ran every time we launched. But after a considerable struggle we were together again, Dan was on board, and we could get down to the main task of eating up those 40-odd kilometres.

Back on shore, as I found out later from footage shot by the camera crew, an awestruck Tracey watched all this and blurted: 'I didn't know it was this tough …', to which Richard replied: 'I think you have to be mad to do something like this.' I'd felt that way myself on more than one occasion.

I calculated that the first leg of the paddle should be to Jökulsárlón, about 23 kilometres away. Conditions were still good, and I hoped they would stay like that. It was now well into what would be the hours of total darkness in South Africa, but behind us the sun hadn't yet set, and the night sea was quite brightly lit. Quite strange for two good old South African boys like Dan and me.

Dan and I spent the late afternoon and onward, until midnight, paddling in thick mist. (With the sun staying up for 23 hours, we had considerable flexibility, time-wise.) Our first landing place, at Kalfafellstaður, should have been a straightforward, small-surf beach landing. The problem was that we couldn't see 10 metres ahead. I had no idea where to land safely. I didn't know if the crashing waves were rolling up a sandy beach or crunching into rocks. Although we'd done only a short distance, the effort had taken its toll, and we were cold and uncomfortable.

Tracey was getting into her new role of selecting landing spots she believed appropriate. It was good to have someone supporting me by checking variables such as weather, wind, swell and, to a lesser extent, tides. It meant that I didn't have to be consumed by it 24 hours a day. Tracey was still learning, though, and I had to have faith she would pick things up as time went on. The shape of the coast, swell size and, importantly, swell direction would begin to take on a whole new meaning for her. She would see how the combination of a few things could change a calm bay into a thunderous surf crunch zone.

That night, Tracey had said she found a possible landing spot and a route for the vehicles to get close to the shore. We stayed in touch via cellphone. When I eventually made the call to land I wasn't expecting complications. I got on the phone to Tracey, but she could not confirm the exact spot with the GPS or with the map. I needed this information, as it would save a lot of effort if we could land near the vehicles. The mist was so thick that we had not seen land for the last hour of our paddle. I used my gut feeling to guide us nearer to land, avoiding breaking surf and possible surprises.

I made the call to head for land and try something I hadn't done before. If Tracey could not find her exact position on the map, then

I would try use the signal of the two-way radio as a beacon. In this mist, the reception would be no more than 500 metres in a straight line. If I could get through to Tracey on the radio, it would mean the beach area was no more than a kilometre in length, which was a lot but still manageable.

Bradley had spent a fortune on maps from the Geographical Centre in Reykjavík, and these maps proved their worth that day. Sometimes the smallest detail can present you with a multitude of options. I knew there was a river and a prominent rock on what was essentially a straight beach trending in a southwesterly direction. The increase in swell size, as well as the louder sound of crashing waves, made us sure we were nearing land.

It was very difficult managing the radio and the cellphone while trying to paddle. If we got it wrong and were caught by bigger waves, then we could be washed up on rocks. I got Tracey on the radio, and asked her to shine our powerful Maglite torch out to sea. Dan and I stopped paddling for a while, trying to see the beam from the torch.

Vasti had seen me land my kayak many a time at Gordon's Bay and Betty's Bay. She had learnt what constitutes a gap in the surf, as well as the route of least resistance to shore. It was exciting for her and Tracey as they combed the shore, looking for us. But what saved us eventually was the sound of Vasti's high-pitched call, which squeezed under the mist and coasted along the surface to Dan and me. I turned the kayak in her direction and slowly brought us closer to land. The first landmark, the rock, made its appearance to our left, exactly the area I was aiming for originally. And then the river mouth showed itself too, and we discerned the blurred figures of the crew, Vasti and Peter standing on the shore.

The logical route to land would have been as far as possible from the rock, but, after watching the one-metre surf-break for a while, I settled on the risky option of coming right alongside the huge rock, timing it so that we missed the impact zone, and then gliding into the river mouth. I could hear Tracey saying something on the radio about landing where she was pointing the torch. It wasn't anywhere near where I had brought us in, but it showed me she was willing to try to make a call. If she weighed up what I had done, she would be better the next time. It isn't easy if you don't have experience.

The group was jubilant as we paddled up the river mouth. I think everyone was relieved. We all knew that a landing in these conditions could have turned out differently. We ended up shivering and groping through thick mist. I had just one request for Tracey: ' Can you get the heaters on in that car, please?'

And so we struggled along. But our tails were up now. Thanks to the calming presence of Vasti and Peter, things were settling down in the team. As Peter said: 'The moment you start getting down and beating yourself up, it's going to get worse.' There was no doubt that kayaking among amazing ice floes, and surviving, did great things for your spirits. Dan and I had argued so much in the past few days, but now he expressed our feeling very well when he said in all sincerity: 'Thank you, boet, this is a privilege.'

CHAPTER 10

SOUTH COAST: BRUTAL AND BORING

*'It was a worrying situation. We were going
to get there before the team did, and, the last
time this had happened, Dan and I had been in
danger because there had been no one to help
us land safely in the thick mist.'*

N ext morning, we headed down to our landing place to check
it out and see what the chances were for a launch that
evening. We also wanted to see if we could get one of the
vehicles down there so that we would have some help in getting
away. Tracey wasn't optimistic: there was only the one road down.

And, to get to the beach, the vehicle would have to be got over the river somehow, which would be a battle, four-wheel-drive or no four-wheel-drive.

Tracey, meanwhile, had yet another headache to contend with: the team had just about run out of bread, which it consumed at the rate of about two loaves a day. She succeeded in finding some, although each loaf cost about R17 (over US$2, more or less double the South African price). But bread, frankly, wasn't really on my mind at the moment – daylight had revealed that not one river, but several, separated us from the beach, each as unpromising-looking as the others. The big question was whether the water was too deep for the vehicles.

I was impatient with all this: I wanted to get back on the water as soon as possible, while the good weather lasted – which, in Iceland, was not something to depend on. Thanks to bad weather and the damage to the kayak, we were a month behind schedule. Now we had the chance of making up some of the backlog with our third consecutive day on the water, maintaining our newfound momentum. Originally, I had planned to do the trip in a series of five-day stages, but reality had made mincemeat of those calculations – I had been wrong every time. But what I would get right, I resolved, was the most important part: finishing it.

It would be a short paddle – 25 kilometres – to our next destination, Jökulsárlón. This is probably the most famous landing place for kayakers on this entire coast. There is a glacial river and a lake with huge icebergs in it, and when some of these icebergs have been melting for a while they actually roll over into the sea … and we were going to be landing right in between them! I mean, any adventurous kayaker would give his eyeteeth to do that – who else would be able to tell his grandchildren tales about landing between icebergs?

Tracey was still on a learning curve after her abrupt 'promotion'. She had just acquired the art of 4x4 driving, which she loved, but she still needed some instruction on the correct use of the GPS device. I gave her some rather curt instructions, which I regretted later; my only excuse is that the tide was coming in, which meant that we had to get going. Peter said nothing, preferring not to stick his oar into an already overheated moment.

The launch went off smoothly, and Dan and I got down to the paddle to Jökulsárlón in high spirits. Conditions were perfect, and we enjoyed smooth going, with Dan making a strong start. I was under no illusions, however, that the finish would necessarily go just as smoothly. Jökulsárlón was rightly famed for its beauty, but it was a very dangerous beauty.

We were still a long way from Jökulsárlón when Dan started flagging. I guessed that he had started off a little too strongly, and now he was rapidly tiring. I egged him on with a mixture of sympathy and exhortation; I knew it was not just physical fatigue but a mental battle for Dan to overcome the limitations his cerebral palsy placed on his stamina.

We managed to reach Jökulsárlón in fairly good time, however. Now we had to find a landing place – and soon. It was beginning to get dark, and the darker it got the more difficult it would be to spot the treacherous blue ice. We managed to reach the entrance to the glacial lake, and I spotted the first piece of ice in front of us. It was only a small piece, but we didn't need a close encounter with it.

On shore, meanwhile, Tracey was worried because the team hadn't been able to spot us yet. She had concluded that it was necessary for us to get across the mouth of the river and land on the beach to the west to avoid the worst breakers. But we couldn't make contact.

Eventually the team spotted us, but we had to run the gauntlet of icebergs before we could get to the western beach. Then, before we knew it, we had capsized. To say it was disheartening would be an understatement, and it was a real struggle to get back in – especially for Dan, whose muscles stiffened as the temperature dropped and he became more tired. He was plunged in gloom, because he felt his performance just hadn't improved. It wasn't really surprising: we had had two strenuous paddling days in succession for the first time in about two months, and inevitably we were not in top form.

Anyway, we struggled across the river mouth and landed without incident. Dan's spirits picked up after the adrenaline rush of the last half hour and the frightening but exciting landing. When the team turned the camera on him next morning he declared: 'We were definitely at the most exciting place I have ever landed a kayak … [When] we came in late last night it was a different tide, and the icebergs now are busy literally rolling out in this river out to sea. What I didn't think we would do was actually go out and paddle with this raging river combining with the rolling icebergs. I think it's going to be an exciting launch.'

On the way to Jökulsárlón's fine hotel, where we were putting up, Peter gave Dan a wise pep talk, his last before his departure: 'Many, many days to go, so you just have to keep the mind and effort on the thing; don't get down, the moment you start getting down and beating yourself up, it's going to get worse … You know what your focus points are, and you have to build up to get to that point, and, once you're through that, I think you're going to be fine. You've had a bad day, when you've hoped that it would have been better; now you're going to have to focus on the next day. Just go on, that's all you can do. Let's go home, get some supper and have an early night.'

Vasti and I took Peter to the local airport so he could catch a flight to Reykjavík. I felt a little sad as we returned; she would soon be leaving as well. I was going to miss her very much, and I think we were all going to miss her calming presence.

Meanwhile, the team planned the night's paddle, 30 kilometres southwest to our next landmark, Ingólfshöfði, which lay on a long, high spit of land with a lighthouse at its southern end. Night paddling had by now become our norm. We had got some advice from Gísli Friðgeirsson, the grandfather of Icelandic paddling, who had told us that, when he had paddled around Iceland, he did most of it at night. I could now see why.

Once again, Dan and I had to deal with cold and fog. It seemed that low-pressure systems brought calmer seas, but also cold at night. I think Peter and Vasti had been surprised to hear us say that temperatures had risen dramatically. The snowy start to the journey had melted away almost entirely in our memories.

One night, after seven hours at sea, I remember being dazed at how the coastline lacked reference points. It was like we were paddling to nothing. I was desperate to see some land through all this mist, even though we did nothing but complain about the uninspiring black-sand beaches and dunes when we could see them. Nevertheless, I couldn't have been more wrong about Ingólfshöfði. It was really special. The breaking surf added huge stress for me as I guided the kayak in along the 76-metre-high rock face.

Ingólfshöfði is celebrated as the spot where Iceland's first settler arrived in 874. The story goes that Ingólfr Arnarson came to Iceland after being forced to leave Norway because of a blood feud. After a second trip to the island, he and his brother-in-law, Hjörleifr Hróðmarsson, decided to make it their home. Together with their wives and slaves, they trekked westward from this spot. Hjörleifr was later murdered by his Irish slaves. According to the *Book of Settlements*, Iceland's official record of the people who came here, Ingólfshöfði became the focal point for any new settlers.

Now, 1100 years later, two fools in a kayak were attempting to land here too. We were exhausted, but little did we know what still awaited us on the ride back to warmth and rest: 4x4 adventure, Iceland style!

When the team had done a recce down towards Ingólfshöfði, they had made contact with a local landowner, one Einar, who offered us assistance if we ever needed it. According to Einar, there was a road to an old harbour near the lighthouse, which would be a good landing place, and the road was passable at high and low tide. The sea was flat and, all in all, it looked like a good night for paddling.

But on the way back, both of our Toyotas got stuck in a river bed. The water level was high because of the tide, and the vehicles were not being driven in 4x4 mode. Tracey put in a call to Einar, and he came out at 03h00 with his trusty tractor to pull us out of the mud – something his father had done for tourists for years.

We were blown away by his energy and by his willingness to help us out of the quagmire. Geezlike, if only all locals could treat tourists like this. This loving feeling did not last, though. As I sat huddled in the front seat of the Land Cruiser, trying to warm up, Zahir came to me with a surprise: the farmer wanted to know how we would be settling our bill. Cash or credit card? Einar, all businesslike and professional, whipped out a credit-card machine from the tractor dashboard and swiped a few hundred US dollars off my account. It was a bit of a shock, though I made sure Tracey got a receipt.

All good things must come to an end sooner or later, and now it was time for Vasti to go home after 10 amazing days. It was a sad thought for me, all right, but I reflected that it had been time well spent. She'd got a taste of what we were doing, and even helped to pull the kayak out of the water. She had enjoyed it, too, and regretted having to leave.

I took her back to Reykjavík, which was no loss of travelling time because the winds were too strong to allow a launch. The rest of the team made sure the kayak was safe at Ingólfshöfði. (They took no chances: Tracey and Dan even dug a trench for *Inspiration* to rest in until we needed her.)

Ahead was the impressive glacial plain of Skeiðarársandur, remote, bleak and crammed with rivers swollen with spring runoff rushing towards the sea. What was planned was a 01h00 start the following morning on a two-legged paddle totalling 62 kilometres; at the halfway mark, the team would put up tents and make food, and we would sleep for a few hours before taking on the second leg, to Skaftárós.

For the first part of the trip, we would have a six-hour window from 01h00 when the wind would be southeasterly, and around 07h00 it would turn into a westerly. It would be a stiff trip, but there was no other way to do it, and a recce had shown that there was a usable road down to the landing place so that the team could set up the tents and prepare hot food.

Dan looked forward to the early-morning start with some foreboding, because the sea seemed pretty choppy, although he consoled himself with the thought that perhaps it would have calmed down by the time we launched. By contrast, I was in a buoyant mood. Thanks to the wind, I had been able to stay an extra day in Reykjavík after putting Vasti on the plane. It was only on the way back that I realised just how important that one day on my own had been to me. The fact is that I like it on my own, which is perhaps one of my strengths. Anyway, I was feeling positive again, and I was really looking forward to the night's paddle. I was glad that I was the old Riaan Manser again.

Just after midnight, we set off back to Ingólfshöfði. This time, Tracey mastered the waterlogged road like a real pro, but Zahir bogged down. Einar had to be called in once more, and it was 08h00 before the team was assembled at the beach.

But the surf was too heavy for us to launch. So there we sat, hoping for the best – in vain. At 10h30 things were no better; we wouldn't be able to stay on the kayak, and I didn't think it was going to get better. Disheartened at the thought of the time, energy and money we'd wasted, we headed back for some much-needed rest. About the only good thing to say about the whole expensive venture was that this time we didn't get stuck.

With no immediate prospect of a start, we decided to make use of the downtime to travel vertically instead of horizontally for a change. I have a fixation about getting to the highest points of the places I visit, and had heard about Hvannadalshnúkur, Iceland's highest peak, from our friend Vilborg, who is an official mountain guide. She put me in touch with Einar Sigordsson, owner of Glacier Guides, who agreed to take Darren, Richard and I up the mountain, which lies within Vatnajökull National Park. In typical positive style, Darren agreed to carry the camera and all its associated gear. No one gives much thought to what it takes to film someone summiting a mountain. Cameramen probably have a more difficult time than the climbers.

Richard and Darren quickly discovered that I had space in my backpack, and loaded their ropes and crampons into my bag. It made thinks more difficult for me, but these guys needed to be 'working' for the entire journey, and cumbersome gear would hamper them from getting the best shots.

The first 300 metres were medium-gradient and fast. I found myself breathing heavily and perspiring profusely. Essentially, I hadn't used my legs for any strenuous effort in months. My overheating related directly to wearing too many warm clothes. Mountaineers make every attempt to avoid perspiring, as it becomes more dangerous the higher you go. Your body takes more time to regenerate heat than it takes to lose it.

We continued upward through tundra, and moved into rocky and sometimes difficult volcanic terrain. The barren vastness began to expand with every metre of altitude. Space began to seem infinite the higher we went. We approached the Vatnajökull Glacier, at an elevation of 1 000 metres, and got our first sight of Hvannadalshnúkur itself. It looked about 30 minutes' climb away, but in fact took another seven leg-busting hours to reach. We climbed and climbed and climbed. Totti, our guide for the day, joined us together with a safety harness, in case one of us fell into a crevasse.

Hvannadalshnúkur is 2 119 metres above sea level, and is definitely the murderous 15-hour hike they say it will be. The crevasses are big enough to quietly take a minibus to Hades. Darren has a very dry sense of humour and a constant smile, and it was strange to see him turn dead silent and expressionless. He later said to me that the climb was the hardest thing he had ever done. It was tough going for me as well, probably more so than it looked from an outsider's perspective. I kept the humour going until we had about 100 metres left to ascend. With the sun beating down and the gradient near-vertical, jokes didn't seem funny any more.

We were all buoyed by the achievement of reaching Iceland's highest point. From this rare vantage point, we could see the Grímsvötn and Eyjafjallajökull volcanoes, the Vestmannaeyjar Islands and even tiny Surtsey Island. The southern coastline was covered in thick, puffy cloudbanks, but we could clearly follow the line of the coast heading eastward. I told Darren and Richard that they would speak of this moment fondly for the rest of their lives. But it was also something I would have liked Dan to accomplish, although on that day I think he preferred the relaxation and quiet time the warm guesthouse offered. This time with Darren and Richard on top of Iceland is one of my fondest memories of the journey. Definitely a bucket list effort, if you ask me.

The winds finally died down, and, after a week off the water, we headed for Ingólfshöfði once more. By this time we really were a match for Einar's dreadful watery road, and we got to the beach without any trouble. Dan and I were psyched up and ready to go. The sea state was still anything but ideal, but I decided to risk it and launch. Of course, we still had to make it through the breakers. The formula was as before: keep the bow facing into the breakers, or the water would smash us into the rocks. As soon as we were clear of the breakers, we'd head south and then west.

Sure it was dodgy, but this trip was full of dodgy moments. I was still pumped up and feeling positive, and so was Dan, although he was having a problem with some blisters on his hands and was afraid they would make him flinch and lose his balance while paddling. But his spirit was all right: 'I'm feeling good. Obviously there are always nerves before, but it's better nerves than usual, so I just want to go.'

My worries turned out to be groundless, and before long we were on our way. About the only thing that went wrong was that Brad the cameraman didn't get a particular shot his colleague Darren wanted because, at the crucial moment, he was dive-bombed by a flock of skua gulls. As he explained, 'In the end, this one got like really aggressive, and he was coming straight at my face and at the same time, he was dropping poo on me, but he was like banking and shit, and flying all over me, and I just gave up – my life was in danger …'

With this minor Icelandic drama out of the way, the team headed back to camp to refresh themselves before tackling the trip to the rest point. It turned out to be a bad decision. Dan and I made such good time that we were far ahead of schedule, but Tracey didn't realise this because for some reason my GPS beacon wasn't working. The result was that when I radioed her that I was only 40 minutes away from the rest point the team still had some considerable distance to travel.

It was a worrying situation. We were going to get there before the team did, and, the last time this had happened, Dan and I had been in danger because there had been no one to help us land safely in the thick mist. This might not seem all that perilous, but the reality was different. Landings are always potentially dangerous, and can be even more risky in a double kayak because of the extra weight and thus the decreased manoeuvrability, with both the boat and the paddlers in danger of being knocked about if they capsize.

The team was still about half an hour away when we got to the rest point, and all we could do was hang around, getting colder and colder. After about 40 minutes, they finally appeared on the beach. I was really annoyed; having to wait and freeze like that was really, really not fun.

But there was a pleasant surprise awaiting Dan. Two old friends, Phil Beier and his dad, Guenther, had arranged to visit him along the way, and here they were with the team, having arrived early. Phil and Guenther had known Dan since he was young and were extremely fond of him.

Unfortunately, this stop had reaffirmed the disdain that the crew had built up towards me. I was trying hard to avoid conflict and to reassure everyone, especially Dan, of their importance to the success of the journey. It was troubling, though, to finish a paddle as the villain once again. It made me feel that human beings are cowardly by nature. Like hyenas, they feel powerful in a group, but when alone they seem to have no backbone.

Dan and I had had a sincere chat the evening before. I was making a big effort to communicate with him about everything I was feeling. One of the things I mentioned to him was that I felt he was letting other people do things for him. I had, on the last three occasions, packed his sleeping bag and dry clothes for him; I thought it would only do him good to do it himself. Dan had told me he wanted to take more responsibility and show independence. Now, I don't know what I should have done, but I told him that we could start immediately. Packing the next day's halfway kit – sleeping bag, dry clothes, and so on – would be his responsibility. I did not remind Dan again and left the ball squarely in his court.

It was a foolish mistake on my part. When we landed, Zahir and the others had just arrived on the beach. I helped them set up the tents and then collected my sleeping bag from one of the vehicles. I was cold and tired but managed to change quickly into my dry gear and fall asleep.

Later, I heard a commotion outside the tent; Dan was frantically searching for his stuff. Tracey asked him where his kit was, and he replied that he thought I had it. Tracey then came on Dan's behalf to ask if I had taken his gear. Of course, I began to doubt myself, and immediately double-checked that I didn't have it. Then I went back to sleep.

When I awoke, I found that Dan had slept in the vehicle. He was grumpy and uncomfortable. When I asked him where his gear was, he said he couldn't find it. The crew, especially Tracey, were sulking, but I couldn't understand why.

It was only when I got back in South Africa and reviewed the footage shot for the documentary that things began to make sense. The inner workings of the team dynamics and the team's lack of impartiality came to the fore at this moment. On camera, Tracey explains to the viewers how Dan has to suffer in the vehicle while Riaan sleeps snugly in Dan's sleeping bag.

Once we were back on the water, I asked Dan about his sleeping bag; his response was, firstly, that he had never once mentioned that I had his gear, and, secondly, that he would set the record straight that evening. But, by this time, the hyenas had found their victim. Dan had guests and was too preoccupied to address the issue in the open, which was fair enough. The battering I was taking seemed never-ending.

That evening, Guenther kindly took the whole team out to dinner at their hotel. The team had fun, I think, and appreciated the gesture immensely. I enjoyed Guenther's wisdom, and took away what I considered valuable tips and advice. He is someone who knows more about leadership than I probably ever will. What did disturb me, though, was something he had saved for me on behalf of Dan.

'Riaan, I'm asking you to stop one thing. And that is to never tell Dan again that he is privileged. He has told me it bothers him immensely when you tell him this. Please never ever bring this up again.'

I listened in amazement, I must admit. I was stunned that Dan could have expressed such feelings. He and I had had very sincere, very emotional discussions. What reason did we have to withhold truth from one another? I felt emotionally swamped, and was filled with doubts about the sincerity of those around me. I agreed with Guenther that I wouldn't bring up the topic again. In hindsight, I feel embarrassed that I didn't stand up for myself. The fact is, Dan has been privileged, and nothing can change that.

Thinking back, I can only marvel at the distance between me and the team. I woke every morning rejuvenated in my commitment to Dan and to what I had promised to do in Iceland, while on the other side of the spectrum a constant effort was being made to vilify and gang up against the 'enemy'.

In spite of all my forebodings, we reached Skaftárós without incident. Our next destination was the halfway mark at Vík, about 70 kilometres away. We had planned to finish the whole expedition in 90 days, after which I would fulfil a long-standing obligation to take part in the Western Cape's famed Windhoek Berg River Canoe Marathon. Instead, we had got only halfway, and all of us were pretty much at the end of our tether. So we decided that the team would have a break at Vík to recharge their batteries, while I would dash back to South Africa for the Windhoek Berg River Canoe Marathon and then dash back for the second half of the expedition.

Seventy kilometres was a long haul, but not an impossible one if it was done in two phases, as we'd just proved. This time we'd do it in three. Dan and I would paddle the first 30 kilometres and land near a lighthouse at a place called Mýrnatangi, where the team would be waiting with food and a tent so that we could grab a couple of hours' sleep. After that, we would land again 20 kilometres further on, refresh ourselves and do the final 20 kilometres to Vík. Tracey calculated that the team would probably put in a 24-hour stretch, but what the hell, everybody was wound up to do it.

On top of everything else that had happened, it looked like we were now headed for a showdown with Cooked in Africa. Over a few telephone conversations and emails, Justin and Peter had decided it was time to lay down the law with me, to the point of even threatening their withdrawal from the project. You can imagine how I felt – exactly what I didn't need. But it was par for the course on this adventure.

They had sent me an email requesting that I take over the staff salaries and the entire expedition expenses. I really believed that they felt I was being generous in my willingness to assist. But what they were teaching me – and I didn't realise it at the time – was that people like me, the trusting kind, are usually taken for everything they have. We end up the fools.

Our original agreement was simple. We would each cover our own costs, no exceptions; similarly, we would split all income from additional sponsors of the documentary, no exceptions. Since they had failed to get money in, they told me the agreement was unfair. They should be allowed to get money in just for them and their expenses. Now, obviously this wouldn't be fair. Who would cover my costs? How was I going to make a living if I was spending my own money to make this expedition bigger and better? They thought I was being arrogant. Nevertheless, I offered to carry the entire expedition expenses, which were by now at the million-rand mark. Over and above this concession, I said I was willing to pay their staff salaries. They just had one stipulation: I should pay them the money for salaries directly and they would keep the staff on their books. Why, if I were willing to do something so generous, would they not be as transparent as possible? They knew everything about me – my income, my staff salaries, and so on. Of course I wouldn't agree to that. What idiot would?

The conversation that followed, via telephone, was again a hugely stressful one for me. We were planning to go paddling, and everyone, including the crew and the Beiers, was standing around waiting to get going. The scenery of Myrdalssandur was stunning, and kept the guys relaxed. I strolled off to take a conference call with Peter and Justin. I explained to them that I was prepared to assist even more with the finances, but that they also needed to be reasonable. It took Justin to raise his voice at me only once, something I didn't think he would ever do, for me to tell him how I felt. What he didn't realise was that he was not the reason I was in Iceland. He and his crew knew very little about what I had done in the last 10 years. I had earlier asked Darren if he had read any of my books or knew where I had been and what I'd gone through. He replied that Justin had told them to read up on me and they all read some websites and stuff.

Well, of course these guys must be wondering why I think I can make the decisions! After all, they had no respect for me. If Justin didn't, why should they? They didn't realise what it took to embark on an expedition like this, and they didn't respect the fact that I had some experience in this field. They couldn't have; they knew very little of what I had achieved in the past. And having this conversation with Justin made me realise that he had no respect for my expertise in this kind of stuff either. It seemed that he didn't want a working relationship, but rather a 'telling you what to do' one.

Toyota had loaned us a Land Cruiser and a Hilux in exchange for Justin's cameraman and sound man shooting some promo videos for them. The guys were leaving for the shoot that Thursday, and we expected them back the next Monday. Hearing Justin shouting at me at the top of his voice, obviously in front of all his staff in Cape Town, I realised that I needed to cut my losses sooner rather than later.

Calmly, I made my position clear: 'Justin, when your people go up to shoot near Reykjavík this weekend, don't bother sending them back. I don't need you and your threats any more. Tell them to pack their bags and go home. I've got more problems than you can imagine.'

Man, I didn't need this drama. All I wanted was to share a story about a brave guy who, against all odds, amazes everyone in the world with his courage. Right then, the story had nothing to do with that.

Before we left on the long paddle to Vík, we said goodbye to Phil and Guenther. They knew Dan far better than any of us, and their parting comments made a lot of sense.

'I think for Dan it's a huge experience, because he's never had a challenge like this in his life before,' Guenther said on camera. 'It's also having to relate to Riaan, to understand what Riaan requires when he's out on the boat, to know that, when he asks him to do something, he's got to do it and to keep on repeating this whole issue. And for him it's not easy, because his balance is not perfect when he's out there.

'So he's got to concentrate on that and sometimes, of course, he's also a little afraid of what's happening and so, consequently, he doesn't remember what he's been told. So, one has to keep on going at it and giving him like a plan to understand, "This is what I expect of you and make sure you do it". But I think there's a better understanding between the two of them now, and I think it looks like they're going on a good trip.

'Everything that's thrown at him out here – hey, he can do it. He's a very capable person, there's no doubt about that. But at the end of the day, you've got to take your hats off to what these two guys are doing, it's just absolutely incredible and it's really, really tough. I don't think I'd be able to do something like this, you know.' We'd be the first to paddle around Iceland in a two-man kayak, and Dan would certainly be the first to do it with a serious physical disability … of course, we were still about a thousand kilometres away from setting those two firsts, but at least we were well on the way.

We got going without any mishaps, to the tune of my usual exhortations, of which both Dan and I were heartily sick by now: 'Watch the waves, watch the waves! Wait, wait, wait. After this one you can jump in, OK? This one's gonna hit you hard, go aggressively into it, aggressive, aggressive! Good stuff! You've got to go hard here; you've got to go hard! Hold the weight up against the kayak. Do you know what I mean? Just go.' And so on and so on.

And so we went, first south, then west, over a delightfully calm sea. But after a while I noticed that the kayak had taken on quite a lot of water. I set Dan to pumping it out while I paddled. I wasn't too worried – there didn't seem to be more than four or five litres on board, which meant it was a slow leak. Since we'd been paddling through calm water, I reckoned that the leak hadn't been caused by the working of the kayak's hull, but by a small hole somewhere. If Dan kept emptying the water out, we should be OK, and we'd make it to Vík, and that long-anticipated break from the forces of Nature.

Which reminded me … Vík was not strictly the halfway mark, geographically speaking, but it was close enough for our purposes, and reaching it meant a lot. It's all very well having a final destination, but it helps a lot to have some intermediate destinations as well, to keep your spirits and determination high. That was why we were doing that long, long paddle, which would probably take us to 04h00 or 05h00 next morning, which would break the camel's back, as far as the south coast was concerned.

I called Tracey: 'Tell you what, if we make it to Vík, you guys are going to have a party when you land. That's what you're gonna have; nobody goes to sleep. Tracey, will you get some beer and some whisky for the guys?'

'Ja, OK!' she said enthusiastically.

But Vík was still far away, and in the meantime we had more immediate problems … one of which was that the makeshift brace I had rigged for Dan's legs at Húsavík had somehow disappeared. This was quite serious, because the brace kept his knees apart and thus helped him to balance. After some experimentation, we found a substitute that worked quite well, and we went back to paddling and pumping.

The south coast was forcing us into a 'wet' start almost every paddle session. If we had any surf to contend with, no matter how small, I made sure to psych up Dan beforehand. I love a surf launch; it sets the tone for the day, as well as getting you loosened up physically and mentally. Most front-seated paddlers hate taking the brunt of the surf, though. For the guys at the back, it's merely a bit of a splash or spray. It was an adventure for Dan every time we set off through surf.

Dan and I had had a reasonable paddle the previous night, one that was meant to have been the half of an 80-kilometre-plus plan I had conjured up: a monster day that would see us to our halfway mark at Vík.

After the first 35 kilometres, we landed at Mýrnatangi, which allowed the team easy access to us from the main road. Although I still had ample reserves of energy, I allowed myself to be lazy and entertain the thought of resting for the rest of the day and only paddling again the following day. To be truthful, I might have succumbed to this laziness if it were not for the weather: gale-force winds and huge six-metre surf were forecast for the next few days. It was almost hard to believe, considering we had just finished a night paddle in flat calm.

Reaching the halfway point was what I needed mentally at that moment. I was feeling very unmotivated, and needed more of that 'I'm on the way home' talk in my head. This was a slogan I'd adopted in Tunisia during my Africa bicycle circumnavigation: after the halfway mark, every stroke is two metres closer to home. I think this is what kept me aggressive and fired up when the sea got rough. The sea doesn't care for your story, your tears or your plans. The sea has an energy that you can feel even when standing on shore. The ground trembles when huge waves break on the pebbled shores. The main beach at Vík, with finger rocks just offshore, would make a chilling backdrop to what was going to be one of our most 'exciting' landings of the entire journey.

We had a snooze that morning. Right afterwards, Tracy told me she believed the conditions were ideal for paddling. My desire to get to the halfway point probably squashed any concerns I had welling up inside me at this time. The south coast of Iceland is very similar to what I had experienced in Madagascar: unhindered swell pulverising long, unprotected beaches. Conditions can change in an instant.

Dan and I set off in the shadows of Mýrnatangi's gigantic caves, unaware of what lay before us. The wind was blowing from behind us with considerable force, and was picking up with every minute – an eerie reminder of that fateful day when Dan was lost at sea. It was only at the 20-kilometre point that I mentioned to Dan how concerned I was. In fact, I steered us closer to shore in case we capsized and found ourselves separated from the kayak. The positive aspect of the rising swell, wind and surf was that we almost doubled our average speed. I was unrelenting in making sure Dan stayed focused. We capsized twice, and each time I swam with Dan around the kayak nose to get him back into his seat.

The mist was growing thicker, and the temperature plummeted from a balmy 10 °C to -3 °C. Anyone could have predicted the wheels of this chariot were about to come off. I estimated the swell at four to five metres in height, and the crests of breaking waves were easily one metre high. We struggled to stay on board the kayak. By the time we were near Vík, Dan was totally fatigued. I had invited effort on his part that he probably hadn't thought possible. But no encouragement was going to help him now. He was slumping sideways, with almost no control of his upper body. I managed to prevent us falling out on several occasions, but it became almost impossible as we drew within landing distance.

We could see huge crushing surf smashing into Vík's half-finished breakwater. The kayak was almost six metres long, but it looked tiny in the churning water. From the crest of a wave to the trough below us was nearly double the kayak length. To the west – the direction the wind was blowing us – the coastline was jagged volcanic rock. The breakwater had created a bigger hazard than I thought it would. Even the lulls between the monster wave sets were big enough to smash us onto the rocks.

When I think of what we had to do to get Dan safely to land, I am amazed we did it so efficiently; there was nothing elegant about it. It was almost impossible to communicate with the crew on the beach and then look blindly from the back of the gigantic swell, all the while trying to balance us. The guys on land had little idea of what took place during that long 45 minutes as I tried to keep us in the boat while searching for the courage to bring us through the most dangerous situation we had yet been in. Dan could hardly stay in the boat; he was panicked beyond words and crying with fear. Each time we tipped over, the wind pushed us further to the west, toward the rocks and away from the beach landing spot.

Maybe it was good that Dan didn't understand the true danger we were in. We were blown a kilometre past where we hoped to land. Richard frantically radioed suggestions for a better landing place, and Tracey was a shivering wreck every time I asked her something on the radio. I had very little energy left to keep us from falling out and then to help Dan back into the kayak. The last time we fell out I physically had to get Dan back into the boat, the surf breaking over us. I held onto the kayak with one arm, and with the other gripped Dan's life jacket so he wouldn't be carried away. When I tried to push him upwards onto the kayak, I went under and swallowed a lot of water. The kilometre that we had to paddle back *into* the wind took nearly an hour and sapped my remaining energy.

I tried to decide when to take us into shore, but kept chickening out. As it was just before midnight, and our last drop of light had gone, I ran out of time. I could feel the relief when we eventually went for it; it was as though a burden had lifted.

Timing is a gamble in a heavy kayak that takes a dozen or so seconds to get to a reasonable speed. For any sea paddler, this is too slow to attempt surfing a big wave with safety. If you don't get it right, the wave could smash right on top of you.

It was unfair on Tracey and Richard to have to carry the burden of trying to tell me via radio where they thought the sea was calmer. They had no experience of this kind of sea. Later, when I saw the footage of that day, I understood how utterly panicked Tracey was.

My decision, about three seconds down the face of the wave, surprised me. I believed we could ride the kayak very close to shore. I managed to steer us out of trouble on the first wave, which proved a blessing, as it placed us perfectly into the path of a wave strong enough to tumble us coastwards. After taking off on this wave, I made the call to bale out so that we wouldn't nosedive and have the kayak topple over Dan. We spluttered and gasped in the icy water, the kayak washing dangerously over Dan's head at one point.

The danger wasn't over, though. If the rip sucked us out to sea, we would be in critical danger. I could feel and see the rip a few metres to our right. We had to stay clear of it, no matter what. The timing was again fortuitous, and, incredibly, I managed to get Dan safely to shore. As a swell approached, I took a firm grip of his waist and ankle, pushing him forward with the breaking wave. Dan kept washing forward with the wave into safe, shallow waters. A wave crashed over me, and, for a few seconds, I thought I was caught in the rip. The following sets were of the 'non-negotiable' type, and, fortunately, everything went to shore.

Dan and I both crawled from the sea. My lower back was cramping as I lifted him up. We had little breath left for an immediate philosophical take to the cameraman, but I spluttered a soft and subdued self-congratulation. *You've done it, halfway! Well done, well done!* The crew surrounded Dan and made sure he was OK. I sat alone on the nearest rock watching them all, offering myself another due congratulation. After all, no one else would.

But the bottom line was that we had made it to the halfway mark. It was 25 June, precisely 91 days since we had set off from now-distant Húsavík on the other side of Iceland.

CHAPTER 11

Halfway point

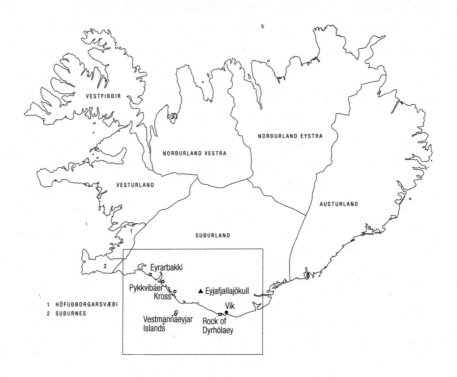

'I could see the reconstituted team finally settling into the rhythm of the expedition. Dan and I seemed to have found our groove at last ...'

As it turned out, the laughing and singing didn't take place at Vík: we decided to make up some of the time we had lost. So now the plan was to go on to the actual geographical halfway mark before the team took its well-deserved break and I dashed back to South Africa for the Windhoek Berg River Canoe Marathon. In other words, it was watch-the-weather-and-hold-thumbs time again.

I was really looking forward to the break. The trip so far had really taken it out of me, and here I was, committed to doing the Windhoek Berg River Canoe Marathon – a tough paddle, one of the premier kayaking events in South Africa.

I reckoned Dan could use the break as well. For months he had been pushing his body, and on top of that he had been grappling with immense mental strain. Remember that, apart from anything else, he was a novice who had been flung into the most gruelling kayaking venture imaginable, even for a veteran, without having had the opportunity to work up to it on smaller trips.

We set off again after a much-needed rest day, not planning to do anything ambitious. We had only a short window when the wind was expected to stay reasonable, so we were content to plan a 20-kilometre paddle to just past the Pétursey River. After that, we would see; it would be nice to go on and complete a 35-kilometre stretch – we would have a tailwind that might help us to cover more distance – but at this stage we weren't banking on anything. What we really hoped is that we could make it to Reykjavík before I left for South Africa. In the meantime, every kilometre covered brought us nearer to that goal. So if the time-window stayed open for longer than was estimated … but we would just have to see.

Our landing place at Vík looked less terrifying than when we'd come ashore there, and we launched without too much trouble. Dan and I were feeling pretty good as we dug our paddles into the water; the sea conditions were fine, we had an easy paddle ahead and a helpful tailwind, and we were going to be doing something very special.

The most spectacular tourist attraction along this part of the coast is the so-called Rock of Dyrhólaey, which is actually a rock arch that visitors gape at from the shore. We weren't going to do that; we were actually going to paddle *through* it. I only hoped that, when we did so, the cameras would roll as scheduled, that their batteries would last instead of conking out without warning, as camera batteries tend to do, so that the team would be able to get some good footage of us from the shore.

Before too long, we had reached the river mouth, 17 kilometres from Vík, and pushed on again for the remaining two or three kilometres or so to our landing place, at a farm called Stóraborg. Passing through the Rock of Dyrhólaey had been everything we had expected. We had taken our kayak to and through an amazing natural wonder, something very few people had done – even Icelanders. It was a special day all right.

Having reached Stóraborg, I got ambitious and called Tracey about going 11 kilometres further to another landing place while the fine weather lasted. But she told us that there was no road access at all to the 30-kilometre mark. I didn't complain. It had been a delightful day's paddling, which we had really enjoyed. Sufficient unto the day … 'Cool,' I told her, 'we'll land here.'

At this landing, we tried out a new technique that I had thought up for getting ashore. Unfortunately it was better in my mind than in reality, and didn't work so well. I wasn't too disappointed; you win some, you lose some. Dan was in fine form, alert and trying hard to overcome some of the problems he'd had from the start. For some reason, he hadn't slept well the previous night, but as he said later: 'I feel good; I'm also keen to just get some kilometres under the belt.' That was the sort of spirit that counted.

Next morning, the sea conditions were still good, and we set out on what we hoped would be the last leg before I left for South Africa. We were going to give it a good try, but, to be honest, I wasn't as enthusiastic as usual. I was very tired, so tired that I hadn't even felt like getting up.

The plain fact was that I had taken a mental and physical beating in the last three months, and now it was catching up with me. But I knew I would feel a bit better once I got into the rhythm of paddling.

The plan for the day was to travel in three stages. The first would take us right past Eyjafjallajökull, whose eruption had caused so much trouble recently, the second past the Vestmannaeyjar Islands, and the third a little further along in the direction of Reykjavík. I got a bit worried when I found myself short of breath. Was my heart up to doing the Berg River? The canoe marathon placed a huge strain on your cardiovascular system, that was for sure … I found myself struck by doubts.

The Vestmannaeyjar archipelago, like so many other places in Iceland, has an ancient and sometimes violent history. The story goes that, around the year 874, Iceland's first settler, Ingólfr Arnarson, set off after a bunch of escaped Irish slaves who had murdered his brother-in-law, Hjörleifr Hróðmarsson. He chased them to Heimaey (home island), the largest island in the archipelago, and killed every last one.

The only positive aspect to this gory tale is that, in the process of hunting down the errant Irishmen, Arnarson gave names to various places and landmarks, which endure to this day. The unfortunate slaves left their mark, too; 'Vestmannaeyjar' derives from 'Vestmenn' (West Men), as the Irish were called in those days.

The archipelago seems doomed to suffer death and/or disaster at intervals. In 1627, three Barbary pirate ships sacked several coastal settlements and islands, including Heimaey, stealing what they could and taking some captives. One of the latter was a woman named Guðríður Símonardóttir, who was later sold at the slave market in Algiers. But Guðríður seems to have been one of your typical

Icelandic survival experts, because she managed to make her way home via Tunisia, Italy and Denmark, and ended up marrying the noted Icelandic poet Hallgrímur Pétursson.

After that, the archipelago enjoyed a few hundred years of peace until 23 January 1973, when Heimaey's Eldfell volcano came to life. Tons of hot ash rained down over everything, and a tide of lava threatened the little town of Heimaey. Most of the local fishing fleet happened to be tied up in the harbour. The island's 5 000-odd inhabitants were evacuated that night, but half of the town was incinerated and it looked as if the harbour was doomed as well.

The inhabitants fought back by spraying huge amounts of sea water on the lava, enough of which cooled and solidified for the flow to be diverted away from the harbour. When the eruption ended about six months later – by which time the island was about two square kilometres larger – the inhabitants were not as devastated as one might have expected; their attitude reportedly was that, while it was terrible that half the town had been destroyed, the important thing was that their livelihood was safe, and that only one death had been recorded. I tell this story because it gives an indication of the type of people you find in Iceland.

Dan, who seemed to have found his sea legs, as you might say, saw that I was feeling low and came to the rescue: 'Don't doubt yourself, hey!' he admonished me. 'I'm really starting to enjoy myself a lot more. The funny thing is, I'm more … after those long chats we had, and those sort of shit days, I'm more aware of the scale of the challenge, you know what I mean? So it's a good thing … I think I'm making progress.'

'I think you are, for sure,' I replied.

'Nowhere near where I should be,' he said jauntily, 'but I'm going *somewhere*.'

Our first stage ended with a landing at Landeyjahöfn harbour, from where ferries depart on the 30-minute ride to Heimaey. We had a quick lunch break here before tackling the next stage, to Kross, 42 kilometres from our starting point. From there we could go on to do a night paddle. This last leg was a bit of a tall order, but we decided that we would see how things developed.

In the meantime, it was pleasant to be paddling in the comparatively warm daylight hours for a change, and I felt pretty good. I even ended up singing, although the words were hardly inspirational and I don't think Dan liked it much (please understand that I could hardly blame him). But things really were going very well. Here we were, nearing the 40-kilometre mark, and earlier we'd all been thinking no further ahead than doing about 30 kilometres for the day.

My only concern was that my hands were taking some strain. I was worried about arriving at the Berg River with blisters, and so in the end we didn't do the night paddle. Kross seemed like a good place to stop, not only so that my hands and blisters would have time to recover, but also because the team members were very tired. It made no sense to push things to breaking point when there was no urgent reason to do so.

So it was at Kross that we called a halt for a few days and went our separate ways. I caught a flight back to South Africa, not that I was going to get much rest. In a day or three I'd be battling some of the best kayakers in South Africa on the Berg River, but thankfully not in either of our heavy and rather battered *Inspirations*; my bright-green Windhoek Lager boat was waiting for me back home. Dan and

Richard were heading to London and a spot of physiotherapy at a place he knew well from previous visits. Tracey, Zahir and Brad were going to stay on in Reykjavík, seeing the sights and taking it easy.

Make no bones about it, the Windhoek Berg River Canoe Marathon lived up to its reputation as the toughest river race in the world. My week 'off' was a whirlwind: after I landed, I attended media events, collected my very fancy new boat, and started the race the following day. The day after finishing, I boarded the plane to fly back to Iceland, a physically battered and bruised man. It was crazy.

My lasting memory of the week was all the inspirational people I met. In spite of the difficult conditions, no one was shy of smiling or offering a word of support. The South African paddling community had supported me on my Madagascar journey, and was behind the Iceland expedition, too, so I had many of them come up and chat with me. They usually asked if there was anything they could do to help. I didn't know many of them personally, and they surely didn't have to offer their help. There was one special group of eight or so paddlers from the KwaZulu-Natal Midlands, led by famous Dusi River champion, Martin Dreyer. But the true hero was a guy by the name of Hennie. He came in hours after everyone on each of the first three days, and on the last day he came in four hours after the second-last paddler. The prizegiving ceremony was nearly finished, but everyone in the hall went outside and applauded Hennie as he slowly made his way over the finish line. He had paddled for almost 10 hours on this last day, but not once had he considered giving up. He wanted that medal, and it didn't matter what it took. Everyone was amazed.

It was good to get back. The team seemed buoyed by their individual rests. My friend Troy flew in for a much-needed visit, and

ABOVE: Here we are preparing for a paddle, with the camera crew busy in the background. Tensions within the team were rising at this time, and the group dynamic was definitely not what I wanted it to be.

LEFT: Coming ashore in Héraðsflói Bay in relatively calm conditions. Although it was late April by this stage – well into the Icelandic spring – the sea was never less than frigid and forbidding.

ABOVE: Dan strikes a serious pose as I display the visitors' book at one of the guesthouses we stayed at. In fact, this was how we came across the names of Geoff Hunter and Nigel Foster, the kayakers who had first circumnavigated Iceland back in 1977.

ABOVE: Héraðsflói Bay is a place of vast spaces, its wide, black-sand beaches formed by the deposition of volcanic debris carried down by the many rivers.

RIGHT: Powering a two-man kayak weighing 250 kilograms, all up, through the frigid water was something new and tough for a hitherto lone kayaker like me; wrist and elbow pain was guaranteed, as I soon discovered. I began to think I must have been crazy to believe I'd be able to manage 10 000 strokes a day for six months.

THESE PAGES: This is what too many of our landings looked like. We groped our way in, unable to see the land or what the huge three-metre surf was crashing onto. Rocks or a beach? The only thing to do was hold your breath, cross your fingers and hope for nothing worse than a wetting.

The river deltas were grand in scale, with
pitch-black basalt beaches and snow-
covered mountains rearing dramatically in
the distance. The enormous vistas sometimes
reminded me of just how insignificant we are
in the greater scheme of things.

ABOVE: Hvalnes lighthouse, east of Höfn, just after midnight. By mid-May, when this photo was taken, it was light almost 24 hours a day. Ordinary time now meant little to us, allowing me to work out paddling schedules that gave us the greatest safety and the best chances of getting up a good speed.

ABOVE: It was difficult for Dan to pull the heavy kayak out of the water, but I often gave him the job. Of course it was a struggle for him, but I resisted the impulse to take over.

RIGHT: We set off on our first midnight paddle, with just enough light to see the rocks in our way. Getting off wasn't easy; when the sea is foamy it invariably means trouble. With rocks always nearby, we couldn't even attempt to launch when the surf was anything over a metre high.

ABOVE AND RIGHT: Secure in the knowledge that we had a spare, I was foolish enough to leave the kayak on the beach at Hvalnes. We paid a heavy price for my folly. Raging winds and stormy seas smashed the boat around like a rag doll. When we got to it, the strongest parts, including the reinforced bow and triple-layered seams, had been badly damaged. The photos on these pages show some of the damage the boat sustained.

ABOVE AND RIGHT: The mangling of the kayak
sucked up a lot of our team's morale and,
more importantly, valuable paddling time. I put
a brave face on it and got stuck into repairs
the same day. Conditions weren't ideal, but I
managed to get the spare boat seaworthy in a
few days. Now we could carry on, but we had
lost almost a week. Until the damaged kayak
could be repaired in Reykjavík, we would have
nothing to fall back on in the event of a bad
landing or a collision.

ABOVE: Taking award-winning photographs in Iceland is practically a case of point, shoot and collect your prize. In this mirror image, Dan is practically walking on water!

LEFT: The Stokksnes launch area marked the start of the dreaded south coast. We knew that long, black-sand beaches with huge surf and strong winds awaited us. To take my mind off this prospect, I climbed onto the carcass of a sperm whale that we came across.

ABOVE: The crew of the Höfn rescue boat was kind enough to follow us for a few kilometres to allow our team to get some footage. I thought the rescue boat would give me a reassuring feeling, but in fact it made me very nervous!

ABOVE: Dan charms every woman he meets without even trying, since he is a model of note – as this post-landing photograph shows. Few people can look that good after a rough beach landing.

LEFT: Even when things are bad, you just have to keep smiling!

RIGHT: Launching the kayak was always a challenge. Dan would first wade out into the surf, and I would follow with the kayak. Then came the tricky part: choosing the right moment to climb on board.

TOP: On our paddle to Jökulsárlón (the name means 'glacier lagoon'), one of Iceland's most famous and scenic spots, we encountered a lot of brash ice, the remnants of icebergs 'calved' from the edges of Vatnajökull Glacier.

ABOVE AND LEFT: When one of our vehicles became bogged down in waterlogged conditions near Ingólfshöfði, we were fortunate to get assistance from Einar, a local farmer, who used his tractor to pull our vehicle out of the mud. His help did not come cheaply, though!

Chez also arrived to lighten the load on the team. We were just past the halfway point and probably had another thousand kilometres to go. If we averaged what we had done over the preceding two weeks, then we could quite confidently pay the deposit on the brass band for the final fanfare. At that point, I was hoping for a mid-August paddle back into the harbour at Húsavík, where the mayor, the friendly townsfolk, and of course our friends and family would be waiting for us. Winter was behind us, and there were many reports of whale sightings. One of the boxes I wanted to tick before we reached the finish was to paddle alongside a whale.

One problem, though, was a swollen infected foot that I'd been living with for a month or so. Because the dry suits are moist inside, cuts and grazes take a while to heal. My white and puffy feet attracted so much attention that a journalist from Iceland's biggest newspaper nearly based his whole article on them when he interviewed me on my return from the Berg River marathon. He said his colleagues had heard I was suffering from an infection caused, he believed, by the 'dirty' water back in South Africa. I set him straight, and his article instead focused on the amazing paddling Dan and I had done in the preceding two weeks.

I planned to hit the water running, so to speak, to continue our momentum. I called ahead to the team in Hvolsvöllur and asked them to prepare for a paddle. I was tired and my hands were blistered raw, but I wanted to tick off one more day. The conditions were good, and I hope the crew wouldn't mind filming this. It should make for a good story, I felt: me paddling 250 kilometres of tough river and then wasting no time to get back into the circumnavigation of Iceland.

On 21 July we were back at our last landing place, near Kross. There Dan and I got our heads down; weather permitting, we would launch in the small hours next morning, and, if things went well, we would get to a landing place about 50 kilometres away. While we slept, the team made the final preparations. Now, at last, we were on the second half of our long journey!

Dan was up and about by 03h00, a little earlier than me, to give himself enough time to get ready. It was cold, but the wind had dropped. He was in a good mood, and ready for the day. As he remarked: 'It's nice to be able to look at the map and see those dots getting closer and closer.' That was about the way I felt, too. My body hadn't had much rest in South Africa, but my spirit had been pumped up again.

The plan was that Dan and I would do a short paddle to a place called Þykkvibær, take a rest, and then tackle the 30-kilometre leg to where the team would be waiting, at Eyrarbakki. We got off all right, and that was the last the team heard from us for several hours.

After about three hours, so they told me later, they began to get seriously worried; they didn't know where we were, or even whether we'd stopped for a rest at the halfway mark, or decided to press on. A phone call from the local Coast Guard station, to say they hadn't heard anything from us either, did nothing for the team's peace of mind. They decided that the only thing to do was to drive to the halfway mark, near a lighthouse at Loftsstaðir, to see if they could spot us. This wasn't easy; the coastline around here is remote and surrounded by private land, with plenty of locked gates. An alternative route had to be found.

After a long struggle, among other things with one of Iceland's many rivers, they managed to get down to the beach, about two kilometres northwest of the lighthouse. Where *we* were was, of course, another story. The last they had heard from me was when Dan and I were about 18 kilometres southeast of the lighthouse. After that, there was nothing, in spite of repeated text messages and radio calls, and the

GPS spots were unreliable. All they could do was sit tight and hope for either a message or a sighting.

Then, after seven long, stressful hours, I managed to make contact. We needed help, and fast. The good weather in which we had started had turned very ugly, and Dan and I had been battling through it with all the grim determination we could muster. But now we were nearing the end of our tether. We needed to get to dry land, and fast.

'Riaan, can you hear me?' Troy asked.

'I can hear you,' I said. 'What're the instructions? Quickly, please. We're in a bad situation. Quickly.'

'Man, keep on going,' Troy said. 'You've got probably 500 metres to go, before you enter a little bay where you can land safely.'

I sighed with relief. 'Fixed on where we are now, straight on?'

'Yes, straight on.'

'Copy that,' I said, with even greater relief.

'The first day back, and this is what I get,' Dan said mock-ruefully as we forced our burning muscles to make the final effort to the landing place. That just about summed up the day.

Anyway, all had ended well. We'd done 40 kilometres, which was pretty good.

I think the day's adventure had also enlightened the newcomers, Troy and Chez. Earlier, Troy had done a map appreciation and calculated that we probably had a month and a half to go to the finishing point, but now they had had their first real inkling of why it had taken us so long to get as far as we had.

'Their biggest enemy now is not even themselves, because they've got the determination,' as Troy put it in an interview with the film crew. 'It's the weather. I mean, you can't even really judge when they're going to finish. Because even if you work it out, like doing 50 kays every second day, they should finish by 26 August. But you can't work it out that way. The weather's just way too unpredictable.' Too true.

And there would be more of that, lots more. We were going to encounter many more windy days and rough waters as we headed up the west coast. We would have no choice but to take them on. Oh, well, if you can't stand the heat (or the cold, in this case), stay out of the kitchen.

On the positive side, I could see the reconstituted team finally settling into the rhythm of the expedition. Dan and I seemed to have found our groove at last, and Chez's expertise was making a big difference. He calmed Tracey down when the pressure got to her, and he helped Dan to strengthen himself so that his paddling improved. Dan was now more determined than ever.

CHAPTER 12

ROUNDING REYKJANES PENINSULA

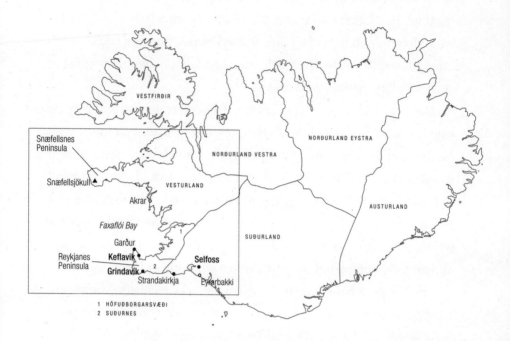

'That night's paddle was a magical experience.
The stormy waters of the past few days had
subsided into total calm, and we were treated
to a sunset that went on and on ...'

O ur next stage was a 40-kilometre paddle from Loftsstaðir to a tiny place called Strandakirkja, which is among Iceland's least-visited destinations. Visitors to the area are usually bound for Reykjavík or the coastal town of Grindavík, further to the west, although the locals make energetic efforts to attract the tourist trade.

We had a strong motivation to make those 40 kilometres in good time. The following day, the Springboks were playing Australia in the first Tri-Nations Test, and the team – particularly Dan and I – were determined to find a place in Reykjavík where we could watch a broadcast. We were optimistic, since Icelanders like their sport; if such a facility existed, we'd find it.

Dan and I are both rugby fanatics. I'd been watching and playing rugby since I was a kid, and Dan grew up in a rugby family, with his brother Bob becoming a Springbok. The chances were that it wouldn't be a great match, and that Australia would win, but what did that matter? We were going to enjoy it, not just us but the rest of the team as well. And from then on it would be shoulder to the wheel. At that stage we had been in Iceland for four months, and should have completed the trip. But we were still only halfway.

But things looked good: the weather was relatively warm and conditions were calm. Barring catastrophes, we should make good time. Which we did, with Dan and me spending a lot of the time talking rugby. Tracey, Chez and company were waiting for us at Strandakirkja; the landing place was a bit rocky, but the team took it in their stride and we got the kayak up to a safe spot on the beach. We decided to leave it there instead of going over the rocks higher up with it ('My foot doctor would be horrified if he saw me walking on these,' Dan grinned).

The addition of Troy and Chez had made a big difference, and for Chez in particular it was a happy time. As he remarked, he and Tracey had been engaged since February, and 'you don't realise it, but you get sort of used to emails and SMSes and phone calls. And then, actually seeing somebody for the first time after four months … It's the first time I really, really felt that I had a girlfriend again.'

Next morning, we had everybody up at 06h00, followed by frantic washing, shaving and packing, and then we were on our way to

Reykjavík. Our immediate destination was the city's one and only sports bar, which we still had to find, after which we needed to beg the owner to open early. The match was due to start at 10h00 local time, and that's about the time that most Icelanders get going with their day.

And so the great search began as soon as we hit Reykjavík. By 09h00 we still hadn't succeeded, and we were getting worried. But in the end we made it. Unfortunately, it was a bit of a disappointment; the Bokke were lacklustre and the Aussies won. But, as Dan quite correctly pointed out, that wasn't the point: 'We've got to support the Bokke, hey. Imagine if we didn't have people supporting *us*.' That was the bottom line, all right.

With the most important part of the day's proceedings behind us, we went on to the hostel at the next day's stop, Grindavík, where we were to spend the night. It was a rather eerie sort of place, which Tracey reckoned had started life as a fish factory. Not that we worried much about it. We had slept in worse accommodation, and we had greater things on our mind, starting with a return to Strandakirkja for a 40-kilometre night paddle to Grindavík. After that, we would set off around the boot-shaped Reykjanes Peninsula on the 140-kilometre journey to Reykjavík. From there on, we would be free of the exposed southern coast and heading into whale territory as we paddled northwards.

First we had to find a suitable landing place at Grindavík, though, and next morning Tracey and Chez did a recce of the harbour and its surroundings. Just east of the harbour was a little bay with a beach, which Dan and I could use instead if the sea conditions allowed. But the final decision would depend on what the sea was doing; just then, the bay had some fierce breakers crashing into it.

In spite of Iceland's famously changeable weather, it was still much the same when we headed for the launch site that evening (a relative term, of course, since full darkness does not occur at that time of the year). There was a possible landing spot about halfway through the 40 kilometres we had to cover, the only place where the team could actually reach us in case of emergency – there were impassable lava fields all the way along the peninsula – and Tracey suggested we take my sleeping bag with us, just in case.

We struggled over the rocks to get to the beach where we had left the kayak. The rocks were very slippery, and I held thumbs that no one would fall and get hurt – that would have been all we needed. But everybody made it safely, and the kayak was where we had left it, unharmed and ready to go to sea.

So far, so good. We started preparing for the launch. By now it was going on for 21h00, and I calculated we had about a seven- or eight-hour paddle ahead of us. Well, the hell with it. We had things to do and places to go. We had reports that the weather would improve a little up to about 02h00. After that? Well … when in Iceland, do as the Icelanders do, and prepare for the worst.

The terrain ahead was considerably different from what we had been experiencing in the past 400 or so kilometres. Instead of the endless black basalt beaches, there would be coves and inlets where we could find shelter from the surf and the swells. So we were definitely better off, and if all went well we wouldn't have the crash landings of the past two or three weeks.

'Be aware of the swells coming on your left-hand side here,' I warned Dan, 'because those are the ones that wobble you. So it would be good if you do glance now and then, now I feel confident because I know you're seeing them, OK?'

When we got out on the water, the going was tough enough to suck out much of our good mood of the past couple of days. The swell was very big, and the sea was all over the place. No doubt even more of our good mood would have been sucked out if we'd known about the completely unforeseeable problem the team had run into. They had neglected to fill up with petrol, and now the vehicles were virtually running on fumes. There was nothing to do but turn back to Strandakirkja to refill. After a nerve-wracking drive, with everyone worried that the vehicles would cough and come to a halt, they eventually got to a garage, Tracey – so I was told – having made the deathless prediction that 'it's the most exciting thing that's happened all day'. She was wrong about that.

Dan and I were making good progress. It was now 23h00, and thanks to a good tailwind we were averaging nine or 10 kilometres per hour, so that it looked as if we might reach Grindavík two hours earlier than we had calculated. While we stroked away and talked about food – Chez had made some good pasta, and Dan promised to prepare his own special ginger-flavoured version, which he had cooked up at Höfn, and which I had enjoyed very much – the pumps at the garage spat out my South African credit cards.

The team became worried, as their watches showed midnight was approaching. They were nowhere near the landing site. Needless to say, we weren't very pleased when we arrived and had to hang around, fighting off hypothermia. Tracey had informed me that they were still at least half an hour away, and stranded into the bargain.

'I'm tensing up, hey,' Dan remarked, which was a considerable understatement that applied to me as well.

But the fuel situation was solved, thanks to a desperate expedient on Tracey's part. She flagged down a couple of passing motorists and offered them a deal: if they would pay for the fuel with their Icelandic credit cards, she would refund them in cash. In typical Icelandic fashion, they were happy to help, and the team roared off into the deepening twilight, hell-bent on reaching the landing place.

They arrived about 03h20, in the proverbial nick of time, just as we rounded the eastern arm of Grindavík Bay. The twilight had finally thickened into darkness, and we were wrapped in sea mist so thick that we didn't know which direction to head in, although we weren't quite lost, since we could see the lighthouse on the point. Iceland has more than 100 lighthouses scattered around its forbidding coastline, and a damned good thing, too.

When Tracey told me they'd arrived, I told her to flash her head-lights. She did so, aiming in the direction of the lighthouse, and I spotted it right away.

'I can see you,' I said. 'OK, cool! I'm going to come straight to you. You'll be able to hear me.'

And that was it. We beached and secured the kayak and headed for Grindavík and our eerie accommodation for hot water, equally hot food and, above all else, dry, warm clothes. Dan and I were pretty satisfied. The weather conditions hadn't been ideal, but they had been manageable, much better than during the last paddle, and we'd put another 40-odd kilometres in the bank, so to speak. Dan said he was feeling strong, although earlier he had got tired – he hadn't slept well before leaving and had popped some anti-inflammatories, which had made him drowsy. But now, he said, 'I'm cool … strong. Strong like mother Russia before the war.'

That night we set off again, this time to a perfectly sheltered bay at a place called Hafnir, about 35 kilometres up the coast and halfway along the 'sole' of the Reykjanes Peninsula. The team was running like clockwork, and we launched smoothly, although there was a large enough shore-break for the local surfers to take to the water. We goggled at them. *Night-time* surfing? And in water colder than a pawnbroker's heart? Well, no time to goggle too much. We had to get through the same surf. 'Paddle hard now, paddle hard!' I shouted. 'We're gonna try and time this one. Paddle hard, paddle hard, paddle hard.'

We went through the surf like a dose of salts. 'Nice!', I said. 'Sjoe!' Dan said with satisfaction. '*That* was awesome.'

'Awesome,' I agreed. Because that's what it had been.

As we bored into the twilight, and the surfers packed up for the night, I found myself thinking about the Reykjanes Peninsula, which is harshly beautiful in its own right, but, more importantly, is the source of life for the Icelanders. The peninsula lies in an active geothermal area; volcanic activity below the surface is harnessed to heat up the plentiful water supply and supply no less than 87% of the country's energy needs – all of it completely natural and 'green', if a trifle smelly at times. No nuclear power stations producing toxic radioactive waste, no coal-fired plants belching clouds of sulphur-laden smoke into the atmosphere; the Icelanders, uniquely in the world, live in harmony with their environment. How different the world would be if other countries could satisfy their energy needs in such a natural way!

That night's paddle was a magical experience. The stormy waters of the past few days had subsided into total calm, and we were treated to a sunset that went on and on, as if it were reluctant to allow the three short hours of darkness after 23h00 to fall. It was an enjoyable paddle, any way you looked at it, and the mellow mood was still on us when we reached the landing place, where we bit into the team's peanut-butter sandwiches.

Next day was a rest day. As if to make up for the good conditions the night before, the weather served up gale-force winds and a blanket of white clouds. We remained cheerful. Normally I'd fret if the weather was bad, but now I laughed it off. In the past couple of days we had covered 80 kilometres. Now we would rest up and do the 75 remaining to Reykjavík. If we could keep up this rate of progress, it would be perfect.

I made use of the break to take Troy to the airport and see him off. We would miss his quiet and supportive presence. Dan, meanwhile, spent the day training with Chez. Fitness *per se* wasn't his problem; Dan needed some core training to help him to sit up straight in the kayak and reach forward when paddling. This would improve his balance, his biggest problem because of his condition and the most difficult one to overcome.

The rest of the team joined in, and Dan really appreciated it. As he said, 'It's nice to have a group of people doing it, so that you get each other's *gees* going.' That was a key word; in Afrikaans, *gees* means 'spirit', and South Africans of all language groups use it, whether they are talking about team spirit, individual spirit or just plain dogged determination. It was more than just a gesture of solidarity, though. The team members were humping the kayak around every day now, and they needed to be as fit as possible. Chez worked them hard, to judge by Darren's heartfelt groan at one stage, but it was doing everyone good.

Next day, the winds hadn't abated much, but we were so full of that famed *gees* that we decided to go ahead anyway, although we weren't planning on doing anything more than a 23-kilometre paddle to a village called Garður. We wanted to keep up the momentum; every kilometre we covered was a kilometre nearer to the finishing point. We would be helped, we hoped, by a powerful tailwind gusting to 30 or 40 kilometres per hour at times. Then the following day, we anticipated another strong tailwind, which would help us to do a big crossing to Reykjavík. It would be a bit risky because we'd be far out at sea, but that was the way things went, and we hadn't done a big crossing for a while.

It didn't quite work out that way, which did not surprise us, being by now veteran Icelandic travellers. The tailwind was strong, as we had expected, but it swung around to become a headwind. We buckled down to the job, but it felt as if we were moving in slow motion; in effect, we had to put in 40 kilometres' worth of effort to cover the 23 we were supposed to be doing. It was a particularly tough time for Dan, because the headwind made it even harder than usual for him to brace forward, and of course this affected both his balance and his paddling. For the first few kilometres, there was considerable growling between us, but then Dan hit his stride and had one of his best paddling days so far.

On shore, meanwhile, Darren's whole face had swelled up to such an alarming extent that he and Zahir had to go to Grindavík to get some medication. What caused it, no one knew. We were aware that Darren was highly allergic to fish – a dangerous affliction in a place like Iceland, where seafood is virtually the staff of life – and Tracey joked that perhaps the smell of the former fish factory where we had been sleeping had got to him.

Where Dan and I were, though, there wasn't much to joke about. We were wet and cold, and averaging a miserable four kilometres per hour or so. We needed to work out a way of doing better, but what? We just had to keep going, grinding our way around the 'toe' of the Reykjanes Peninsula's boot at a point called Garðskagi, with its inevitable lighthouse, and heading southwards towards our landing place at Garður.

The team beat us to Garður, and while Tracey and Chez relaxed and kept an eye open for us as we toiled along the coast, sniping at one another, Zahir and Richard wandered off and struck up an acquaintance with some anglers. One of them gave his rod to Zahir, who promptly started pulling several mackerel. Zahir and Richard agreed that, under the circumstances, they wouldn't invite Darren to join them.

Dan and I finally came power-paddling into the little harbour and wasted no time getting ashore. The main priority now was to get back, eat and rest up, because tomorrow was to be the day of the big crossing of the bay off Reykjavík.

Early next morning, we said a rather grumpy goodbye to the former fish factory, after struggling down its steep stairs with all our kit. Dan and I had our thoughts firmly focused on the crossing that lay ahead: 42 kilometres due northeast from Garður to Akranes, well beyond Reykjavík. Akranes was originally settled in the 9th century, and is quite populous by Icelandic standards, with more than 6000 inhabitants. Fishing is, naturally, of first importance to the local economy, but Akranes has been home to a cement factory since the 1950s and an aluminium smelting plant since 1998, and the commercial sector services a large part of the surrounding regions. We were told that more growth was expected because of an expanding industrial sector and the 1998-vintage Hvalfjörður Tunnel, one of the longest underwater road tunnels in the world. But what really gets the inhabitants' water hot, however, is soccer. Their local team, Íþróttabandalag Akraness, or ÍA, has long been high up in the Icelandic league, and a former ÍA midfielder named Siggi Jónsson used to turn out for Sheffield Wednesday and Arsenal.

Not that Dan and I had much time for discussing such considerations just then. A big bay crossing is rather dodgy at the best of times, because you're far out to sea, which means it's impossible to make an emergency landing in case of injury, a leak, bad weather or anything else. This one would be even more difficult because we would have to go further out than normal, to avoid getting run down by ships. There is heavy sea traffic along this part of the coast, with ships plying back and forth between Reykjavík and other ports, such as Akranes. Dan and I were acutely aware of the fact that, in the mist, our kayak would not be very visible.

While we were on the water, Tracey intended to dash into Reykjavík to buy new maps she needed for the trip ahead, but I reminded her of the importance of being at Akranes before we arrived. There is a lighthouse on the point of the bulbous peninsula, but not at Akranes itself, which is nestled in a little bay. If the mist was thick, we would have trouble landing. She said not to worry; the team would be there before us.

We left in style from Garður's pier – no battling with the surf this time! – and set off with a tailwind for help, GPS in hand, and hearts full of determination. Dan was particularly focused: 'I don't want to over-think it. It's gonna be long and tough and hard, but let's give it a go. Come on, we're here to paddle!'

In Reykjavík, Tracey bought maps – two covering the Snæfellsnes Peninsula, the next big piece of Iceland jutting out into the frigid North Atlantic, and three of the Westfjords region (Vestfirðir in Icelandic), the huge bulb-shaped peninsula that has so many bays and inlets it looks like a hand with a triple ration of fingers – and the team set off for Akranes. It was an exhilarating drive, firstly, because actually leaving Reykjavík behind was a big psychological milestone, and, secondly, because Iceland's capital looked so different when we first arrived. Then it had been a snowbound place; now, in springtime, it looked totally transformed. After four months of hard times, it was a great boost to their spirits.

Out in the bay, things were a little less exhilarating. According to the GPS, we were going in the right direction, but Dan wasn't so sure. I decided to believe the GPS. But the fact was that, on a trip like this, the best way of navigating is to have sight of the land, because then you can work out where the wind is in relation to your destination, and take it from there. On the other hand, if we made a mistake and didn't travel economically with the wind in our favour, we'd have a problem when we were, say, 10 kilometres out. So I just hoped that I was right in trusting the GPS.

It wasn't all worrying, however. Along the way we came across a vessel full of whale-watchers, who got quite worked up about spotting this particular bit of wildlife and hung over the side, frantically taking photographs. We exchanged greetings, shouted, 'Send us the photos, OK?', and went on our way.

Several hours into the paddle – and it was a tough one – Tracey came through on the radio to give us the GPS coordinates of a good landing spot she had found on the beach at Akranes. We started looking forward to landing and putting our heads down … but only after supper. We agreed that our main hope was that there was something good to eat (there was – Chez was making chicken tortillas).

'Just to the right of the lighthouse and the big harbour,' Tracey's voice came crackling over the radio. 'Half an hour? Sure, OK, bye.' Aha! That was what we wanted to hear. The six long, cold hours we had spent at sea had really affected Dan's dodgy leg muscles, so that when we came ashore he could barely stand. The crossing hadn't been much fun, but, what the hell, we'd got there in one piece. He wasn't happy, although still full of determination: 'I still lose concentration, man,' he fretted, 'and ja, it's bothering me … I don't know, I can't talk about it, I've just got to do it.'

Needless to say, Dan and I slept well that night. But when Day 111 of the expedition dawned we were greeted with gale-force winds. To make matters worse, Darren's suspected fish allergy had worsened to the point where we were getting worried. We bundled him off to the Akranes hospital, where the doctors confirmed that his condition was definitely not terminal, while Tracey and Chez set out to find two possible landing sites for the next leg, which might well be the longest of the trip so far.

What I envisaged was a 45-kilometre paddle and then, if we had enough energy left, another bay crossing, this one across part of Faxaflói Bay, between the Reykjanes and Snæfellsnes peninsulas. That would give a total of about 75 kilometres. Sheesh! I didn't even want to think about it. I would be quite happy just to do the first 45 kilometres. But you never knew …

Finding possible landing sites – in fact, even reaching them – wasn't easy for Tracey and Chez. They had to struggle over badly demarcated farm roads for which the new maps weren't much help. Tracey radioed me during the search to tell me of their difficulties. I told her that one option for next day, weather permitting, would be a two-part trip, so, if she could find a suitable place at around 25 kilometres, that would be OK for the time being.

A little later, Tracey came back with an expletive-studded message to the effect that the roads were a mess and she couldn't get to a landing spot she'd identified: 'They showed a road on the map, but this is not exactly a road,' as she put it. She and Chez would have to double back. But then, at a place called Akrar, she found a first-class spot at the end of a road on which all driving was banned.

The rain began pouring down as she and Chez headed back, and along the way she missed a turn-off. Coming on top of everything else, this was just too much, and Tracey blew her top in no uncertain terms. But a night's sleep got her back on an even keel, and things seemed to be favourable: Darren was recovering from his rash at last, and the weather looked good, as did the waves and swell.

We were now safely in Akrar, and this presented us with what I had hoped we needed: the opportunity to paddle in almost any weather. The days were growing shorter, making it crucial that we make the best use of the available daylight. This section of coastline was jagged, and would offer refuge in many places. I was confident I could get Dan and me to a good landing spot every night, even if that meant not always meeting up with the crew. I had repacked our gear to accommodate this possibility. Tracey had also gone ahead and booked flights for Nigel Foster and Geoff Hunter, the kayaking legends, who had agreed to join us in a few weeks. I wished she had told me she was going to do that, because Vasti had already booked and paid for the flights. This put further strain on my finances, which I had to sort out later. Well, we couldn't miss them. We had been told that, from here, we would be more isolated and alone – fewer roads, fewer people, fewer resources.

Snæfellsjökull, Iceland's smallest ice cap, lay ahead as our next beacon of progress. Popular in the past with hippies and the spiritually inclined, for us the sight of this Lady of Iceland would represent progress and a goal. The south coast of Iceland lacks spectacular landmarks, so we were looking forward to our first sight of the glacier. Locals say the majestic mountain is visible from as far as Reykjavík, nearly 100 kilometres away across Faxaflói Bay.

Snæfellsjökull is apparently guarded by a half-man, half-troll creature called Bardur. The story goes that, after serious disagreements with his family, Bardur became so disappointed with humanity that he decided to separate himself for good. So he walked into the glacier and has lived there since. Those who believe such stories also believe that your best chance to spot an elf or a troll is on the glacier.

We checked into a hostel midway between Akrar and Snæfellsnes for a few days of recovery and fun and games. The crew played soccer with the local kids, but, when they were moved into the hospital-style dorm-cum-basketball court, all hell broke lose with a game of indoor rugby. Dan and I were, if I may say so, untouchable. Our strategy was simple. It was direct rugby, draw an extra defender and then Dan would cut straight up the middle for the diving try. Strategically placed high-jump mats allowed Dan many a graceful swallow dive, gently but purposefully rubbing salt into the opposition's wounds. I enjoyed spending some fun time with the guys. I could change nothing about what had happened on the first half of this journey. But I could try to enjoy the rest.

FHM magazine in South Africa wanted to do an article on how Dan and I had changed physically. They suggested we show how we had beefed up in the past four months. It was strange to be asking two guys to show how they had beefed up when we'd both beefed *down* by over 10 kilograms each! But that was the photographer's challenge. My standing joke with Dan was how many second and third looks he gave himself in the bathroom mirror – sort of a 'well done' second glance, and then a 'making sure it's all still there' third glance. Our team thought Dan would be 'shredded like a tuna salad' by the time he got home – if he didn't over-indulge in the cakes I had bought for his birthday.

But first we went for a birthday paddle of note. We started rather late from our last landing spot, at Akrar. We hoped for a swift paddle in the glassy paddling conditions, so arriving at Geldinganes lighthouse before midnight was the likeliest of outcomes. I was selfish, though, to want the birthday moment to be between him and me first. We made good time, and soon, in pitch darkness, had the flashing lighthouse in our sights. The presence of another lighthouse, at Arnarstapi, further to the west, nearly made us arrive late. By 22h00 it was dark, and it became easier for me to navigate in the crisp, clear, night air. Geez, it was scary but stunning to be so far out at sea with the land of Iceland wrapping around us like it did.

By 23h00 we were no more than half an hour from landing, so I offered Dan many breaks, which must have puzzled him. I normally schedule a stop very strictly and without exception. In my mind I believed I was going to offer Dan a really special birthday. At midnight, Dan's 31st year of existence would begin. And where was he celebrating it? Out on Faxaflói Bay, in sight of Snæfellsjökull. It was chilly, and a warm pub with cold beer and pretty girls might have seemed more attractive at that moment, but it was a birthday moment like none other. I wished Dan happy birthday and encouraged him to make the most of the year ahead. After all, he had certainly shaken up the world so far in his 30 years of existence. He needed to build on what he had gained on the journey, not let it slip away. I had been guilty of not capitalising on my opportunity in full when I returned from the bicycle trip round Africa, so my advice came from experience.

We arrived back at the hostel, and this time I didn't aim for the shower first. I had a surprise for Dan. He had told me how much he loved the Norwegian cakes made by Daima. I could see his mouth water just mentioning them. I had bought him three or four of these cakes for his birthday, and handed them out one by one. The point was he couldn't believe he had a whole one to himself; now I was handing over one after another. It was lovely seeing him so happy.

To try to keep the hungry wolves at bay, I had bought an extra cake for us as a team to share. It's sometimes unfair, I thought, when someone in a team gets a gift but ends up sharing it with others. I wanted Dan to enjoy this treat and remember his birthday in Iceland forever.

Dan made use of the break to work on his fitness level by going for a walk instead of catching a nap – 'just to keep the blood flowing', as he explained, 'keep my legs strong, also to be active. I'd love to have a lie-down now, but it's not going to get us round the island quicker.' Dan's reasoning was that this would give him a completely different kind of aerobic fitness: 'I can paddle longer than I can run, which seems obvious, but you think that, if you're just doing a lot of cardio in paddling, that all your cardio will be so, which is not correct, as I found out.' He had been thinking in terms of a leisurely stroll, but then Chez got in on it and stepped it up to something more vigorous. Dan didn't mind: 'It's good … Legs are burning a bit, I had a little bit more gas in the tank there than I thought I did. Probably doesn't look pretty on telly, but who gives a shit, hey? It's going to get us round the island faster.'

Dan was going to need every scrap of fitness, I knew. If we were to finish this trip before we all grew long grey beards we'd have to ramp up our average pace by more than half in the next month … starting the next morning with a 37-kilometre paddle. This would be our first step towards circumnavigating the Snæfellsnes Peninsula, one of the trip's pivotal landmarks.

After the excitement of Dan's birthday, we took the day off – sort of, since the camp had to move up to our next port of call and I had to dash back to Reykjavík with Darren to deal with some administrative matters. In my absence, Tracey turned up with a fellow South African named Johnny Cramer, who ran a youth hostel in Grundarfjörður, a picturesque little fishing village cradled by impressive mountains on the northern side of the peninsula. He offered us free accommodation when we got there, for which we were naturally very grateful.

Next day, we headed for the Hellnar slipway. It was crucial for us to keep to our schedule so that we reached the finish at the end of August. Every day mattered now, especially while we had good weather.

CHAPTER 13

HEADING NORTH

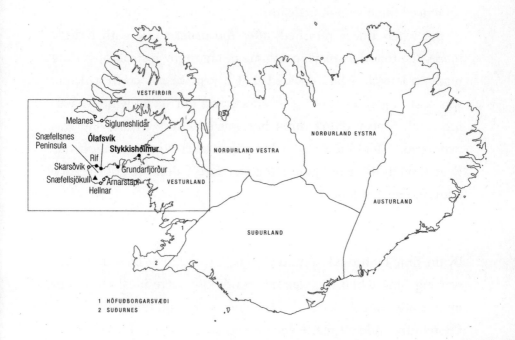

'The most majestic sight for me was the male killer whale, with his dorsal fin rising two metres above the water.'

While Dan and I prepared for our journey round the Snæfellsnes Peninsula, I asked Tracey to head north on a recce to find us a suitable landing spot near Melanes, in the Rauðisandur district of the Westfjords. Melanes lay near an abandoned farm called Sjöundá, the scene of a notorious double murder in the early 19th century. Two farmers, Bjarni Bjarnason and Steinunn Sveinsdóttir, murdered their wives for reasons they presumably regarded as valid. The courts did not agree, however, and sentenced the two men to death.

But when Tracey returned, after the usual battle with terrible roads, she found us playing a game of tag rugby instead of getting ready to launch. I had decided that it just wasn't worth it. There was a strong gale warning in effect, and our likely window was too small. Tracey didn't mind her wasted effort; in fact she was overjoyed. 'Well,' she said, 'at least that takes some stress off me. Even though we're not going to go forward today, I've got so much admin to do, it's cool.'

By the time I returned from Reykjavík, it was 22h00. I felt that I was wasting time while the weather conditions were ideal along our immediate route. In Iceland you do not look a gift horse like this in the mouth, and so I made a snap decision: we would undertake a 30-kilometre paddle that very night to a little bay called Skarsðvik, near the western tip of the peninsula. It was a hard thing to ask of my travel-worn and overtired team, but they responded nobly, the way a team should.

In due course, we launched from next to the Arnarstapi light-house, just a hop and a skip from the Snæfellsnes Glacier. I was as stiff as a plank – my body was taking too much strain, and I'd not been sleeping well or eating enough, matters I knew I would have to attend to – but my gut feeling had been correct: the sea conditions looked as if they would make for a great paddle. While we stroked into the twilight, the team set off to meet us at Skarsðvik. To mark the occasion, we fastened our national flag securely to the kayak, just to make sure passing seals and whales would have no doubt that these crazy sea venturers were two good old boys from behind the Boerewors Curtain.

Just before we launched, we did a quick interview for South African television, and I think a few of our comments pretty much mirror what we were all about at that stage:

DAN: OK, why am I doing this adventure? It's an interesting question sometimes when you're standing here at six, seven in the morning and it's freezing cold.

RIAAN: When Dan said to me that he wants to come back a different man, I think he's going to achieve that, without a doubt.

DAN: Was it a worry about my disability, and how I was perceived and how I perceived myself? So what I needed to do was to find a vehicle in order to effect a change in my life.

RIAAN: We sit in this little world, where we think the world's on top of us and we can never ever get out of it. The bottom line is that there is somebody, not even one person, multitudes of people, in a worse situation than you. Once you realise that and actually understand it, everything becomes easier for you in your life. Think what Dan's putting himself through, and you'll realise your life isn't that bad …

Actually, the interview also helped to remind us about why we were doing this in the first place – sometimes you tend to forget that under the pressure of more immediate concerns – and we felt positively re-energised. And, just to help things along, I had decided that the best way to get us through the coming ordeal was for us to listen to the latest Tri-Nations match on my iPad. This might sound crazy, listening to a sports match in the middle of Iceland's nowhere, but you have to remember that Dan and I are rabid rugby fans.

The day started well all round. Dan and I got off to a good start on our (or perhaps I should say 'my') ambitious paddling plan, and the team, including the now-recovered Darren, were in an upbeat mood as we got going. But the good cheer didn't last all that long, on land or at sea. Tracey found it impossible to track down the next night's accommodation, because the tourist season had arrived and almost every place she tried was booked up for both bed and sleeping-bag space. The only exception demanded a high price that was far beyond our modest budget. Finally, she found us a place to sleep.

After the customary battle with the surf, we were safely launched and on our way, feeling good and stroking strongly, feasting our eyes on the beautiful landscape passing to our right. However, it was difficult to make much headway; after four hours, we'd done just 12 kilometres – our worst time ever. The coastline didn't help either, thanks to a multitude of small rocky islands that didn't show up clearly on the GPS. We couldn't be sure which of them were stand-alones and which were linked to the mainland. Slogging into a dead end was the last thing we needed, so I kept us well out to sea, which of course added more distance to our paddle.

Dan was doing well, though, and I made sure to encourage him. When he was interviewed later, he explained: 'Riaan said to me that my paddle stroke was the best when we were going into the wind. So he said there were times there when he was very pleased with my paddle stroke, which I was chuffed about. It's not a picnic out there, even in good conditions … 99.99 recurring per cent of the people would say that I shouldn't be here. Doctors, physios, but I am, so damn, I'm going to finish it and I'm going to enjoy it.'

It had been a long, bitter struggle for him, but he seemed to have slipped into the groove – although in the course of the paddle he was seized by an urgent need to empty his bladder (the result, he later

186

explained, of drinking coffee before eating breakfast). On land, this situation would have been easy to remedy by simply finding a handy bush, and on a boat just by leaning out over the side, but on a kayak such things become complicated. The only way out was for him to pee in his suit, which was pretty embarrassing.

And then, finally, we were heading towards a golden beach – such a drastic change after the endless black ones we had encountered so far – where the others were waiting. It had been a long, long day – eight hours on the water, averaging a measly five kilometres per hour. We were fagged out, and there was no question of carrying on with the ambitious distance I had planned for this paddle. But tomorrow was another day. Weather permitting, we would cut across the corner of the bay ahead and make for the next landing point, a short paddle of about 25 kilometres.

We had time now to reflect for a moment on just how far we'd come, not just in terms of kilometres (and they were many more than it might seem from totting up figures on a map) but also as regards our approach. I wasn't pressuring Dan as much, and Dan's feeling was that 'a diamond, you know, it can't be polished without friction'.

But there would be no rest for the wicked, or, in our case, the weary – 1 600 kilometres down, but hundreds more to go. So we rested up that day – a beautiful one, incidentally – and then at 18h30 set off on our third paddle in a row. It was a tall order, but we weren't in Iceland to fool around. Fish swim, birds fly, paddlers paddle. We were going to press on until we'd finished that stretch, aching bodies or no aching bodies. And then the one after that, and the one after *that*, and so on until we staggered over the finish line at Húsavík.

By launch time, the glorious weather had turned distinctly inglorious.

Dan and I fought our way through the surf in the customary clouds of spray, exhortations and imprecations, and then got away to a strong start. Now the only question was whether we had enough endurance left to finish what we'd set out to do. Well, there was only one way to find out. Dig those paddles into the water, man, and never mind that aching back and those blistered fingers. Perhaps we weren't dedicated adventurers so much as obsessive masochists. But, well, most people have this sort of thought about themselves from time to time.

On land, Tracey grew more and more worried as time went by without any word from us. While we were drinking in our majestic surround-ings – I remember us passing some incredible rocks, big, black volcanic boulders with razor-sharp edges – she was trying to drink coffee and eat waffles with some friendly expatriate South Africans. Her enjoyment was spoilt by the fact that she had last spoken to us two hours earlier, at which time I had predicted that we were probably another two hours out. Now, with her watch showing 23h30, we should be somewhere in the vicinity of the landing place. But were we? And if, in fact, we were, should the team not be at the landing place?

Actually, we had made it in good time, although we were really tired out after fighting headwinds all the way. When I got through to Tracey, I asked for just one thing: 'Just please don't get lost …' She and the team said a hasty goodbye to their hosts and hit the road … but not to where we were.

'Where are you guys driving currently?' I asked. 'Are you going to keep driving for a lot further? Because I thought that bay was a little bit closer … Tell me where you guys are planning to drive.'

'I don't think it's a lot further,' she said. 'It's just after the lighthouse.'

My heart sank. 'No, no, no, no. We're past the lighthouse, Trace.'

We were completely burned out, and there was still one more paddle before we tackled the approaching 60-kilometre dash. We got into our bags and slept like dead men, and when we got up again we felt refreshed enough to put the rough passage behind us and tackle the sea again.

The next leg was only a short paddle – 15 kilometres to Rif – a good starting-point for the 60-kilometre run to Melanes. A little after 23h00 I got on the radio to Tracey, to tell her that we were just passing the village of Hellissanður, which meant we would probably arrive in another 45 minutes or so. That turned out to be right, and when we arrived around midnight they were waiting on the beach for us, bearing some very welcome hot coffee to drive the chill from our bones.

Dan's legs were in poor shape after four consecutive days of tough paddles, but he was in high spirits. 'Thanks, man,' he said, 'it was a great day.' And so it was – one of our most memorable experiences so far – and a good omen for the big bay crossing that now lay ahead.

Believe it or not, Iceland has a South African mafia. We'd heard about them for the last few weeks, and didn't know whether to fear for them or to embrace the idea of entering their lair in Grundar-fjörður, a beautiful fishing village on the northern shore of the Snæfellsnes Peninsula.

We went with our gut feeling, and the South Africans really came to the party. Sheilagh Smith, who owns the Framnes Hotel, gave our crew free run of the place: from Jacuzzis to electric massage chairs, for 10 days we made hay while the weather was bad. She and her twin sister, Fiona – who had originally brought Sheilagh to Iceland – even gave a dinner for us and some other South Africans, such as June Scholtz. June had left South Africa in 1989 to come and pack fish for six months. She met a mountain of a man named Siggi, and, 23 years and three children later, has never left. Johanna van Schalkwyk is another South African who originally came to Iceland with a childhood sweetheart. She fell in and out of love with the country a few times, but eventually settled on her lifelong dream of teaching, and is now married to Grundarfjörður's mayor, who also joined us for dinner. It was Johanna's ex, Johnny Cramer, who had made his youth hostel available for us to stay in.

Naturally, the special treatment we received made the team feel 'at home'. But, as I added when Sheilagh made a toast to us, they also made us feel extremely homesick! The bottom line is we had the biggest and most dangerous bay crossing ahead of us: 60 kilometres of open sea and temperamental weather. We needed this support, care and sincere comprehension of the task we have taken on. Viva South Africa! Viva Iceland!

While we recuperated and prepared for the crossing, it was a good time to think back on everything that had happened so far, and to reflect on what it all meant. Later, when I saw the footage the film crew had shot of our unrehearsed ramblings, I realised for the first time how much we had revealed about our thoughts and feelings:

DAN: Before I went into this journey I was completely undercooked, and underestimated what kind of effort it would take to get around this place.

RIAAN: I went into this journey with passion, and the reason I'm here with Dan is only because of that, that passion for Dan to be able to achieve something that absolutely nobody said would be possible.

DAN: I think sometimes that lack of urgency on my part is very frustrating for Riaan, and also for me.

RIAAN: *Obviously, the one I think that's most obvious is the relationship between Dan and myself. We're paddling partners, for goodness' sake, man, we spend, you know, days just a metre and a half away from each other.*

DAN: *I underestimated my disability, in the sense that, because I've grown up in a situation where I didn't think much of it, I didn't see it as a problem …*

RIAAN: *Trust me, I'm the only guy that knew what it meant the first time Dan was separated from me out at sea, when I had to try and turn the boat around and I had to say to myself, this can't be happening, and you're not phoning the Skinstads to tell them that Dan's died. I mean I literally was thinking that as I was trying to turn around to get him.*

DAN: *I struggle with balance in my hips, and that's the essential form of balance that you need in a kayak.*

RIAAN: *Maybe I was also just a talker, you know, saying, shucks, I know that there's going to be a big responsibility on my shoulders. And the reality was that I didn't know what that responsibility actually entailed.*

DAN: *You know, I wear my heart on my sleeve. I say what I feel. There've been a number of occasions where we've had altercations.*

RIAAN: *I've had to change my approach too, in some degree, and the way that maybe I approach the things that I tell him. And I think that's maybe taught me a lot, too. And I'm glad that he's actually changed his approach, the way he responds to it. And understanding what I really, really … What Riaan Manser, the human being, has taken on, on this journey.*

DAN: *Or the fact that, one, I've been handed a major, major opportunity. Two, he's proved that he was willing to risk his life for me on a number of occasions. In fact, every time that we go out in conditions that are even just a little bit less than pristine or calm is a risk.*

RIAAN: Once you've taken stock and you get a little bit of confidence, and I mean, OK, a great amount of confidence when we look at a map now. Dan and I also just realised what is ahead of us now, a humungous bay crossing, 60 kilometres plus, and with weather that's so temperamental. And obviously people know what our situation is, as a paddling partnership, that it's not ideal for the two of us to be out there.

DAN: A diamond, you know, it can't be polished without friction, so let's hope that this is a stepping stone, for me, for Riaan, and for everybody involved.

RIAAN: Iceland has changed from that day we got here till where we are right now. It's a whole, whole new world, I must tell you, in the last two, three weeks. Probably, the thing that I've realised is that we're gonna see a different Dan arrive back.

Interesting to look back and see where we were mentally at this stage of the journey. It has never ceased to amaze me how lucky I have been on my journeys. Sometimes I have dodged danger, or good fortune has just arrived on my doorstep. I know I'm pretty good at seeing past the negatives (irritating to some) and creating a picture that is rosier than reality. I was lucky again during our stopover at Grundarfjörður. I had agreed to splash out to hire a helicopter so that the crew could get some aerial shots of Dan and me. In four months of paddling, we hadn't spotted a single whale – not clearly, at least. That would soon change.

Dan and I kitted up for the film shoot as we would for a normal paddle. We planned to do some 'acting' for the cameras. We had agreed on four locations to shoot, which meant we would be paddling around a fair bit – even though it was a rest day. Darren the cameraman and I met with the pilot and the camera rig operator just before we jumped in the kayak. Our paddling route was clearly set out for us so that the crew could get the best footage possible. We were set to go. As I started dragging the kayak over the pebbles, I heard Tracey's voice.

'Riaan, Riaan, Riaan.'

'Yip. What's up, Trace?' I replied as Dan got into the kayak.

'There are two killer whales out there, just behind the rocks, about a kilometre out to sea,' she said breathlessly.

My heart raced and my hands tingled with excitement. To hell with the shooting plan; this is what I'd dreamt of. Now Dan could get a taste of marine wildlife first-hand. What had started out as an almighty production expense was turning into a possible dream shoot. Even though I have an excellent grasp of the importance of finance in making a documentary, I had to think twice about the idea of parting with more money in one day than some people earn in a year. I didn't feel easy about it. But how do you think I felt as Dan and I headed straight for the killer whales? I was thanking God. If ever I would have wanted a helicopter camera crew in the air filming us, it was then.

We got superb footage, although the water was very dark. The whales mimicked the movements of dolphins, and sometimes were only three metres from us. The most majestic sight for me was the male killer whale, his dorsal fin rising two metres above the water. A youngster about four metres in length popped up right next to us, its mouth and eyes clearly visible. It was an unbelievable day, and unmatched when it came to what other 'rest' days had offered us. Killer whales with us at sea!

Now the open-sea crossings we had planned for awaited us. We had to recover from this adrenaline rush, rest, and then give our all on a 12-hour paddle.

And, with our souls freshly purged, we prepared for the mother of all paddles. If it worked as planned, it would show just how much fitter and stronger we'd become since setting off on our expedition. But, of course, there was a big 'if'. The crossing of any big bay holds some serious potential hazards, and if anything went wrong we would be further away from help or safety than at any other time during the journey.

A great deal would depend on the conditions we would face at sea. By now, we knew only too well that the Icelandic weather was not to be taken for granted under any circumstances. I was really hoping that we'd have a tailwind from the start. According to the forecasts, the wind would be right behind us, which would give us a relatively comfortable initial 10 kilometres.

We had been held up at various points by all sorts of things – from bad weather to simple exhaustion – but this was a good time to start that last burst of effort that would take us to the finish by the end of August, 20 days away. A big challenge tends to generate a big effort, and we were on the brink of our biggest challenge: 65 kilometres from Rif to Melanes in one stretch. A smaller challenge, but a significant one for me personally, would be to keep myself dry – I had just discovered a hole in my dry suit. We whacked together a makeshift repair job as fast as we could, because there was no time to waste.

Everything was feeling whirlwindish for me. We had been paddling huge distances every day, sleeping little, and keeping our heads down. After having committed to Tracey and all the others who were expecting us to finish on 27 August, we didn't want to let anyone down. I hoped that our dream date would stay intact. I had a few things riding on this.

Chez had visas and flight bookings that made it almost impossible to stay past 27 August, unless of course we applied for extensions to both his UK and Icelandic visas. This would be expensive and risky. I believed we could make the call once Dan and I had reached the Westfjords. I could feel the stress building, on top of my responsibilities on the water, but I had to take it in my stride. I knew some tough decisions, ones that would leave some people unhappy again, were on the way. But *I* was the one who had to make those calls. No one else could do it.

The day of the big crossing was upon us. Fortunately, the South African contingent from Grundarfjörður turned out at the crack of dawn to encourage us. Our launch spot was at Rif beach, flanking the new harbour. I had the unenviable task of making the final decision whether to go or stay. Everyone was watching and chatting, unknowingly putting me under pressure to say the words 'let's go'. Of course, I didn't want to disappoint people who'd come out to support us, and, more importantly, I wanted to give them something in return for hosting us for more than a week. Looking at the sea that morning, you would have said something like, 'It doesn't look that bad. Surely it'll be OK.' The conundrum for me was that we didn't need conditions that were temporary; we needed conditions that could see us through for more than 12 hours. I needed to gaze into my crystal ball and make the call. An hour and half later than expected, we set off. It was special to have our friends from Grundarfjörður waving goodbye to us.

This day was a very long and tough one, though more for the boredom that comes from performing repetitive motions, hour in, hour out, than for the physical exertion. The total distance of 65 kilometres was equivalent to some 33 000 paddle strokes. I anticipated that we were going to become mentally and physically numb.

I encouraged Dan with an exercise I'd employed before on long, mentally taxing efforts like this. It involved breaking the day into four segments, and seeing each quarter as a stand-alone entity. Start by aiming for time sessions: see what you can achieve in 30 minutes, and then again for the next 30 minutes. (This is easier than trying to paddle for five hours straight, which wasn't even halfway across the bay.) Make the halfway point the larger goal, and reassess or discuss your goals and progress when you get there. Once you have covered three quarters of the distance, it should feel as if you are being sucked towards the finish line. It's a theory, but it works.

I had a rush of childlike enthusiasm at the halfway mark. We were out at sea, on a kayak, 32 kilometres from any land. That's pretty isolated. I pulled out my emergency phone and decided to make a call to Vasti because I knew her number. She wasn't available, so I suggested that Dan call Bob. It was fun saying hello from this unique spot, and I think Dan appreciated the gesture. There were no numbers saved on the phone, but I remembered the number for Talk Radio 702, as I'd done lots of interviews with John Robbie and other presenters. I decided to call the station. Jenny Crwys-Williams was on air at that moment, and I felt out of my skin to share this special place with her. I think they were discussing female fertility treatments when I called, but Jenny, gracious as always, took it in her stride. We chatted for a while until the phone credit ran out. I think the fertility expert came back on straight after me. (I know some readers will ask the question: how can you let the credit run out on your 'emergency' phone? It's a good point. I'm only human, and did discuss the error of my ways with myself that night. Nonetheless, the paddle was majestic and ended memorably.)

I have had the fortune of travelling through the mountains of Morocco and Ethiopia, which are magnificent in their own right, but the cliffs that line the southern coast of Iceland's Westfjords region really take your breath away. The cliffs of Sigluneshliðar rise

640 metres directly out of the sea! Moving towards and past this monstrosity is slightly unreal and at times dizzying. As Dan and I sat below the cliffs to have a Lucozade moment, we tried not to glance upwards too often. It made me lose all sense of where I was and become disoriented. Dan noticed a flock of birds rising out of a jagged piece of the mountain and pointed it out to me. The flock was moving at high speed but it looked like slow motion because of the scale of this mountain.

Amid all this awesomeness, we had the additional privilege of spending an hour with an eight-metre basking shark, the second-largest fish in the ocean (after the whale shark). It was Dan's first experience up close and personal with such a large creature. Unbelievably, the big fellow didn't just chill with us, he also chased us at one point, and, as if to wrap the day up with him in control, gave us a goodbye hit with his tail – right where Dan sits. We were two quietly stunned kayakers at that moment, I can tell you. We finished off a glorious and proud day at sea. We were brave seamen who had rolled the dice and hoped for the best – sort of. It sounded good; it felt good.

But I was still couldn't answer the nagging question: was the end nigh? There had been so many hurdles and stumbling blocks on the journey that I couldn't have imagined finishing so soon. But we were determined to finish what we had started.

What I didn't know was that, on shore, the team had suffered a serious last-minute problem. They had a long way to go, because the road wound in and out of the fjords along the way, so it would take them six and a half hours to get to our landing place at Melanes, near the abandoned farm at Sjöundá, and they had to be there and waiting when we arrived. But, five minutes before they were due to leave, Chez did a last check of the trailer's tyres and found that the casing was coming off one.

This left them in a tight spot. All they could do was grit their teeth and push on, hoping that the tyre would hold up until they got to Stykkishólmur, the nearest town of any size, where it could be replaced. The danger was that it would suffer a total collapse in the middle of Iceland's plentiful nowhere, which would mean that they would most likely miss the landing. Even if they *did* get to Stykkishólmur, the time spent on replacing the tyre might still mean that they would be too late to meet us. They would just have to carry on and hope for the best, which did nothing for anybody's nerves. Neither did the road, which was terrible and frequently consisted of little more than a meandering dirt track that ran between the mountains, and frequently up and down them, so that they rarely were able to go faster than 60 kilometres per hour.

As it turned out, the tyre was the least of their problems. The vehicle-killing road also did for the trailer's suspension. This was pretty serious. The trailer carried all our gear, not just the stuff we had started with but all sorts of things we had accumulated in the past four months. We were on the verge of entering the remotest and most underpopulated part of Iceland – which is saying a lot, even by South African standards – where replacement gear would be almost impossible to find.

The fact was that, after well over 1500 kilometres of travel, our equipment was starting to show signs of failure. Before setting off on our 65-kilometre jaunt, Dan had struggled to switch his camera on. He and Brad managed to get it going, which was a relief; on the next phase of the journey, through the most inaccessible sections of Iceland's coastline, we would depend heavily on the kayak-mounted cameras to record our adventures. But it was a sign of the times.

As we neared our landing spot, the team was beginning to panic, because it was looking more and more as if we were going to beat them to it. Tracey's last GPS spot, almost two hours earlier, had put us about 18 kilometres from Melanes. If her calculations were correct, it meant that we now had only about five kilometres to go, whereas the team was still about 45 minutes away.

Tracey was now pretty sure that the team would not make it to the rendezvous in time, so she quickly formulated a Plan B. This consisted of calling a local farmer and asking him to go to the landing place and wait for us. It wasn't perfect – we'd still need the team when we arrived – but it was a lot better than nothing; at least there would be someone to welcome us and help us with the boat.

It sounds easy enough to talk about now, but two months earlier a one-shot paddle of over 60 kilometres, and in distinctly less than ideal conditions, would have been inconceivable. It had cost us a lot of pain and effort to reach this point, and so that paddle stands out as a milestone in the Iceland trip. It was a particular milestone for Dan, and I made no bones about it.

'You have to understand what you really, really achieved today, Dan,' I told him.

'I haven't yet, so far,' he replied.

'I want to tell you that today you absolutely amazed me.'

'Thank you, brother. I appreciate that … I put in a huge effort today. I really put in my all today. Well, I can always give more, but I gave it a full go.'

'You wanted your brothers to be proud of you; I tell you what, I wish they were here now. Forget about the ending! This is awesome, china … you have no idea what you've done … You were a machine today. So, I'm just, hey, man I'm blown away!'

This might sound a little over the top. But Dan needed to hear it. He had risked so much and suffered so much, and he had come out on top. I had no doubt that we would still squabble at times before we crossed the finish line, and that I would still nag him about some things until he hated the sound of my voice, but this day had been a triumph for him, and for me.

Despite all the anxiety, the team made it to the landing place first, and were there to meet us when we rode the surf onto the beach. It was a good end to a good day in all respects. We still had hard times coming up – that we were sure of – but we felt ready for them.

CHAPTER 14

THE FINGERS OF THE HAND

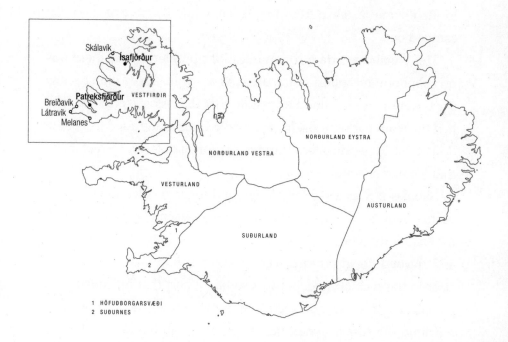

'Please just look out for us, and please just keep alert … It's a dangerous area. I've got winds bringing that swell in and breaking up here, plus the current going … It's going to be a hell of a journey around that corner. It's one of the most dangerous parts of Iceland's coast.'

Tracey's efforts to find accommodation ran up against the stone wall of the Icelandic reality that August was the prime tourist season, and that beds of any sort were like hen's teeth. In the end she managed to organise just two, and by common consent

201

they went to Dan and me, given our gruelling 65-kilometre paddle from Rif. So that night we slept very comfortably in a guesthouse located some distance from the beach, while the rest of the team camped out.

This created a certain communications problem, since there was no cellphone reception in the area. As a result, Tracey didn't know if we were planning another paddle that day. As a precaution, she had the team pack up, just in case, while Chez made good use of the downtime by getting local farmer Asthor Skooleson to repair the trailer's suspension.

Skooleson was a typically tough and ingenious Icelander. A few years earlier, he had been seriously injured when his car skidded off the road – the same road on which our trailer had been damaged – and crashed down a nearby cliff. Skooleson had managed to jump clear in the nick of time, but was so badly hurt that he ended up a paraplegic. This did not keep him from farming or, in this case, repairing the suspension of our trailer, although he warned that his repairs were only temporary: the broken part needed to be replaced as soon as possible.

It was obviously good advice, but I decided not to take it. The weather was so perfect that Dan and I wanted to get back on the water right away, in spite of our aches and pains. We couldn't call Tracey, so we creaked our way into the vehicle and set off on a death-defying trip of about an hour and a quarter to bring the news to the team.

I was in a bad state as we drove towards the sea. I was so deep-down tired that driving was a real battle; all I really wanted to do was stop the vehicle and get out. Then I told myself: *Calm down. You've been here for so long to try to achieve the total thing; if we don't make it towards this end, we're stuffed, you know what I mean? Everything we've worked for is coming down to this time now!*

The team took our decision in good spirits, perhaps partly because it was such a lovely day, and also, I think, because for the first time we really felt the finish was within reach. I had by now set a provisional date of 2 September to reach Húsavík. This was perhaps optimistic, in view of the weather problems we were sure to encounter, but the important thing was that a firm target had been set, something to work towards.

Up to this point we would never have even contemplated setting a date, so uncertain were we of our progress. We had been grinding away for so long now that sometimes it seemed we had embarked on a journey without an end. Yet I couldn't fault Dan's remark that 'It's a bit surreal to think of an end now. It was just the other day that we were about to leave.'

That day's paddle wouldn't be a long one, a 35-kilometre leg to Breiðavík, the first part of a 75-kilometre stage that would take us west and then north around the first finger of the deeply serrated peninsula of Iceland's extreme northwest, the forbidding Westfjords region. The area is popularly known as 'The Hand', because that is exactly what it looks like when you see it on a map.

Breiðavík is an abandoned farm tucked into a cove just north of the Látravik lighthouse, Iceland's – and therefore Europe's – westernmost point. Isolated though it might be, it has its claims to fame. One of these is a parsonage dating from 1824 which in summer serves as a guesthouse. Another is the wonderful bird cliffs at Látrabjarg (Nest Mountain), said to be the most magnificent in the world. On the way there you can visit the Hnjotur Museum, a private aeronautical and folk museum whose exhibits include well-preserved Russian Antonov biplane ... not that we had the time for sightseeing, unfortunately.

That was the good news. The bad news was that after Breiðavík we would be entering into very tough country indeed, with cellphone reception fading out completely the further north we got, and the roads, such as they were, cutting across the bases of the various fingers rather than reaching their tips. This meant that, for extended periods, we would be out of contact with the team, both visually and electronically. Dan and I would really be on our own.

Just to make it a little worse, more equipment failure surfaced while we were kitting up. This time it was Dan's dry suit, whose zip was malfunctioning and opened up when it was supposed to close. A malfunctioning zip might not sound important compared with some of our other preoccupations, but, although it was summer, the water remained freezing cold, and the suits were essential for preventing hypothermia in the case of a ducking or worse. Our suits had saved us several times already. The problem was that Dan didn't have a spare suit, yet daren't paddle without one – he would be as stiff as a plank in no time. But about all we could do was to be very careful about zipping it up.

I had hoped that the previous day's beautiful weather would continue, but no such luck. The sea was choppy and the wind and current were against us. We were clearly going to have to work for every kilometre we clocked up. Before we launched I said a few words, each one straight from the heart: 'Please just look out for us, and please just keep alert … It's a dangerous area. I've got winds bringing that swell in and breaking up here, plus the current going … It's going to be a hell of a journey around that corner. It's one of the most dangerous parts of Iceland's coast.'

Not very inspiring words, but, in my experience, bad news is better than no news. Battles are won or lost in your mind: the killer is uncertainty, which has led to many more defeats than you might think. Now the team members knew exactly what we – and they – would be up against, and could start preparing themselves mentally and physically to face the worst hand that Iceland could deal them.

We punched through the massive surf, battling to keep the kayak's nose pointing straight into it. If it rolled us over and smashed our boat it would be a disaster, because the other kayak was still under repair in Reykjavík. The surf seemed to get bigger the deeper we got into it. Getting on board was a desperate struggle, especially for Dan. Eventually, though, we were paddling towards the open sea with every ounce of strength in our bodies. Breiðavík, here we come! But my earlier suspicions were confirmed. For the first hour and a half in particular, it was pure hell.

On land, meanwhile, the team started packing up; all going well, they would reach the landing place at Breiðavík in about an hour and a half, and set up camp for all of us – no more worries about trying to find accommodation, since, apart from Breiðavík, there weren't any guesthouses in this part of the world. From now on, the support team's principal preoccupations would consist of hoping for good weather, finding launch sites and setting up camp there. It almost made us nostalgic for that strange former fish factory at Grindavík. Well, maybe for the rest of the team – Tracey had managed to snag beds for Dan and me at the guesthouse.

By now, Dan and I had run into some problems of our own. Our only working kayak was beginning to succumb to the strain and had sprung a leak, so that every so often we had to interrupt our momentum and sponge up some of the water. Perhaps 'momentum' is not the right word. Things were so rough that I suspected we were actually drifting backwards. The only remedy was to put on more speed, which was easier said than done. Another worry was making contact with the team at Breiðavík; the sun was setting, and it seemed likely that we were going to get there in the dark. OK, not Africa dark, but dark enough to make things difficult.

To my dismay, I found myself sinking into negativity – me, the one who was always chivvying Dan to greater effort. I took a deep breath and set about getting my mind right: *It's easy, you can do this. This is not above you. This is not beyond you. This is absolutely what you can do. This is what you do, this is what you do. It's what you do. Get your mind right, stay positive. You work, you work. Come on, Manser, man, come on, man!*

That helped. When Dan said uneasily: 'Shouldn't we get going again?' I replied: 'Danny, hit it hard, hey!'

When we finally fought our way around Látravik's sharp point, we eased off a bit because we were finally shot of the current that had been giving us so much uphill, and had time to enjoy the scenery, which included the 400-metre-high cliffs of Látrabjarg, home to one of the largest puffin colonies in Iceland. As many as 1.2 million puffins gather here every summer to breed. It was a truly staggering sight, and the amount of noise a million-odd puffins can put out is phenomenal. 'Unbelievable!' I heard myself saying. Dan remarked: 'It's taken us forever to reach these cliffs, but, now that we're here, it's pretty humbling ...'

I pulled myself back to the present. We'd averaged only four kilometres per hour; with Iceland's midsummer now past, there would be a few hours of solid darkness, and we still had to find the team and land. 'OK, Danny,' I said. 'Let's get going, it's getting dark.'

On the beach, Tracey was grinding her teeth. By her calculation we should have arrived two hours earlier, but we hadn't, and no matter how much she tried her cellphone it remained as dead as a doornail. Then I managed to get through by radio. That could mean only one thing – we were close by. Now, lights were needed to guide us in. Ordinarily, the team's vehicles would have provided the illumination, but the guesthouse owners had insisted that only their vehicles be allowed on the beach. That meant they would have to get up in the dead of night. In typical obliging fashion, the guesthouse owner, Brina, got her husband and another man to come down with their cars.

About 500 metres out, I radioed Tracey and asked her to show some light. She grabbed her torch and aimed it seawards, and at first I couldn't see it because an outlying strip of coastline was in the way. We paddled closer, though, and at about 200 metres out she spotted us.

Dan and I managed to land without much trouble. This was just as well, because we were really knocked out. I looked at my watch. It was 01h15 in the morning, and we had left at 18h00 the previous evening, so that 'easy' paddle had taken us more than seven very rough hours. Coming on top of the 63-kilometre paddle, that left our batteries pretty flat. I was just very, very glad that the team was there to help us, and that I could look forward to a soft, warm bed.

Dan was in pretty bad shape, too, but his tail was up: 'Heavy day today, hey? Yesterday the challenge was the distance, and we came up trumps there. It was my best day so far. Today, if I can be so bold as to say it, we had to be bloody brave, hey. I'm still me. I'm still, like, a happy guy, but I'm far more, you know, aware of dangers and consequences now.'

Brina seemed tickled to have two travel-worn lodgers and their colleagues camping down on the beach. 'I felt today like a very old mother,' she grinned.

'Why?' I asked.

'Because, you can't go to bed without the kids coming home!' she laughed. 'Oh, my God, I'm so glad to see you!' And I knew that, being a warm-hearted person and a veteran of the Westfjords, she had been worried about us, even though we were total strangers.

'Come on!' she invited us in, and gave Dan a kiss. As I've said before, the man's a charmer second to none.

After a wonderful night's sleep – well, for Dan and me anyway – we set off again. We thanked our hosts for everything, and they wished us good luck. As we rode back down to the beach for the launch, it transpired that Dan had picked up a nickname: *'Trolli'*.

'Because I like you, I'll tolerate a nickname, but I don't really like it,' Dan said.

'What does "*Trolli*" mean, buddy?' Brad asked.

'It means "troll",' Dan replied. Needless to say, this caused some hilarity. In Norse mythology, trolls were dodgy types – ugly and slow-witted creatures who lived in remote mountains.

There was not much laughter, however, when it came to getting our ailing kayak down to the launch site. So much water had accumulated inside that it took all hands to shift it. The only one to be excused kayak duty was Dan, who needed all his strength to make his recalcitrant body do what he wanted. He had taken a beating like no other cerebral palsy sufferer, and the physical stress was beginning to tell. But Dan did his thing uncomplainingly. He wasn't on this trip to whine about his physical problems.

We were set to tackle the rest of the Westfjords, jumping from finger to finger of 'The Hand' and working through our problems and crises with whatever we had available. We could take short cuts across the fjords between the fingers, but the team would have to drive at least halfway up each one to meet us. All sorts of things could happen in the process. They could run out of fuel, run out of time, or, worst of all, lose contact altogether.

And just to make things worse, my GPS device suddenly stopped working. We had had trouble with the GPS spots before, but it had never been all that important. But this was another matter, seeing that we would be doing some very isolated paddles; it was very important that the device worked properly. We swapped our spots, and I suggested that Tracey find out if there would be any communications from our landing place on the Selárdalsheiði Peninsula, about 40 kilometres away. But, despite this technical hitch, I could see that the team's spirit was good.

The main problem, however, was the water that was getting into the kayak. To my mind, it was seeping in via the rudder cables, so I decide to apply a good layer of Vaseline around the cable apertures. That way, the cables could still move in and out, but most of the intruding water would be repelled. I hoped that would do it; from the beach, the sea looked nice and flat, and so it was, but it looked a bit different from where you sat on the kayak, mere centimetres above the surface. Anyway, we would just have to see.

We got off to a smooth start, with no problems from the surf. The sea was a little rough, but this would normally have been no problem. Now, however, the kayak made slow going. My Vaseline applications hadn't helped; there was still a lot of water coming in somewhere, and we couldn't bail it out fast enough while struggling with the chop of up to 60 centimetres. We were so busy that we hardly had time to spare for an occasional glimpse of the stunningly beautiful fjords we were crossing.

While Dan and I forced our overburdened craft northwards, Tracey and Chez delayed starting on the long, meandering drive to the landing place until they had dealt with the urgent requirement for more lasting repairs to the trailer. They repacked the entire contents into one of the vehicles and set out to organise some help from the locals to get it properly fixed. This done, and the trailer in for repairs, they headed for the landing site. (It turned out that the repairs they had done cost more than the value of the trailer.) Thanks to our deliberately later start, to make use of the calm-weather window, it was going to be another night arrival, and not only a night landing, but a night recce of the site as well.

Eventually, we appeared out of the gloom in a state of some discomfort. The watertight seals of our dry suits had now begun to give way – hardly surprising, I suppose, given the almost daily abuse of the last four months. As Dan aptly put it when we landed, 'Another Icelandic sunset, and we've both got water in our pants'. Well, we would have to live with it. It would be a real danger if we capsized, but otherwise we would just have to get used to sharing our suits with the ultra-chilly water of the Icelandic seas. Not that it would be a friendly coexistence; by the time we stumbled ashore we were very cold, stiff and crampy from the damp suits.

I felt bad enough, but, needless to say, Dan was in an even worse state, so much so that it was a struggle for him just to get off the kayak. Zahir and Tracey gave him a hand up to the camp, where he attended to yet another problem. By this stage, both of us had blisters on our hands, but one of Dan's was particularly angry. There was

210

no question of lying up while it healed; the only thing he could do was slap a piece of sticking plaster on it, in the hope of reducing the friction of the paddle handle, which had caused the problem.

Even with another successful paddle and night landing out of the way, we weren't celebrating that night. We had too much to do and too far to go to begin slapping ourselves on the back. We were all painfully conscious that Iceland's ridiculously short summer was drawing to a close, with farmers busy harvesting in preparation for the long, cold winter months, which would soon see the land cloaked in snow and ice.

Our hopes were pinned on reaching the finish line within another two weeks, before autumn took the land in its ever more icy grip. But to do that we would have to put in a maximum and consistent effort, and just hope that our leaky kayak and dry suits would not let us down any further. As Tracey put it, 'It's go time'.

'Go time' meant another immediate night paddle. Neither of us was really up to it after the exertions of the past few days and nights, but it was an act of desperation on my part. The weather forecast, for what it was worth, predicted that a whole week of storms was on the way, so I decided to make use of the window we had to do a short paddle of about 23 or 24 kilometres. It wasn't much, compared to our recent efforts, but it would put us that much nearer the finish line and help to make up for time we might have to spend ashore if the weather turned really bad – or perhaps I should say 'worse'.

We struggled back into our damp and leaky suits and, with the help of the others, launched our equally damp and leaky kayak. It wasn't too difficult, since the cove was quite calm, but we knew only too well that this was no guarantee that things would be the same out at sea. This was of even greater concern than it had been in the past. With our kayak and dry suits in their present condition, a capsize would be disastrous.

We had struck up a good relationship with the local Coast Guard. 'There's one grumpy guy, one very friendly guy and then one guy is quite bored with his job,' Tracey explained with a laugh, 'but they know me, they talk about the girl they always speak to.' The problem, of course, was that in our present state it was doubtful if they could get to us in time if we got into difficulties.

As I'd feared, conditions worsened as we hit the open sea. There was a current pushing against us – it was full moon and the tides were at their strongest – and all the indications were that the wind was going to get worse. And, of course, at this stage we still didn't know exactly where we were going to land, because the team was still sniffing about in the dark, looking for the right spot.

But the full moon was beautiful when it emerged in all its glory at sunset; it seemed to be very close, so that we could see its textures and craters. Its appearance, I remembered, marked the start of the twentieth week of the adventure. How long ago, yet vividly remembered, that seemed now! For Zahir, I realised, the full moon meant something else: he was halfway through Ramadan. It had been hard for him to fast during the daylight hours, when you considered how the team's activities and the cold weather burnt up the calories, but he had stuck to it.

In the fading light, Tracey and Chez had to get to the area of the landing place along secondary roads cut into precipitous cliffs. Now our lack of reconnaissance came into play: the team couldn't get down to where they needed to be, namely, on the shoreline near a lighthouse. That meant they could not pinpoint a good landing place. They tried to tell us this, but couldn't get through on the radio. By the time they finally succeeded, we had already arrived, while they were still up on the cliffs and nowhere near the beach.

'You're going past us!' I warned.

'Riaan, the beach is closer to the lighthouse,' Tracey replied. 'We've been driving on a cliff. We can't get down to you there.'

'Can you see my flashing light?' I asked.

'Yes, I can see you.'

'Give me instructions,' I said. 'What must I do?'

'Well, we'll follow this road till we can get down to the water, but ja, right now I can't give you instructions until we find a landing spot … We just have to carry on till this road goes down to sea level. That's what we're going to do now, and I'll give you instructions when we find a road that goes down to sea level.'

I was a little confused now, as Dan and I had passed a couple of beaches. I asked Tracey if there was, in fact, a road down to the shore, and she said that, before we left Breiðavík, Brina's husband had confirmed there was one.

Further complications ensued, and in the end we had to turn around and paddle back in the teeth of the current to a potential landing place that Zahir finally located north of the lighthouse, a rocky cove with a little beach at its end. It wasn't ideal – the high ground behind it would present a struggle for Dan, and there wasn't a hope of manhandling the kayak up – but it was the best of several bad choices. The only alternative was to paddle deeper into the fjord.

That was that, then. 'Can somebody just shine a car light or something higher up, so that we can see you?' I asked.

We landed easily enough, and stored the kayak as securely as possible against the cliff face by packing rocks against it, hoping that the winds wouldn't be strong enough to inflict any damage. Then we toiled up to the vehicles. That allegedly easy little paddle had turned into a nightmare, and I was exhausted, physically and mentally. The fact was that I was now very near the end of my tether.

Dan was surprisingly upbeat, considering the physical stress on him and the battle he had to get up to the vehicles. 'It was already windy to start, but Riaan made a good point and he said that the wind in the next couple of days is going to be worse. So we've just got to tough it out for now. He's a master at making little goals … just aim for one rock, one ripple, one bird, one whatever, and little bit by little bit we go, but shit, my balance was tested in the beginning, That oke's a hero at being able to paddle, keep me balanced in bad weather, and then still keep his head when the shit goes down, That oke is incredible.'

Dan had acquired mental toughness and conquered his fear of the sea, dug deep into a well of endurance he would never have discovered but for all this hardship, and made his body do things that no one believed it could. He was picking up the attitude of the kayaker, the mental games that help you to endure. The squabbling of the early days was far behind us. This was not to say that we wouldn't have a few more disagreements before the end, but the perspective had changed.

We holed up there for the next 72 hours while wind and weather raged around us. It was a welcome and in fact very necessary break. After covering 158 kilometres in four days, Dan and I badly needed rest and time for our bodies to repair the wear and tear we had inflicted on them – and for the mechanics to complete the repairs to our trailer.

This interlude also provided time for reflection. The paddle had shown that the team had learnt to adapt to whatever problems came its way. It had also been a reminder that you couldn't plan for everything. Sometimes the planning went wrong, or there wasn't time to do any. If you couldn't take that in your stride, then your goose was cooked. But that's what true adventure is all about. You know what you want to achieve and do what you have to do, come hell or high water. And there might well be a little of that hell awaiting us, because in a few days' time there would be no road access at all for the team in most places. We would have to cope on our own with anything the Westfjords might throw at us.

Three days later, we were on the move again. We got our stuff together, and toiled down the steep, rocky slope – at least it was in daylight this time. We found the kayak where we had left it. Good! All we had to do was get it down to the beach and launch.

But things weren't so good on closer examination. Now that we were launching in daylight for a change, Richard spotted what was clearly a hole in the hull – no doubt the reason why it had been taking on so much water. Clearly, we weren't going to launch that day. There was no way we could go to sea in a kayak that might sink under us; in fact, we'd been fortunate that that hadn't happened already. It was also obvious that a quick patching job down here on the beach was not going to be enough. It was a terrible blow to our timetable as well as to our spirits.

Deeply frustrated, I said: 'Are you guys willing to help me carry the kayak up and take it back to the vehicles? We're not going today.' Of course they were. That was what a team was for – and that particularly included Zahir. I worried about how the struggle to get the kayak up the cliff would drain his waning energy reserves, but he put his back into the struggle as though he had been knocking back three square meals a day like everybody else.

The delay, I could see, had unsettled Dan. 'Don't build your own angst and hype, Dan,' I counselled him. 'It's not necessary.'

215

'No,' he replied. 'No, I'm just thinking of it, because it's been … it's been pretty relaxed the last little while. So I'm just … I'm not over-anxious, I'm just trying to focus more.' That was fair enough. It was pretty much the way I felt.

I could have done the repair work by myself, but time was too valuable to go about it in any way except urgently, so I enlisted the entire team to help. Within 12 hours, the inside repairs – the most important part – had been completed, the hole had been properly patched, and the new resin had set. It would have been nice to take a breather, but the weather window was holding, more or less. That night – well, actually 04h00 next morning, after about four hours' sleep – we launched our revitalised (and now much lighter) kayak. Our destination was Skálavík, about 43 kilometres away. There Dan and I would get some sleep before we started paddling again.

Getting down to the beach in the dark without damaging either ourselves or the kayak was nerve-wracking, but all went well and we were soon on our way. As we left, the team started packing up before heading northwards to identify our next landing place. By my reckoning we had 11 paddles left before the finish. Today was 18 August, and we simply *had* to reach Húsavík on 2 September. That date was set in concrete, because we had invited the media and all sorts of people, from as far afield as Wales and the United States, to be in at the kill. Two very special guests would be Nigel Foster and Geoff Hunter, who had made the first circumnavigation of Iceland by kayak in 1977. We had found their names in the guest book at that farm at Strandhöfn early on in our journey, and had managed to track them down. The idea was that they would join up with us for part of the final paddle to Húsavík – their first reunion since their epic adventure. This was what history was made of – ordinary people doing extraordinary things – and we'd be a little part of it.

So we'd be gunning it – Iceland permitting, of course, not to mention the repairs to the kayak. It was going to be damned tight, and to make it even tighter was the fact that Skálavík would be the last place where the team would be able to reach us. From that point, we would really be on our own in every way.

We were taking a very big chance, Dan and I knew, given all the things that could go wrong, and both of us were a bit nervous about it. But we were playing for very high stakes, and if you want to score big in a game like this you have to put all your money on the table. All the same, I could anticipate the massive strain we were letting ourselves in for. But Dan's reaction was to vow to be more active and more constructive.

CHAPTER 15

HALLDOR AND THE LEGENDS

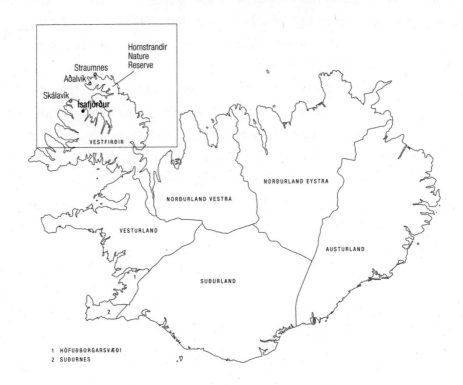

'"It isn't over until it's over" was something I'd learnt in Madagascar in the most brutal fashion. It seemed that this lesson hadn't finished with me.'

This was going to be our toughest challenge yet. We were going to spend the next four days threading our way through the remotest parts of the Westfjords, totally out of physical contact with the team and at the mercy of a whole range of potential perils – all this in a patched-up kayak and leaky dry suits.

We would be paddling round the remotest part of Iceland, the Hornstrandir Nature Reserve in the extreme north, a chunk of huge basalt mountains. Until the mid-20th century, Hornstrandir had been home to a scattering of fishermen and farmers who were tough even by Icelandic standards, but in 1975 it was proclaimed a wilderness area to protect the subarctic fauna and flora.

The first leg of our four-day journey would be a not-too-arduous 35-kilometre paddle from Skálavík to the west coast of the nature reserve. We were aiming for a lighthouse north of Aðalvík on a headland called Straumnes. There we would land safely (we hoped), huddle under our tarpaulin to sleep, and then continue on. We had so much gear to pack into the kayak that space was at a premium – to the point where we were not even taking our tents; we were just going to get into our sleeping bags and pull the tarpaulin over us. If that wasn't enough, we would just have to suffer.

I think the only person who fully appreciated the real risks of the venture was Halldor, a journalist who also owned a kayak club, who had been following our trek around Iceland and had come up to see us off.

Halldor is probably the best sea kayaker in Iceland when it comes to competition. He has an uncanny ability to become one with a kayak out on the water, and can do Eskimo rolls at will. He is tough, and he understood the danger of what we had tackled. I was pleased by the extremely complimentary and supportive words he offered before we said our goodbyes. He said he had always wanted to circumnavigate Iceland, and planned to do it sooner rather than later.

Dan had somehow misplaced his gloves, but at Breiðavík he had acquired some waterproof dishwashing gloves, bright pink things that made our picture in the Icelandic newspapers hard to miss.

Halldor took a photograph of us, and then left us to get on with our preparations. Chez started up one of the vehicles and laid the kit across the bonnet to dry it out a bit, while I sponged out some water the kayak had taken in through a new hairline fracture. All this took time, which ate into our paddling schedule.

Dan, on the other hand, was edgy but confident, and his belief in me was touching: 'Riaan, he's always had my back on the trip, and he's a guy that you can depend on in terms of safety. So I'm in good hands, I've just got to do my job, hey. Putting my one hand in front of the other and getting those kilometres ticked off, and then first prize obviously would be to see the other kayakers cheer ... and that would mean a lot to me.'

Now all we had to do was get through the next few days, and get through them on time ... I could hardly believe that we were so close to the end, and that we were going to do this last spurt through such dangerous country. It was a lot of pressure, but, hey, so many people had supported us, and the best way to show our gratitude would be to get there in one piece and on time.

In the gloaming, we wrestled the kayak towards the water. For the first time in months, it was fully loaded and weighing over 250 kilograms once more. I knew that this would make it harder to manage, because we had to avoid capsizing at all costs.

We were about 12 kilometres from the Straumnes lighthouse, but we had started late. Thanks to the winds and the heavier kayak, we were doing less than four kilometres per hour. It was 08h00, and we had to take a decision. To struggle on like this until we reached the lighthouse would serve no purpose; we would just wear ourselves out to the point where it would screw us up for the days ahead. So I decided to land and take shelter at the first shoreside hut we laid eyes on.

It was a wise decision; we were really tired. We found a rocky but more or less suitable landing place at Aðalvík, where there was a little jetty. We had spotted a few houses when we were about seven kilometres out, and hoped for a sign of life. My encouragement for Dan to aim for this spot was more about the fact that we needed to win every last kilometre we could. The weather was not ideal, but at least we could move forward.

We got ashore and dragged the kayak up onto the rocks. It got bumped around a bit, but was undamaged, as far as we could see. A local couple, Bjorn and Matilda, who knew all about what Dan and I were doing, gave us the use of a one-room shack for the night. It was pretty basic, without even water, but what it *did* have was walls, which kept the wind out, and also a gas heater, which was what we needed more than anything else. Retrieving the gear from the kayak was a shiveringly painful task for me. I could feel winter was almost upon us, and the simple task of bringing all our gear from the kayak to the hut seemed bigger than it really was. Making us dinner was probably the highlight for me that night. I was in need of physical repairs.

I felt a bit downhearted as we lay back and let the heat get to us. We had come unsupported through the first day, but I didn't regard it as a successful paddle, because I had spent most of it having to ask Dan to do as I asked, namely, to put the paddle in front of him.

Dan and I *did* have a special bond. It was a great thought that our relationship was not going to have to endure this ordeal for longer than another seven or eight days. It would be great just to sit around a fire with him, have a cold beer and chat about sport. And, as he had said, what we were going to achieve over here would be pretty mind-boggling.

Next morning, we said goodbye to Bjorn and Matilda and got going again. Before we left, Dan filmed himself, and what he said showed a great insight into what he was feeling:

'Old Riaan and I have been chatting a lot on the boat yesterday and today, and obviously, you know, there's been a lot of times when I've harboured a lot of resentment and he, too. Essentially, what I think it boils down to is that we see different aspects of each other's personality than the others in the group do. Do you know what I mean?

'I think he … I know that I can be lazy a lot … You know, there's a difference, there's a massive difference, between the worlds of sayers and doers. It's a massive achievement to be already here, you know. So, I think what happens is that I get too sensitive when he's, when he carries on being as brutal as he is. But … the honest truth is, that he's probably one of the people that is most qualified to be brutal.

'I mean, you know, he has to be. I mean, he's the guy that, in the freezing cold, went to go and get the bags out of the kayak last night, you know. It's a massive responsibility on his shoulders, to have to worry about the both of us. To know that you know he's the only person that's answerable for me. Underneath a lot of that harshness is a very, very good, good person that wants to help me. It's just sometimes it's difficult to be able to see past that, sort of, that harshness. I need to be more active, and more constructive in what I do, and listen. You can't fix all the problems that you have and all, end all the insecurities in one day, but it's a good start.'

'It isn't over until it's over' was something I'd learnt in Madagascar in the most brutal fashion. It seemed that this lesson hadn't finished with me. Our paddle from Aðalvík started with a sheltered eight kilometres along the peninsula's westerly cliff range. I'd expected a headwind to blow for the next few days, and hoped the dramatic coastline would offer some shelter. After rounding the Straumnes lighthouse, we were taken aback by the strength of the headwind, but remained determined. One kilometre into our easterly direction, I felt a snap on my footpedals and all resistance disappeared. That meant only one thing: a disabled rudder. I swung my upper body around and tried to get a clearer picture of what was wrong. Man alive, it was just a simple rudder cable or swivel malfunction; the securing bolt had snapped in half. I realised that the mechanics Thor had found to assist us had used untreated steel, as well as drilling out the core of the bolt. Our lives had depended on a thin, rusted piece of metal.

I had a good idea how to fix the rudder bolt, but our location drastically limited our options. Fortunately, the sea was pushing us backwards; with some careful manoeuvring, I soon had us tucked into a rock slipway, where I could inspect the damage more accurately. The rudder was only repairable on land, and so we had to focus on getting back to a place where we could repair it properly. With the rudder stowed temporarily on the deck, I had to steer the kayak using traditional leaning methods and rudder controls.

With the extra weight we were carrying, losing the rudder was a disaster. Steering now became a serious struggle, because it was very difficult to keep going forward in a straight line. It made the job twice as difficult, and our speed dropped dramatically. I was dumbstruck. I just couldn't believe we were going to be stuck so near the end. After a closer inspection later on, I realised that Bjorn's basic tools would not help at all. This was miracle number one. Miracle number two was that the final ferry of the season was leaving Aðalvík within the hour. It could take us back to Ísafjörður, where, I hoped, Halldor and his kayaking colleagues would help me repair this vital piece of equipment. However, I was going to have to break the bad news to Tracey. The finish would have to be moved a week later.

Miracle number three, though, was just around the corner. After 10 years of extreme testing, I have realised that I automatically see the positive and the opportunity in many a bad situation. The rudder problem had delayed us, it was true, but it had also created the opportunity for Dan and I to spend time with Geoff Hunter and Nigel Foster, the original 1977 kayakers. Geoff Hunter had arrived from England, and Nigel Foster was supposed to fly in from Seattle. We were battling to find out what had happened to him. Everything seemed to be unravelling at a rate of knots. Zahir and Brad went off to Reykjavík to collect Geoff, to try to find the missing Nigel, and to pick up the second kayak for them to paddle in (it was still in Reykjavík, in the warehouse where it had been stored after the repairs in Höfn).

In Reykjavík, Zahir and Brad nearly went mad trying to find Geoff. Thanks to Zahir's foresight in getting the car washed – for the first time in five months – before leaving for Reykjavík, Geoff spotted the expedition logo and flagged them down. Right! One down, one to go. Nigel was still missing.

Miracle number four was to have had Halldor as our go-to guy. There was no one better in Iceland. For the repair, Halldor roped in his friend Peter, who was said to be able to fix anything – and certainly looked it. Peter replaced the rudder's snapped hollow steel rod with a stainless steel one, which is exactly what I would have used back in South Africa if I had been repairing it, and then resined and fibreglassed it in place. And basically that was it. When the resin had cured, we had only to hang the rudder back in place and secure it with the existing two screws on top of the bridge.

While the resin was setting, we inspected the kayak itself. I had a good look at the bottom and found that the repairs I'd done had stopped most of the water. I kept on looking and found there was a big hole we hadn't seen previously. The remedy was straightforward: sand the hull in the appropriate places, apply square patches to stop the leak, and reinforce the hull around it. All being equal, it would be enough to see us through to the finish line. I was tired of repairs and more and more speed bumps!

While the kayak was being repaired, the conversation naturally turned to Geoff and Nigel. Halldor was kind enough to say that having people like us and Geoff and Nigel come to visit was like having the best golfer in the world visit the local golf club. My reply to that was that we could learn a lot from the local kayakers – I just hoped we wouldn't tire them out with all our questions. 'I hope you do!' Halldor laughed. I felt pretty good. Perhaps things were starting to fall into place, I thought. Then Tracey called to say that Nigel had been located. His transatlantic flight had been cancelled and he had returned to Seattle, but he was leaving for Iceland the next day.

When Geoff, Zahir and Brad heard that Nigel was on his way but wouldn't arrive for a couple of days, they decided to leave Reykjavík with the second kayak and rejoin the rest of the team. We, on the other hand, were lounging about while Peter finished the repair work, enjoying the respite. Doing nothing constructive can be very therapeutic at times. This was the place where the souls of keen kayakers probably went when they died, and if the rudder hadn't broken we would have bypassed it in our rush to get to Húsavík! Perhaps the gods of good fortune had decided: *Well, if you're going to break your rudder, this is the best place to do it.*

What made it even more pleasant was that the team brought Geoff to Ísafjörður that evening so that he could have dinner with us at

Halldor's home, something I was really looking forward to (more good news, of course, was that Nigel had caught his flight this time around).

Meeting Geoff was a great experience. He is a pleasant, humorous fellow who is as modest as our host; he laughed it off when I told him in all sincerity what a pleasure it was to meet a legend like him, and thanked me for the opportunity to meet me. He told us that he had never returned to Iceland after his and Nigel's record-breaking 1977 trip: 'I've wanted to come back, but, you know, you get married, you have children and … But it's lovely to be back.'

Inevitably, the talk turned to the 1977 expedition. 'The Customs didn't believe we weren't going to sell the boats, and you know, I said, you know, this is like a car … We're just travelling in this, and anyway, we convinced them, so off we set and we came south. The same direction as you're going. Across the Vatnajökull, which was a hard time and you won't know all about that. Oh, dear.'

'We're just so relieved to have that south coast behind us,' I said. 'Now, when people tell us we've got tough times, we just always think back to the south coast!'

'Yes, are you still friends?' Geoff asked slyly. Dan and I laughed; obviously, he and Nigel had also squabbled on the way around Iceland. 'Ja,' Dan said, 'of course!'

'It's tough,' I remarked, 'you know it's tough beyond basic outsider's observation.'

'Oh, yeah, yeah, yeah, you're living so close to someone, you know,' Geoff reminisced, 'and with Nigel and me, we hadn't met before, but we'd both canoed. It's just such a lovely experience together, but you know, you're there to save each other's lives, really. So, even if you don't like each other, you've got to stick together.'

'One hundred per cent,' I agreed. Geoff's and Nigel's experience had paralleled our own. However, I had all along believed Nigel and

Geoff had paddled in a double kayak. They hadn't, in fact. *Dan and I were the first on the planet to attempt to do this.* Any sane paddler wouldn't take a chance in a double kayak, they said; if your partner packs up, it will mean death for two of you. I understood better now why Halldor had said those kind things to me the other day. What I believed people just looked past as a mere detail was actually significant. Dan and I were an unlikely pair, that's for sure.

Next day, Nigel made his belated appearance, and was reunited with Geoff in Iceland for the first time since their famous circumnavigation of 1977.

'You're an absolute legend, just for getting over here from the States,' I told him, and he replied: 'I really, really wanted to get out to see you guys and to wish you well, because you're doing such a cool thing! Iceland was very special, because, well Geoff was ...'

'Because I was there,' Geoff grinned.

'... an experienced paddler,' Nigel said to laughter from the rest of us, 'and I was kind of naive. Geoff would go cruising in circles around me while I was paddling along, pacing myself so that I would manage to do 40 miles in a day ... He must have been going crazy! And eventually I got annoyed with him, for some reason, and I started paddling hard, and suddenly realised, well, he won't get me more tired by paddling hard, he'd lose ... And so, Geoff taught me how to paddle.'

Later that afternoon, we went out on *Inspiration 1* and *Inspiration 2* with Nigel and Geoff – Nigel with me, and Geoff with Dan. I still stick to my observation that we are not tough these days. These guys were way braver. I would catch myself staring at them and imagining the drama and discomfort they must have endured 34 years earlier. We were privileged to have them offer their time so willingly. The kayak Halldor had all four of us sign that day summed it up. Halldor said no other kayak in the world would have four of the seven Iceland circumnavigators' signatures on it. It was a very special time.

We had ticked a few boxes, but were essentially a week out of the planning. Dan and I needed to take whatever transport came our way to get back to where our rudder broke. We didn't think that we would find ourselves in a vicious storm out at sea. The boat that transported us to the southerly point of Aðalvík Bay did not drop us on shore. They literally dumped us out at sea in the midst of a gale, complete with waterspouts bombarding us from all sides. It was a challenge just to stay in the kayak. On the GPS, I registered our average speed for the first hour as 1.3 kilometres per hour. Madness! But this is where I hope I taught Dan the art of small goals – no matter how pathetic they seem at the time. It turned out that all we needed to do to get out of the full force of the storm was to round the next peninsula, which was just 1.3 kilometres away.

The goal that day was 'to get going', nothing more. Once we were back in familiar Aðalvík Bay, we agreed to find shelter in the little village where we had had assistance a few days earlier.

ABOVE AND LEFT: Our journey up the west coast of Iceland involved rounding the Snæfellsnes Peninsula. This impressive bit of the island is crowned by Snæfellsjökull Glacier, one of Iceland's most celebrated sights. Here, as we prepare for a beach launch near Arnarstapi, Dan waves goodbye to some local well-wishers.

ABOVE: We spent a few days at Grundarfjörður, on the northern coast of the Snæfellsnes Peninsula, where the rocky coastline is interspersed with long stretches of beach. The locals – including some South Africans – made us most welcome.

LEFT: A rusting trawler stranded on the beach at Látrabjarg, in the Westfjords region, is something of a local landmark and a reminder of the unpredictable nature of the sea conditions around Iceland.

ABOVE: Our journey round the starkly beautiful Westfjords meant that Dan and I were out of reach of the team for several days. We had to rely on our wits, courage and sheer determination.

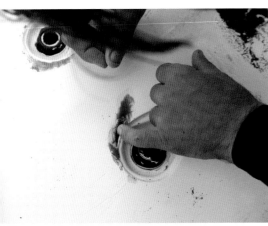

ABOVE AND RIGHT: The coast of western Iceland has a forbidding beauty, captured in these shots of the Snæfellsnes Peninsula.

LEFT: After the damage to *Inspiration 1* at Hvalnes, we had switched to *Inspiration 2* Rough seas and difficult landings inevitably took their toll, forcing me to repair several small holes in *Inspiration 2*.

TOP RIGHT: By mid-August, the Icelandic summer was fast drawing to a close. The sea conditions were only going to get rougher, and we were facing the most difficult stage of the journey.

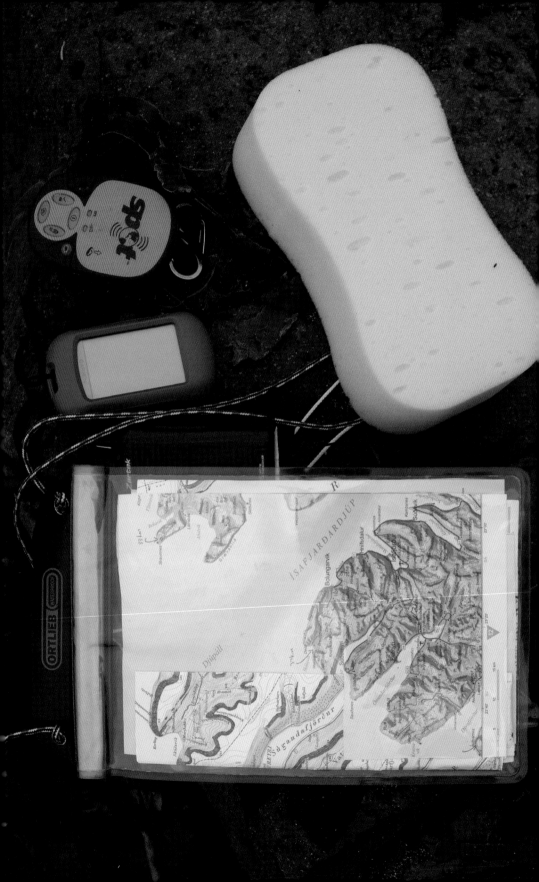

LEFT: Throughout the journey, we relied on our GPS and cellphones to stay in contact with the team, particularly when it came to coordinating landings. I always studied the map to memorise the route ahead and note the location of the rescue huts dotted along the coast.

ABOVE: A weathered farmhouse near Þingeyri evokes the loneliness and hardship of rural life in the remote Westfjords. Life in these parts requires toughness and endurance.

THESE PAGES: Paddling around the Westfjords was a true test of character. These photos were taken at Breiðavík, near the tip of the Látrabjarg Peninsula.

ABOVE AND LEFT: Keeping a sense of humour can turn the toughest moments into great memories. Laughing at yourself shifts your mind's focus from your failings and allows more scope for your talents to thrive. I wanted to laugh more on this journey, but tensions in the team made it difficult at times. By the time we'd rounded the Westfjords, both Dan and I were physically and emotionally spent. I think the strain shows here in his face.

ABOVE: Manhandling a fully loaded kayak – weighing upwards of 250 kilograms – is difficult at the best of times. When you throw in strong winds and monster waves, the boat can become a lethal weapon.

And suddenly it was over. Dan and I stepped ashore on the beach at Húsavík.

THESE PAGES: Our return to Húsavík was an emotional moment. The townsfolk turned out in force to greet us – what a great bunch of people – and Dan was reunited with his family. Amid all the euphoria, I felt an underlying sadness, and wished Vasti had been there to greet me.

CHAPTER 16

WILD WILD WEST

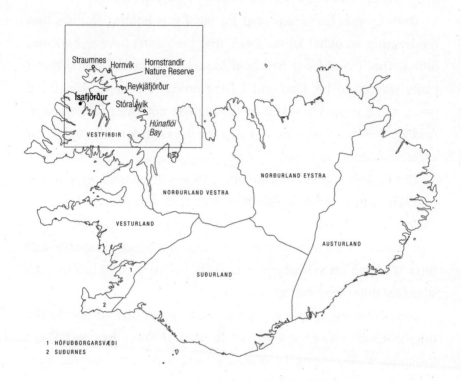

'The weather had turned very bad, with
strong winds and sheets of rain that struck
horizontally, like volleys of icy bullets.'

O ur plan was to head off on exactly the same route we had
been following when the rudder broke. We would round the
lighthouse at the tip of the Straumnes Peninsula – probably in
some tough sea conditions again, four or five hours of slogging into
the teeth of the wind – and then find shelter there. Maybe there would

be another rescue hut … The rest would let us recover enough to put in a really big distance when the weather finally got better.

That day was like a new start for me. I was holding thumbs that the weather wouldn't let us down, that I wouldn't have to bark any orders, that I could just be Riaan Manser and be the friend that I really wanted to be. Dan and I were going to achieve something great, and I wanted to end it on the highest note we could manage. And we were so close now … *Just a few days left, hey*, I thought. *Just a few days and we're home!*

The broken rudder and the effort to get it repaired were in the past. The hut at Aðalvík was bare and cold, but provided enough shelter for us to have a decent eight hours of rest. I prepared what was probably my favourite dinner to date: a mixture of noodles and tuna. It wasn't up to Michelin standards, perhaps, but it had us both silent for more than half an hour!

Next morning, after a few cups of coffee, we started tracing our original route out of the fjord. As we headed along the coast, Dan's thoughts were ranging far ahead, all the way to the famous Dusi Canoe Marathon in KwaZulu-Natal.

'Do you think I could manage the Dusi?' he asked.

'It would call for a bit of a practice, Dan, but, of course, yes. Why not?' I replied.

'I had an idea a long time ago to do the Dusi on a triple, with Bob and Andy. But can you make three-man boats?'

'Ja, you can, of course,' I said. 'I'll be you guys' second,' I replied enthusiastically.

About 20 kilometres later, this nice-ish day became nasty-ish. Before we began to cross Fljótavik fjord, I had to make a call whether we should aim for the nearest rescue hut or continue on around the peninsula to Hlöðuvík. The wind was 50 kilometres an hour from the front and the sea was as tumultuous as ever. As disappointing as it was, I told Dan we weren't going to risk it. Our balance was problematic at the best of times, and we could do without a disastrous capsize so near the finish.

Even for a colour-blind guy like me, the rescue hut stood out like a sore thumb. Although it was icy cold inside, there was a primitive paraffin stove. I probably didn't know how to use it properly, and the hut soon filled with thick smoke. Without a clean flame, we couldn't cook a warm meal, so I set up our usual gas burner and made some pasta. It filled our bellies and lifted our drained spirits.

It was an uncomfortable night by normal standards, but we were not normal people any more, and for us the hut was cosy enough compared to some of our previous stopovers. As a result, we slept in a little, which was pleasant, but also a bad idea, because we missed the early-morning period when it was calm enough to paddle.

The weather had turned really bad, with strong winds and sheets of rain that struck horizontally, like volleys of icy bullets. Instead of being merely a bit bumpy, the sea was seriously choppy, and it seemed likely we'd also encounter a mist so thick that that we wouldn't be able to see more than 15 or 20 metres ahead of us. With a schedule as tight as ours, it looked unlikely that we'd reach Húsavík by late August.

I blamed myself again. I was annoyed at my laziness and willingness to find excuses. It had been cold and difficult to sleep, but that was no excuse to lose our window of opportunity. I should have woken up earlier! There was no other choice but to go for it, horrendous weather or not. We were in a bay that looked relatively calm, though the icy wind blowing down the valley at our backs suggested we'd have a tough time out at sea. The trick of judging what is happening out at sea is to compare the horizon when you landed to the horizon when you're about to leave. I had hoped to use the outgoing tide to our benefit, but I also understood the turbulence that occurs at the ends of peninsulas when the tide is ebbing. In a small kayak, it can feel as though you're in a washing machine.

It turned out to be as turbulent as I'd expected. I was fired up, and remember telling Dan that the rough water would last for a short time only. I lied to keep us both focused. I had absolutely no idea whether we would succeed; experience was my only yardstick. What did I know about the Westfjords? Only seven kayakers had ever rounded Iceland's northern tip. Who really understood this part of Iceland?

Pleasant it wasn't. It was freezing, freezing cold and the sea was dangerously rough. Still, we battled on – we had no alternative. Somewhere ahead there was a rescue hut. My faith in the maps and the old rescue huts they advertised had not been proven wrong. I reckoned that if Dan found it hard to fall asleep tonight I would be amazed. He was struggling a bit; he'd found his form in the past few weeks, but 30 kilometres of wrestling with the sea had exhausted him, both physically and mentally ... Not that I was in much better shape. I nagged and exhorted him time after time, and I felt bad about it, but there was no alternative; our situation was just too serious.

After six exhausting hours, we finally discovered the faded rescue hut in a little bay called Hornvík. I apologised to Dan: 'Ay, my body is very, very sore ... You're a good guy, Dan, and I know you're trying. Sorry man – I'm sorry I have to shout at you.'

Flip it, this journey really needed to come to an end so that I didn't have to be 'this' guy, doing what I was doing. The journey, with all its responsibilities, was probably the loneliest I have ever been. On my other journeys, I'd gone without human contact for long periods. Here though, the loneliness was more brutal. Everything I did seemed to be for others; simultaneously, everything I did seemed to make these people hate me even more. And they knew no better. That's lonely.

I hoped that Dan understood in some way. 'No, I know,' he would say. 'I don't take it personally.' I hoped Dan would say great things about me. If that was all he did with what I'd done for him, that would be first prize. If he could have the strength of character to rebuke *anyone* for criticising or insulting me, then this journey would have been worth every tear and every cent.

It was freezing cold at Hornvík as we clambered up the beach. We stumbled around and found the rescue hut. It was empty and cold. I searched further up the valley and found a furnished cabin full of supplies stashed there for the rangers who are the reserve's inhabitants during the summer months. One of the rangers, whose name was Bjorn, was there, and he wasn't too happy at our unexpected intrusion into what was essentially his home. Eventually, with gentle persuasion and humility, we won him over. He made us coffee and food – fish balls with rice in a very fatty sauce. It was needed and good. Bjorn also introduced us to his semi-tame companions – three brown Arctic foxes. Fortunately, hunting is illegal in the reserve.

Next morning was coldish, but not excessively so, and our efficient thermal jackets kept us warm. Some of our clothes were wet, so we hung them on the side of the hut to dry. They were only half-dry by the time we had to leave, and it was no fun to climb into those cold garments. I think Dan now realised for the first time the relative luxury we had enjoyed on the journey. To me, though, the hut was a palace, compared with some of the places I'd slept in during my earlier expeditions.

Before leaving, I tried to send a GPS coordinate to the Coast Guard and the team. I was confident it had worked and hoped it would put at ease the people who were expecting us to finish on the specific day. We got going earlier than the previous day. After a grateful farewell to Bjorn, I dragged the kayak over slimy, rotting, metre-thick kelp beds to the sea. We set off for our next landing point, Reykjaförður, about 40 kilometres away. As we left Hornvík, we could see the exact spot where Iceland's last polar bear, which had drifted on ice all the way from Greenland, had been shot and killed. The previous night Bjorn had reaffirmed something that I could not easily accept: the authorities believed it was best to kill the bear than to spend money on trying to save it. Crazy.

I could feel a deep-seated sense of fatigue as we rounded the tip of the Hornbjarg Peninsula and headed southeastwards. Determination aside, the conditions were really tough. We were not piling up the kilometres as fast as we would have liked, and the heavy physical toll of the past few weeks was getting to us. I had three strategies in mind, involving a short, a medium and a long day. The medium day was the most attractive in that it meant a stopover at the famous hot springs of Reykjaförður. The place is otherwise accessible only by air, so it doesn't get many visitors.

I was tired, and I think Dan was as well. We took a short break just past the halfway mark, and then got down to paddling the last 18 kilometres. We were really looking forward to indulging ourselves in the hot springs – get ourselves warmed up, get into some warm clothes and creep into our sleeping bags.

But we were doomed to disappointment when we finally dragged ourselves into the bay around 20h00 after a really hellish trip – 'one hundred per cent tired', as Dan put it. With the tourist season at an end, the hot springs and guesthouses were all closed. I left Dan on the beach in a sheltered area, and eventually found the baths. We decided to use the changing room as our shelter for the night. The only problem was that it took me almost two hours of running the kilometre back and forth in the freezing cold to bring over our kit. I was hammered, and was acting on autopilot by this point.

We treated ourselves to hot baths before dinner. I made us noodles with dried fish – not the tastiest meal, but healthy and nutritious. Dan and I laughed as we ate, using plastic lids as our eating utensils, the food finding its way into our beards. As tired as I was, I decided to wash our clothes and hang them up outside. We believed we would reach civilisation the following day, but I wanted us to have some clean, dry underclothes just in case. In my opinion, we were ready to wrap up Iceland. One more day and, mentally, we would be into the home straight.

The following morning was horrible – for me, at least. After we awoke, I immediately started packing up our gear and putting the changing rooms back into the condition we had found them. I wanted to get going as quickly as possible, and asked Dan to assist. He was becoming irritated as I rushed around madly, to the point that, when I finished preparing his oats breakfast and asked him not to take his time finishing up, he verbalised his frustration.

'Why can't you just chill and leave me alone? For fuck sakes, we're a team, and you never stop rushing around. It's frustrating me to no end!'

'Geez Dan,' I replied, 'we have 47 kilometres ahead of us today, no guarantee on the weather conditions, the wrong tide, no bale-out spots, a schedule that we cannot break, and I still have two hours' work to do for us before we start paddling. What do you expect me to be like if we are to actually be successful. Don't be so arrogant.'

'I'm not arrogant. You're an arsehole and don't even realise it. You never realise how you always shout at those around you. And that's why people don't like you. You really have some serious personal issues to address,' Dan continued.

Furious, I continued packing our clothing. We were now shouting loudly at each other.

235

'I wish I had never brought you on this journey! There are so many more deserving people out there. People who don't have a fraction of what you have, and you continue to be arrogant. You don't deserve to have been given this opportunity!' I shouted. Every word came from my sense of anger and hurt. How could Dan not appreciate what was being done for him? How dare he attack me personally after everything I'd done for him? The wind was knocked out of me. I had no energy or breath left to say another word.

Dan had the last word, though. As I walked towards the doorway, with his clothes in my hand, I heard him say: 'You could do with someone who loves you.'

I was floored; no one had ever said such a hurtful thing to me. I carried on with the packing, running back and forth to our kayak with the dry bags and paddles. As I stood there, waiting for Dan to make his way over the grass to the beach, I spoke to the camera. I wanted to rid myself of this hurt and just carry on. I like my strength and didn't need criticism of it by someone who didn't understand. I said something to the effect that I hoped Dan would learn something from this journey, instead of *just saying* that he has. To me – the guy who saw him warts and all – he wasn't showing it.

In the back of my mind, I knew I had to release my hurt. As I spoke to the camera, I saw Dan appear over the ridge. At the time, I didn't want to speak about it further in front of him. However, this is what I wanted to say. Dan was right. Because of my family-less upbringing, I never had the privilege of trusting anyone's love. I have never, ever believed that someone loved me unconditionally. As a child, I was hurt so much by those around me, whether they knew it or not, that I probably would never believe anyone who told me they loved me. I believed Dan would, in a sense, 'love' me because of what I'd done for him. But he had chosen rather to hurt and attack me. But, in another sense, he was dead right: I *could* do with someone who loves me.

The 47 kilometres were cold, misty in some places and sunny in others, but mostly we had the wind at our back. For a change, the weather remained good the entire way, and the sea nice and flat, so that when I got the team on the radio, I told them we couldn't land where they were, at Fell. We were going around the point of Fell and across the little bay to the south of it. We'd land at the far end of the bay, at Litla Ávík or Stóra Ávík. Tracey seemed upset with me again, but I didn't care. I was going to prepare myself for the end. The rest of the team had to do the same: stop complaining and get on with it. It amazes me how people can complain non-stop, but, when they achieve something, they want the glory. You don't get glory for moaning. There are no prizes for achieving something with a negative attitude.

After five consecutive days of paddling, though, we'd got considerably further than we'd planned. If we could just keep to the schedule, we would get to Húsavík on time.

We settled on Stóra Ávík, which was in a pretty rough piece of landscape. From here, weather permitting, we would set off next day straight across Húnaflói Bay, paddling 55 kilometres to a place called Skagi, near the tip of the Skagaheiði Peninsula. It was now 27 August, the day we were originally supposed to arrive at Húsavík. The new date was several days ahead, and, barring really unforeseen disasters, we were going to be there in time.

Tracey had to manage the end-of-expedition function at Húsavík, which was going to be quite an event, but not a very long one, because Dan and I would have to fly out the same evening. In addition, she was playing hostess to Marianne Schwankhart, a journalist from the *Sunday Times*, who had arrived from Johannesburg to spend the last few days with the team for a photo essay. I wish Tracey had embraced these challenges and had communicated better with me. My fault was that I just said yes to everything; I should have showed more courage in leading as well. I saw such strength in Tracey. On the beach at Breiðavík, I had asked her about who had knocked her confidence, or doubted her, so much that she, like me, second-guessed everything she did. I believe Tracey is like me in that we grab every gram of external validation of whether we are worthwhile or not.

It hadn't been an easy few days, but Dan and I had discovered more about each other. I realised now – pretty belatedly, and perhaps it was mainly my fault – that, when it came to Dan accepting himself, open talk was required: honest talk about his cerebral palsy, and about the fact that he was different and walked differently, and that people saw him differently. I felt I'd earned the opportunity to be able to talk to him as a friend who didn't have to hold back. Inevitably, I think, his good friends had always tiptoed around him, but I had earned the right to be harsh with him in a kind way. I could be honest with him, more honest than other people, and that was what he needed.

Before we set out, I had promised that I would treat Dan as an equal partner, which meant that I expected him to do his very best at all times, cerebral palsy or no cerebral palsy. That was what Dan wanted, too, the rite of passage every red-blooded young man needs to prove himself to himself. I had been lucky, blessed with a sound body that had allowed me to become a paratrooper and a rugby player. Through no fault of his own, Dan had been denied the opportunity to do anything like that.

This had been his chance to flip a derisive finger at the bodily weakness that had so unfairly been inflicted on him at birth, and show – to others, but most importantly to himself – that he was as good as, or better than, the next man.

Dan and I were feeling good, now that the finish line was just a hop and a skip away. We could start looking back on everything. It had been tough, sure, and I had lost 12 kilograms without having been overweight in the first place. On the whole, I had enjoyed it, although understandably it was a bit of a shock for Dan in the beginning. But most of the time we had stayed in huts or guesthouses, we had had lots of food, and we were strong all the way. So it was no problem, and now we were just keen to go home. But I knew that the memories of this trip, and particularly our trek round the Westfjords, would go home with us and never fade away.

We now had 105 kilometres left, which, among other things, involved a major bay crossing. An open-water paddle far from land is always dangerous, but by this stage it held no terrors for us – a case of 'been there, done that, got the dry suit'. The secret was the first few kilometres.

'The first 20,' Dan said.

'It's the first 20,' I agreed, 'that's exactly it, and it's actually the first kays, to get us into a rhythm.' Although I was pretty well exhausted, I felt so cheerful that I burst into song. Poor Dan. But he was very good about it, and didn't even beat me over the head with his paddle. Well, he didn't really have time – we were averaging a steady seven kilometres per hour.

CHAPTER 17

To the finish line

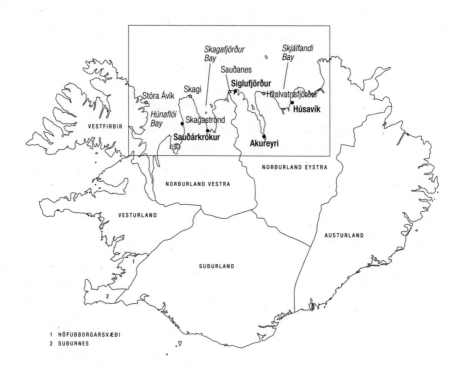

'It turned out to be a lekker day, hey?'

With the Westfjords behind us, the *Sunday Times* giving us their time, and two crucial days of rest, I found myself in an ideal place mentally. I calculated that we had four more hops on our journey before we reached Húsavík. This stretch of Iceland's northern coast is defined by three peninsulas. We would paddle from one to the other, avoiding the deep fjords in between. The distances were a bit extreme, though, given the general unpredictability of the weather and the sea conditions. But although I had disappointed many people by extending the finish date by a week, I could extend it again. Or could I?

While the team began the long and winding drive around Húnaflói Bay to our next landing place, Dan and I forged ahead. I reckoned, perhaps ambitiously, that we would need a minimum of about eight hours on the water to cover the 55 kilometres across the bay. The mist was thick at first. I had monitored the weather reports throughout the night, and the wind was behaving as I'd been led to believe it would, but who trusts weather reports anyway? The bottom line was that this day was another gamble, and I hadn't shared this with anyone. I didn't want to have to explain the possibility that awaited us if the cold southerly wind got above 15 km\h. I often joked with myself that I wanted to be as sure about everything as the rest were around me. No one ever showed any concern for me – maybe to Dan, but never to me. Come to think of it, maybe it was a favour of sorts. I was never given 'more' reason to worry! Perfect, hey?

For this open-sea crossing, I chose to head slightly to the southeast. That way, if we were caught by stronger winds, we would have some emergency landing options. From where we were, far away from land, a strong southerly wind could blow us far out into the Denmark Strait. The strength of the current, though, was the biggest surprise for me that day. When I steered the kayak relative to the coastline, I noticed that we still had the benefit of the powerful tidal surge into this deep bay. This probably made the day. Dan and I paddled well for the first 20 kilometres, but when we reached the halfway mark he was clearly at his limit. Fortunately, I felt stronger than I had in the last two weeks. Maybe the two days' rest had done us good. Our paddle followed a slightly zigzag course, which was longer than needed, but turned out to be safer. Because of the change of direction, the wind was over our right shoulders – almost perfect.

We took it a bit too easy for the last eight kilometres or so, and needed to speed up. It was 20h00, and Iceland seemed to be getting back into winter mode, because it was getting really cold. I suspected there was snow on the way. We'd gone a full seasonal cycle – from snow to snow.

As we neared the landing place, my main objective was to spot the guys on shore and save ourselves time and distance. I couldn't see movement or light. I stopped and tried to call Tracey's cellphone, with no luck – each time it went straight to voicemail. I thought, because of the remoteness, that it must have been the reception. Ten minutes later, I got a radio call from her: 'I SMSed, Riaan. I heard you were trying to call.' I could not reply on the radio immediately as it was safely tucked away and the sea was too choppy. If only the people on shore understood what it took to accomplish a small task such as answering the radio. Tracey sounded irritated; I didn't have the energy to deal with her emotions at that moment. I needed to get us safely to shore. Dan was fatigued, and it took all my remaining energy to keep him motivated. On the positive side, we knew we were now within half a dozen kilometres of shore; the radio wouldn't have worked otherwise.

The problem, as it transpired, was that the team hadn't reached the landing place; they had had trouble getting through a locked gate. But they decided against forcing their way through, I was told later, and had to find another way to get to the shore. My mind had a clear picture of Chez searching for solutions; finding alternative routes is his speciality.

We staggered up the beach, stiff with cold and muscle-weariness. But there would be no time to rest: next day, we would undertake another long paddle, around the tip of the Skagaheiði Peninsula and into Skagafjörður Bay, another amazing 40-kilometre fjord crossing. I hoped the weather would hold. I was making the kind of decisions about weather that I had promised myself I wouldn't make. Just because we were heading for the finish didn't mean that the worst could not happen. As much as I should have been 'enjoying' this, I wasn't.

Next morning, we launched and paddled away as scheduled. Richard and Darren followed us for a while in a rubber duck, frantically filming and photographing us before they had to head back to land. The coastline was like something out of a Hardy Boys novel, full of little nooks, coves and crannies. I wasted time taking us into almost every gap and under every eroded rock arch.

My planning the night before had been ambitious, to say the least. I wanted an all or nothing day. We needed it to bank on the security of finishing on time. The weather forecast was for two good days, followed by a day of poor weather before the final dash to the finish. I believed we could paddle to the tip of the deeply indented Tröllaskagi Peninsula. That would mean doing 72 kilometres in one day. Crazy, I know, but I thought it was possible. Option two was to head directly across the fjord to the nearest land, which was about 40 kilometres away. That would give us 50 kilometres for the day. Option three was to just call it a day and rest up for a monster day the next. I have to admit I felt drained and almost delirious.

I stopped the kayak at the northeasterly point of the Skagaheiði Peninsula, threw my legs over the side and took control of my thoughts. Yip, it was just another paddle. But it *wasn't*. I had had such conviction the previous night about the importance of today's paddle. I couldn't doubt myself now. I explained to Dan why I had stopped, and explained to him how I saw our options for the day, and how each option would affect our finish-day projection. Then I grabbed at a freezing-cold Lucozade and gulped away. I didn't need the physical energy, but I desperately needed the mental bang that glucose delivers.

Dan and I decided on option two. The angles required for this bay crossing didn't allow me the luxury to switch to option one halfway across. Nonetheless, the 50-odd kilometres would do for one day!

I wanted to give Dan a gift that I knew could never be matched: a close-up whale experience. Although the journey was an experience in its own right, I wanted him to have an experience he would struggle to explain in words. I had believed I would fail in this, too. But nature delivered on that day.

I had been listening to music, and so was unaware of the sounds around us. When we stopped for a drink, Dan said he had heard something odd. I listened, and immediately recognised the sound of a whale breathing, which can seem aggressive and bellowing. Dan described it as if we were near a harbour and huge trucks were offloading loads of rubble. It was a very apt description, I thought, of what is essentially water being forced violently into the air. Although I was certain he had heard whale sounds, I didn't get too excited. The water was as smooth as glass and the air crisp. Sound could travel for many kilometres on a day like this. We continued paddling, but I switched off the music.

The small island of Málmey glided past on our right. And then the vision appeared. The afternoon had turned into another of those pinkish, blue-grey scenes of tranquillity. A few hundred metres ahead of us to the left, a humpback whale was regularly breaking the glassy surface to breathe. On my Madagascar trip I had had many interactions with humpback whales, as well as with sharks and turtles. The most dangerous situation was probably when I went too close to a mother whale and her calf. Generally, humpback whales are shy and will not usually present aggressive behaviour. I was confident I could manoeuvre us into a position close enough for Dan to feel the whale's breath. When approaching a whale at sea, your movement must create an almost accidental coming together of paths. Rhythm and timing are key. Never chase a whale; its considerable speed can be very deceptive. Fortunately, this one gave me two breathing sessions before diving, and thus suggested a probable route. I turned us away from the whale and steered slightly landward for 100 metres, explaining to Dan that were going to sit and wait. We needed to be silent and, most importantly, not to tap our paddles on the side of the kayak. If startled, whales will dive deep and disappear.

As if on cue, the whale glided gracefully across our bow, just a few metres away. I estimated its length at 10 metres, with a noticeably unhealthy-looking dorsal fin. I had Dan sit completely still as I began paddling us forward, aiming for an imaginary spot diagonally to our right-hand side so that we would be right behind the majestic beast when it surfaced. And that's how it turned out: Dan and I saw her gliding a metre or so in front of us, gasping for a bigger breath each time. Dan was within reach of the whale as I brought the nose of the kayak right under the animal's tail fin as she flung it into the air before diving. Geez, it was special for me – not specifically the whale interaction, but rather Dan's reaction to it. He brought his hands to his head, fingers through his hair and, with a sigh of disbelief, said 'Oh my woooooord, no ways. No ways!'

It's difficult to explain, I guess, but this was probably the first time I felt I had really given Dan something. It was probably the first time I felt real appreciation, too. Man, I was happy. If only Dan could have seen the size of my smile!

Dan and I reached the shore on the most tranquil day on the water we had yet had. An admirable distance of 50 kilometres signalled the end of our fourth-last paddle. I was in high spirits, and had plenty to say to the nine leopard seals that followed us into the rocky cove. The cameras and Toyotas were waiting for us. I needed a hot shower and some sleep.

So, piece by piece, we conquered Iceland's coastline, but it had taken its toll, and on many levels. When we went to bed we knew that, although the Westfjords were behind us, and Húsavík agonisingly close, we weren't there yet.

Just three more paddles! We'd been doing it for so long that it just didn't seem possible we were near the end.

It was strange – for me, that is – to see the excitement with which the crew responded every time Dan mentioned that his mother and his brother Andy were coming to see him at the finish. Of course, it was natural for the crew to be excited about hosting the visitors in Húsavík, but what amazed me was how no one in the group cared about me, or my welfare, for the finish. No one asked about who would be there to welcome me, the guy who had risked everything he had for them to have this opportunity. Dan never even bothered to ask why Vasti was not coming to see me finish the journey. I believed Tracey had matured on this journey and now understood what was involved in the real world of adventure. I believed she could appreciate the lengths to which I had gone, firstly, to keep her in Iceland, and, secondly, to make her time as comfortable as possible. I guess I was wrong. No one cared.

The truth about Vasti not making it to the finish was something that gnawed away at me. We had no money. We would not be able to cover our rent when we got home. But of course none of the crew cared. Nor did Dan. It hurt. I had spent about R25 000 for Tracey and Zahir to fly to Reykjavík to apply for UK transit visas. It was ludicrous to think that I felt guilty about finishing a week later than planned, outside of their visa expiry dates, when that money could have been used to bring over the person who had suffered back home for six months to make this dream trip come true, the person who had supported me through thick and thin over the last ten years. If there was anyone who had earned the right to be there to see me finish, it was Vasti.

But I buried the negatives, as I always do, and got fired up for our third-last paddle. It turned out to be a cold one. Iceland's worst winter in 63 years was on its way. Fortunately, we had only 25 kilometres to cover that day. My goal was to get within a chipping distance of the next peninsula, which would essentially put us within reach of Húsavík. The weather showed only one day of rough sea within the last three we had available. Our landing at Sauðanes lighthouse was misty and scary, but I had put on the 'no other options' hat by now. The truth was that we had no other options.

Just 85 kilometres to the finish! But there was no undue excitement among the team members yet. There was too much riding on what happened in the next 72 hours, and if this adventure had taught them anything, it was to expect the unexpected. Tracey had the finish to prepare, so I told her to stay in Húsavík for the last three days. Along with Andy, she would organise huge bonfires, Viking style, and arrange to have food and drink on hand for the crowds we hoped would attend.

I could see Tracey was stressed, but this time I did nothing about it. I was saving my energy to finish the journey safely, and on time.

I think anyone would understand how disappointed I was that Dan still saw me as the villain. I had shown myself ready to offer my life for his, but Dan was still talking in interviews about my inability to deal with people and my impatience with him. And, still, I had never said one bad word about him. You have to understand how this affected the positive thoughts I had to muster each day, doing what I was doing for eight to ten hours a day for Dan. But I came back smiling and supportive every single morning.

Our second-last day of paddling dawned. It was crazy to think we had just one more 45-kilometre paddle remaining. As I said to Dan, it was in fact our last paddle: 'The last paddle doesn't feel like a last paddle, Dan, you won't even remember it. Today is actually our last paddle!'

We were heading for a little bay called Hvalvatnsfjörður. We didn't know what to expect, but with the northwesterly swell and an onshore breeze, I believed we had perfect conditions for a safe landfall. More importantly, I believed Hvalvatnsfjörður would make a good launch site for our last day. The conditions were relatively good, but began to deteriorate as we reached the 30-kilometre mark. Dan said he wasn't feeling well and couldn't paddle. Maybe it was nerves or something he had eaten. I didn't mind taking over for the last 10 kilometres, and made sure I used the end of this day to boost him and to remind him of his imminent achievement.

Sometimes you say something to another person that turns out to have more impact in your own life. I remember telling Dan, as we turned into the bay and were about 600 metres from shore: 'Today is not a measure of what you have achieved in Iceland. It is not a measure of you.' I felt bad, as I could see he was emotional. 'Prepare yourself for the magic of tomorrow because you've earned this, Dan. Be strong, be brave!' And then I remembered something that had been a special moment for me in Madagascar: 'Dan, this will be the last time you finish a day knowing you have to paddle again. The last time.' It was getting very real.

'When people say they have a special relationship with the sea now, you *do* have a relationship with the sea now, hey, Dan, you realise that?'

'I do, with the boat,' he replied.

I knew what he meant, and I remembered my own words when I had opened the kayak six months earlier: 'When I take this out, people think that I have some feeling or attachment to this. I absolutely have none ... We're just unwrapping a piece of fibreglass now; when we finish, tell you what, this becomes a living person and part of the journey. This kayak's name is *Inspiration*, so we're going to name it that.'

Then I said to Dan: 'Strange what I started feeling now ... like, sad that this day's coming to an end. Strange, hey. Earlier today I was busy thinking this day is taking too long, now I was thinking, come on, man, this day is coming to an end.'

'It turned out to be a lekker day, hey?' Dan voiced his satisfaction.

I knew what Bob was getting at when he said Dan is a shining light. He is, and I unfortunately had had to bring that gentle, shining light into a rough, unforgiving world that doesn't allow for excuses or 'try agains'.

We did some straight talking as we stroked our way ever closer to Hvalvatnsfjörður, exploring our relationship and delving into our individual motivations.

'I don't want to preach to you … Get over the fact where your challenges are, you know, so do you understand those challenges?'

'Ja.'

'Make a huge effort in other stuff, so you don't have to be apologetic. Show your effort in other stuff, you know, man, it's all *right* … Then you don't have to be apologetic.'

'Ja, ja,' Dan agreed.

'Because you want to do what somebody else can do, that can't do things *you* can do?' I expanded on my theory. This brought back some childhood memories for Dan.

'My mate's dad, he said to me when I was 11, he said you must never forget that you are a special boy,' Dan said.

Enthusiastically, I added: 'And you've always heard people say that, but you haven't believed it, hey?'

'Ja. So now it's just sort of, it's almost like I feel like I'm repaying a little bit of that faith that people have in me, you know?'

'Sure … My harshness has been a part of the jigsaw, Dan, where I'm saying that, we can *talk* about battling yourself. We can *talk* about making the most of the situation … We can talk about it and talk about it, but it's that actual doing that matters, you know, and that's why you've come here and you've done.'

This probably presented the most opportune moment for me to withdraw the hurt I felt my words had caused him a week before. Even though Dan didn't know he had hurt me deeply that day at Reykjaförður springs, I had decided I would apologise to him.

'I didn't mean what I said that other day about the fact that I should have rather taken somebody on this journey that was more deserving.' I paused for a second 'Because you are very deserving.'

Dan was emotional in his response again. 'Thank you,' he said quietly. 'Thank you.'

How dare I have left that thought in his mind? No way. Even if he never apologised, it didn't matter. I was not going to leave a good person with that thought in their mind and heart.

When we got ashore, Dan spoke into the team's cameras: 'We had an enjoyable day, a long day, but we both enjoyed it and tried to savour the moment of the last paddle, because we're racing towards the finish, maybe that'll go away in a blur. We had a good day and a heart-to-heart, and I for one thoroughly enjoyed that.'

'Little bit sad at the end of the day, to see it filmed,' he added.

Dan and I found it difficult to believe that we were on the brink of victory. I had a slight attack of the cautions: 'I've gone through too much in the last little while, from disappointment to worry … just thinking maybe I've bitten off more than I can chew.'

Dan, on the other hand, definitely had his tail up. 'Who the hell would have thought that somebody that's been in a boat for the sum total of about eight hours before attempting Iceland, would actually get around, you know?' he asked triumphantly.

Then Dan brought us back to the present: 'Lots of highs, lots of lows, lots of laughter and lots of tears,' he said into Darren's camera. 'But the fact of the matter is that we're one paddle away from completing something that will change my life forever, and I'm sure will change Riaan forever.'

And the end was nigh; it was unbelievable, actually, as we woke up, drank coffee, and prepared for our last one-on-ones with Darren and

Zahir. The interviews were probably crucial, but inevitably delayed our departure. For good measure, the team had to deal with a flat tyre before they left. But Zahir doesn't blink at small issues like this – last day or not – and had it repaired within an hour.

The delay left us very little time to reach the finish, where the wellwishers were expecting us. More importantly, it left little time for Dan and I to catch our flight to London. Shea, my superstar PA, had worked tirelessly to organise the media and our supporters to come out to OR Tambo airport to welcome us back to South Africa. Every major radio and TV station wanted a piece of the action. We couldn't upset them, and we certainly didn't want to upset Shea!

Our delayed departure from Hvalvatnsfjörður was not the result of slacking on our part. Iceland wasn't going to be beaten without one final battle; the surf was very rough, and, unless it calmed down, we weren't going to be able to get through it. I had to make a difficult judgment call. The urgency for us to get going was immense. Yet, I was hesitant, although I am not by nature a hesitant person, when I looked at what we had to get through to reach the open sea. On the one hand, we had everything to gain by launching; on the other hand, it would be tragic if something went wrong at this late stage.

I wasn't the only one. 'I'm nervous, man,' Dan confessed, eyeing the raging surf – mainly because he didn't want to disappoint the assembled Skinstads at Húsavík. 'These aren't the conditions I expected. I've got to concentrate now, but my mum and Andy have come out a long way to come and visit … the conditions aren't just playing their part now. So it's going to be slow.'

But if we hoped to make the party, we had to set off right away. The two-metre shore-break could easily snap an arm or a leg. The waves thundered onto the rocky shores, making the ground vibrate. I couldn't believe it. I would have to take Dan through the surf, and then return for the even more physically dangerous task of pulling the kayak through. If I failed, the repercussions would be huge, and many people would be disappointed.

The cold water numbed my head and hands as I drove Dan through the shore-break. I needed to get him a bit further out than normal, so I took a minute to get back. Running back up the beach to the kayak was a blur as I tried to remind myself to breathe properly. I turned with the kayak in hand and slid it in one long motion along the smooth pebbles and into a huge ball of foam. I held on for dear life. My wrist and fingers twisted in the kayak handle. Once through the impact zone, it was not plain sailing to collect Dan. I needed him to swim to me in a safe area. I could not risk being smashed onto the shore by the waves. He showed guts and determination as he swam the 20 metres to me and launched himself into the kayak.

Our last day had just begun.

The paddle was a nervous one. As we left Hvalvatnsfjörður, I had to guide us along the cliffs of Geldinganes, with huge swells and thunderous waves smashing into the wall of rock. The problem was that thick mist hindered our view of where we were going. I used a combination of the map and my experience to judge how close we could go as we rounded the peninsula. Two or three close calls kept us on our toes. I kept repeating to myself how much I would like to have an easy run to the finish, but it wasn't to be. We were slowly falling further behind schedule. It's a hell of a thing: a man sweats his guts out for nearly six months and then barely gets to attend his own party!

There was no way we could just strike out across Skjálfandi Bay; I couldn't risk us sitting in open seas without a fully loaded GPS. We had to follow the western coastline of the bay until I could be sure the mist was lifting. But it didn't. I then explained to Dan how we needed to use the swell running into the bay to our benefit. It would save us the time we were losing by not cutting across early.

But things worked out amazingly once again. I hadn't made real peace with this Iceland journey and what it had brought into my life, but I was about to. The moment coincided with my decision to turn left into open water. My inner voice was saying: 'On your African circumnavigation, Riaan, you did something special. You understand our continent like few on the planet do. In Madagascar you learnt new lessons and were humbled by wonderful people again. But in Iceland there is no doubt that you have done and learnt more than both combined. You have done something for someone else. Even if the people around you didn't appreciate what you have done. The bottom line is you have done something great for another human being.'

Geez, I was emotional with myself. I needed to hear those words sincerely from deep inside me because I had not believed them up to that point. I had hated every second in Iceland, but those few sentences changed everything. Now I was eager and ready to take on the dangerous and mist-laden crossing to Húsavík. We had a whalewatching experience similar to the one in Faxaflói Bay, when we encountered a boat cruising in the mist, looking for whales. The tourists on board were flabbergasted at the sight of two bearded madmen, 20 kilometres from shore in choppy, three-metre seas. Dan and I posed for pics, and then began the blur of the final kilometres.

At Húsavík, Tracey was upbeat in front of the cameras, saying how happy she was to have brought everything together. The welcomers were down on the beach, the bonfires were ready to be lit, and everyone was watching the curtain of mist. For Mrs Skinstad, in particular, this was an emotional moment, and I heard later that she couldn't drag her eyes from the water. No other person felt the emotions that she was feeling. Dan was everything to her. The bond between them was beyond a typical mother-son bond. I knew she probably shared the crew's feelings toward me. For her, the finish would represent two things: an achievement, of course, but also the end to the dreadful angst she had endured for the last six months. It must have been tough on her. Of all the people to whom I wanted to guarantee Dan's safe return, above all it was to his mother.

They saw us before we saw them, I found out later. Through binoculars, Andy spotted the speck of yellow that was our kayak. With a sense of great fulfilment, I told Dan: 'You've come, you've seen and you've conquered.' But that wasn't enough. I wanted to tell him more. With the bonfires exploding on the beach and the crowds cheering us landward, I decided on impulse to jump out of the boat into the freezing water and swim to Dan's side to tell him how I felt.

My message was simple. No matter what had taken place on this journey, the fact remained he had done well, he was a hero, and he had made his family so proud.

'Your Mom and your brother love you so much and cannot wait to welcome their favourite son to shore. Look at the effort they have made for you,' I continued.

'Dan, another thing,' I was emotional now, close to tears. 'It has been a privilege for me to be the person that shared the kayak with you while you completed this amazing journey. Take this opportunity and make it happen for you. Your life has changed.'

And then we were there, stiff and cold and tired, and deliriously happy, and Dan was being embraced by a joyfully sniffling Mrs

Skinstad and Andy. Then, as if it were ceremonial, Dan, Mrs Skinstad and myself were knocked into the water by the drifting kayak – a last laugh from the Icelandic seas. Mrs Skinstad has a wonderful sense of humour and kept smiling throughout. She didn't have a dry suit on, but it didn't matter. It was lovely to see how proud they were of Dan. I can only begin to imagine.

At the same time, I was sad, even though the film shows me smiling in the background. I was all alone, the crew hugging and shaking each other's hands, while I pondered what it would have been like to have had someone I loved welcome me and tell me I had done well, I wanted that person to be Vasti. Geez, I was sad. I didn't show it.

Instead, I took care of the kayak and moved it ashore – probably out of habit. Then I did the first thing that had to be done: I thanked everyone, from the crew to the Skinstads and the mayor and his people. The champagne corks popped, like a salute being fired by miniature cannon, to celebrate our safe return. The fellow who wrote that it was better to travel hopefully than to arrive didn't know what he was talking about.

CHAPTER 18

LAST THOUGHTS

I must apologise – if that is the right word to use – that this story isn't the one everyone expected it to be, that it isn't a story in which everyone lived happily ever after.

What value does adventure have in our modern society? Supposedly we now know better and, more importantly, have many more entertainment opportunities available to us than in previous generations. Surely risking it all for the opportunity to say 'I did it' can no longer be rationalised?

A few weeks ago, I could have had this conversation and gladly seen both sides of the argument. The bottom line was that I have realised exactly what we achieved.

The sometimes foolish journeys that I've embarked on have always required some dogged, stubborn and egotistical behaviour on my part to make me persevere, come what may. The circumnavigation of Iceland required plenty of this, and then some. It left little space for poetry and nostalgia, which many believe to be the heart and soul of tough journeys. The truth is otherwise: the grit and the grime are what drive you to the finish line.

The flood of emotion hits home later. It doesn't hit you at the finish line, or on the return flight, or even during the drive from the airport. It hits you when you are alone at home without any hoo-hah or fanfare. The comforting sounds to which you are accustomed create the backdrop for honest and sincere thoughts.

Mine are these: never have I had the privilege of doing something as special and meaningful as I did on this journey. The emotions felt on previous journeys, even combined, don't match up to this one. I told Dan that his family and his friends were so proud of him for the risk he took and for his achievement, but that this faded in comparison to the pride I felt in being the guy who sat behind him the entire way. Without a doubt, this will be the first story I tell my grandchildren.

And it dawned on me how inspirational Dan really is. I had treated him as an equal from day one, both mentally and physically, offering him a seat in the kayak as an expedition partner and not as a passenger. I never allowed him the opportunity for excuses or slacking off. I knew it was the only way, or at least the only way I knew. Now, when I sit quietly and think about it, I sometimes feel ashamed that I drove him to his limits. Dan kept taking what came his way, bought into every scrap of motivation I fed him, and eventually finished something no one thought possible.

I'm inspired. Inspired to do more – for me, for my family, and for others. 'Around Iceland on Inspiration' was exactly what it was meant to be, which brings me back to the question of whether it was all worth it. If Dan takes this opportunity and makes even more of it, then of course it will have been worth it. If I take the lessons learnt and think bigger than before, it will have been more than worth it. But both Dan and I agree that if our story inspires even a few people to take a leap into the unknown, to change their lives for the better, to take risks where they never would have, and to make real the dreams they have dreamed for so long, then this journey and its message is the best way we could've spent six months of our lives.

ALSO AVAILABLE BY RIAAN MANSER

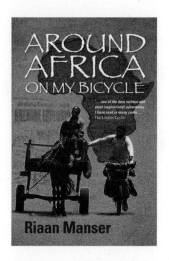

ISBN: 978-1-86842-351-4

EBOOK: 978-1-86842-401-6

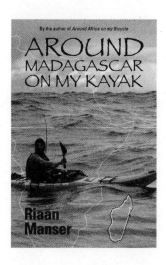

ISBN: 978-1-86842-537-2

EBOOK: 978-1-86842-433-7